IMAGES
*of America*

# TEHAMA COUNTY

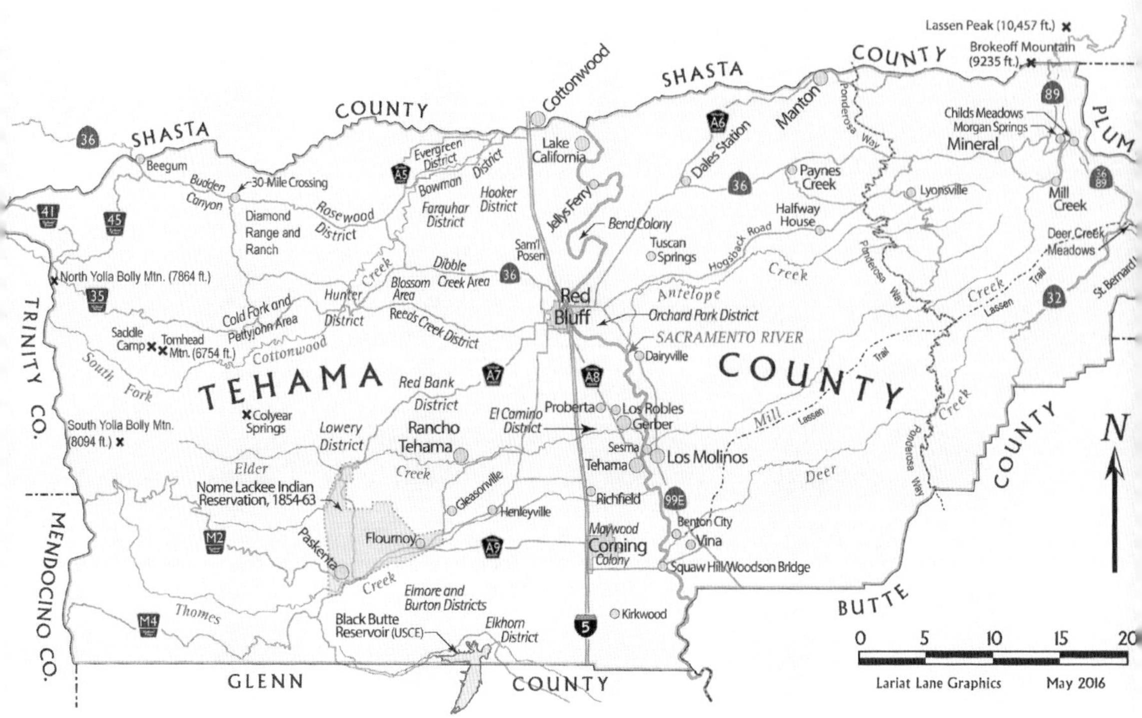


This map shows areas and communities of Tehama County. In 1878, the "Official Map of the County of Tehama" was completed by H.B. Shackelford and F.J. Nugent. It showed townships (Sierra, Cascade, Lassen, Tehama, Red Bluff, Cottonwood, and Paskenta), roads, railroads, original land grants, landowner names, and geographical features. It hangs at the Tehama County Library in Red Bluff. (Courtesy of Linton Brown.)

**On the Cover:** Red Bluff Bull Sale chairman Don Smith (standing) and Loren Miller (on horseback) are looking at cattle on the Miller Ranch, west of Red Bluff. Ranching has always been important in Tehama County. Mexican land grantees and early settlers brought the first sheep and cattle into the area to enjoy the rich grazing where wild oat, bunch grass, and clover grew in abundance. The first branded cattle in Tehama County belonged to William B. Ide, who drove 165 head of cattle to California in 1845. Branded on their right horn was "IDE." (Tehama County Library collection.)

IMAGES
*of America*

# TEHAMA COUNTY

Josie Smith and the Tehama County
Genealogical & Historical Society

ARCADIA
PUBLISHING

ISBN 978-1-4671-1745-6

Published by Arcadia Publishing
Charleston, South Carolina

Printed in the United States of America

Library of Congress Control Number: 2016933098

For all general information, please contact Arcadia Publishing:
Telephone 843-853-2070
Fax 843-853-0044
E-mail sales@arcadiapublishing.com
For customer service and orders:
Toll-Free 1-888-313-2665

Visit us on the Internet at www.arcadiapublishing.com

*This book is dedicated to the ones who came before us, to the ones who are here, and to the ones yet to come.*

# Contents

# Acknowledgments

*We ask that you write a good article and if you don't, there'll be somethin' covered with coal tar and feathers floatin' on the bosom of the Sacramento River.*

—a "warning" to A.V. Hoffman, reporter, *Sacramento Sunday Union*, 1891

With that admonishment in mind, my intention has been to present Tehama County history in terms of its people who did back then what we do now—live. Due to space constraints, much had to be left out or abridged. Still, it is hoped that this book does justice to the history and honors the people of Tehama County (because I really do not want to go "floatin' on the bosom of the Sacramento River").

A history book is a collaboration, and this one is no exception. Special thanks go to the Tehama County Library; Valanne Cardenas, Corning Museum and Chamber of Commerce; Chris Bauer and Darrell Mullins, Tehama County Museum; Arno Martini, Sacramento Valley Museum; James O'Barr, National Park Service; Dr. Michael A. Clynne, USGS Volcano Science Center, Menlo Park; Dr. Eric Ritter, Bureau of Land Management, Redding; and George Thompson, California State University, Chico, Meriam Library Special Collections.

Additional thanks go to Beverly Jenkins, Sharlet Graham, Jim and Sherri Graham, Pamela Wilson, Lamar Bayles, Dan Foster, John A. Bedford, Conni McCoy, Donald Houghton, Larry Moulton, Patti Oakley McFarlin, Linton Brown, Andy and Jill Mark, Jan Larabee, Nancy Leek, Ron Womack, Gavin Marshall, Rich Lorenze of Jake Jackson Museum in Weaverville, and Arcadia editor Liz Gurley.

A big round of thanks goes to Kathy Sibert of the Red Bluff Round-Up Museum—she's a rodeo encyclopedia. I walked in there knowing nothing but walked out wanting to try my hand at an eight-second ride! Okay, maybe that's an exaggeration, but I do want some cowboy boots now.

I am grateful to the historians who have come before me, and the Tehama County Genealogical & Historical Society, especially Opal Thornton-Mendenhall, Gene Serr, Maurice Ness, Carol Mieske, and Alice Jackson. First, they adopted a Butte County person as a board member. Second, they gave me this project. Third, they have patiently been teaching me Tehama County history ever since.

Jervie Eastman deserves recognition for his famous Eastman's Studio postcards. Eastman's Studio began in Susanville in 1920. His postcards (over 13,000) span 70 years (1890–1960) of locations and events in Northern California. His panel truck (later station wagon) is often seen in his postcards.

Finally, I am deeply indebted to longtime Vina historian Frances Leininger for her guidance and especially her friendship. She took me under her wing as her "historian in training." From her, I have learned that ordinary people have the most extraordinary history.

# INTRODUCTION

*Long has it been a contention of mine that to man the thing next in importance to knowing God, and oneself, is to know one's country, one's state, one's county, one's community. To be conscious of the trials and tribulations; the successes and sacrifices; the pleasures and hardships; the tragedy, pathos and, sometimes, the comedy; the romantic past; the promising present and the brilliant future—to be aware of all these human elements, which have contributed to the birth and growth of a county, is calculated to deepen one's interest in, one's sympathy for, one's devotion to, one's defense of, and one's appreciation of the spot that one calls home.*

—Warren N. Woodson

Tehama County is largely agricultural, with river bottomlands, fertile plains, rolling hills, timbered mountains, and a river meandering through it. No one is sure how the word Tehama came about as a name for the county or even what it means. In a *Red Bluff News* account from July 24, 1903, early settler John Harrington recalled that pioneers and Indians told him *tehama* meant "shallow water." He recounted that in the early 1850s, a party of travelers arrived on the east bank of the river near the present town of Tehama. They hailed the Wintun Indians camped on the west side and indicated they wished to cross. A young Indian maiden beckoned the travelers to follow her to a shallow part of the river. She called to them, "te-ha-ma," and indicated they could safely cross there. People traveling in the summer found this a convenient crossing and began using the word "tehama" to describe it.

Native Californians are believed to have lived in Tehama County for at least 3,000 years. They developed into two main tribes—the Yana, east of the Sacramento River, and the Central Wintun, or Nomlaki, along the banks and in the hills west of the river. The Nomlaki Indians were never a large tribe. Prior to contact with whites, the Yana population numbered approximately 3,000 in four distinct groups: the Northern Yana, the Central Yana, the Southern Yana, and the Yahi.

Mountain man, trapper, and explorer Jedediah Strong Smith led the first party of Americans into the region in April 1828. His party of 18 men and 300 horses and mules stopped near what is now Red Bluff before heading west through the mountains to reach the coast. When beaver-trapping parties of Europeans came through the area in the 1830s, they brought diseases to which the Indians had no immunity. Westward expansion and the Gold Rush brought a tremendous surge of miners and settlers to the area in the 1840s–1850s, with further devastating effects to the Indians.

To address the escalating tensions, the 25,000-acre Nome Lackee Reservation was established in September 1854 north of Paskenta. It was the second of five military Indian reservations (along with Tejon, established in 1853; Fresno, 1854; Klamath River, 1855; and Mendocino, 1856) and two "farms" (Kings River, 1854; and Nome Cult, 1856) created in California by the federal government. These reservations were the first of their kind and became the model for future reservations in the nation. Previous policy had been to remove Native American tribes to large swaths of western territory beyond white settlements and government control—"wild" Indian country—with treaties granting them land ownership. In contrast, California Indians were concentrated onto small parcels of government land surrounded by white settlements to be supervised by government agents and watched over by military troops. These reservations had three purposes: to protect Indians and whites from each other, to teach Indians "the habits of civilization" through systematic labor and discipline, and to free up their ancestral lands for settlement. Indians were taught how to work and become self-sufficient in a white man's economy through woodcutting, sewing, ranching, and farming. However, the grain they raised was sold (although some was provided when food they collected ran out), and they were allowed no meat from the cattle they raised—all surplus and revenue supported the troops and agents assigned to the reservation.

Heavy pressure to free up the Nome Lackee Reservation land for settlers, and administrative mismanagement and corruption allowing for the indenturing, exploitation, and maltreatment of the Indians led to very vocal demands for its closure. In 1863, its residents endured a brutal march 65 miles west over the rugged mountains to the Nome Cult Farm at Covelo to live with the relocated remnants of other Northern California Indian tribes.

Spain claimed California as its territory. When Mexico achieved its independence from Spain in 1821, it took California with it. To encourage settlement in the interior, the Mexican government divided a great portion of California into very large grants, or *ranchos*, that were free for the asking. Americans and Europeans could obtain land grants by becoming Mexican citizens (or marrying a Mexican), converting to Catholicism, and occupying and improving the land (building structures and raising livestock). The petition had to include a *diseño*, or "design," which was a hastily sketched map showing the land grant's boundaries and features (such as streams, hills, and trees). Some grantees complied with all or some of the requirements, while others just squatted on land not claimed in land grants. In 1844, Mexican governor Manuel Micheltorena granted seven land grants: five within and two partially in the present boundaries of Tehama County. The five grants within the boundaries were Rancho de la Barranca Colorado (granted to Josiah Belden), Rancho de las Flores (William Chard), Rancho de los Berrendos (Job Dye), Rancho de los Saucos (Robert Thomes), and Rancho del Rio de los Molinos (Albert Toomes). The two partially in Tehama County were Rancho Capay (Josepha Soto) and Rancho Bosque (Peter Lassen). Rancho Capay was partly in Glenn County and Rancho Bosque was partly in Butte County.

In May 1846, the United States declared war on Mexico. In early June 1846, word spread that Mexican officials, concerned about the war and the influx of Americans into California, planned to expel illegal settlers north of Sutter's Fort (Sacramento). A group of settlers including William B. Ide met with US Army captain John C. Frémont before continuing to Sonoma, which was the northernmost reach of Mexican authority in California. At dawn on June 14, 1846, they captured Gen. Mariano Guadalupe Vallejo in his home. Believing they could not count on Frémont, some of the party wanted to abandon the town and retreat. Ide made a rousing speech declaring that he would die before retreating in disgrace. They rallied and named him the civil leader of the Bear Flag Revolt. The Bear Flag was raised on June 14, 1846. Ide issued a signed proclamation that declared California an independent republic. The Bear Flag Republic lasted 25 days. It was brought to an end when US Navy lieutenant Joseph Warren Revere (Paul Revere's grandson) arrived in Sonoma and raised the Stars and Stripes on July 9, 1846.

The war ended in February 1848. Nine days before Mexico ceded the territory of California to the United States with the signing of the Treaty of Guadalupe Hidalgo, gold was discovered at Sutter's Mill in Coloma. This ignited the Gold Rush and brought tens of thousands of people to California from all over the world. California was admitted to the Union on September 9, 1850.

In 1855, residents petitioned the California state legislature requesting that the County of Tehama be formed. Tehama County was created on April 9, 1856, from territory belonging to Shasta, Butte, and Colusa Counties. The first Board of Supervisors meeting was held May 17, 1856, at the county seat in the town of Tehama. The next year, the county seat was moved to Red Bluff, the head of navigation on the Sacramento River and the largest city north of Marysville.

# One

# Northeast

Cattle rustlers were rumored to hide in the riparian forests of the Bend Area, which later became plum, almond, and peach orchards. Because a young Spanish girl knew how to cook, the Queen of Spain rewarded her with a gift of land along the river, but not wanting it, she sold it. It became part of William Benitz's 22,000-acre Mexican land grant known as Rancho de Breisgau. When he never occupied the land, squatters settled there and eventually were able to buy their homesteads from the US government for 62.5¢ per acre. Just to the south of the old land grant, Andrew Jelly bought land and built a road and river ferry there, which operated for almost 100 years.

Hollywood actor Glenn Ford became a spokesperson for Lake California, which was the dream of Dr. Joseph L. Price (1911–1968), who envisioned a community surrounding a 225-acre man-made lake. Dr. Price also developed a variety of almond tree, which he patented as the Price Almond. (Franciscan padres were the first to bring almond trees to California in the 1700s; almonds were grown commercially in the 1860s.)

In the foothills are the old stage stops of Dales Station, named for Creath and Anna Dale, who moved there from the mines of Shasta County in 1908; and Paynes Creek, where Edna "Grovie" Apple was a stage driver as tough and fearless as any man—she once crossed a slough where the water ran over the horses' backs.

On January 8, 1856, borax was first discovered in California (and North America) at Lick Springs by Dr. John Veatch (later renamed and site of the famous Tuscan Springs Resort). Higher in the mountains is Mineral. Snow skiing was introduced to the area in 1932 when Husky Beresford built a ski run and added lights for nighttime skiing, perhaps creating the first lighted ski run in the state. Morgan Springs was developed as a hot springs resort and later sold to become a private ranch where Pres. Herbert Hoover enjoyed fly fishing in Mill Creek.

Timber supplied lumber for mills in the Lyonsville area, and the boards were floated to the valley by flume. In Manton, the Forward brothers (Frank and Alfred) built and operated mills in 1893 and 1906 until they were destroyed by fire on March 26, 1958. Today, the only "teepee" burner left standing in Tehama County is at their old mill site, which is a registered E Clampus Vitus historical site.

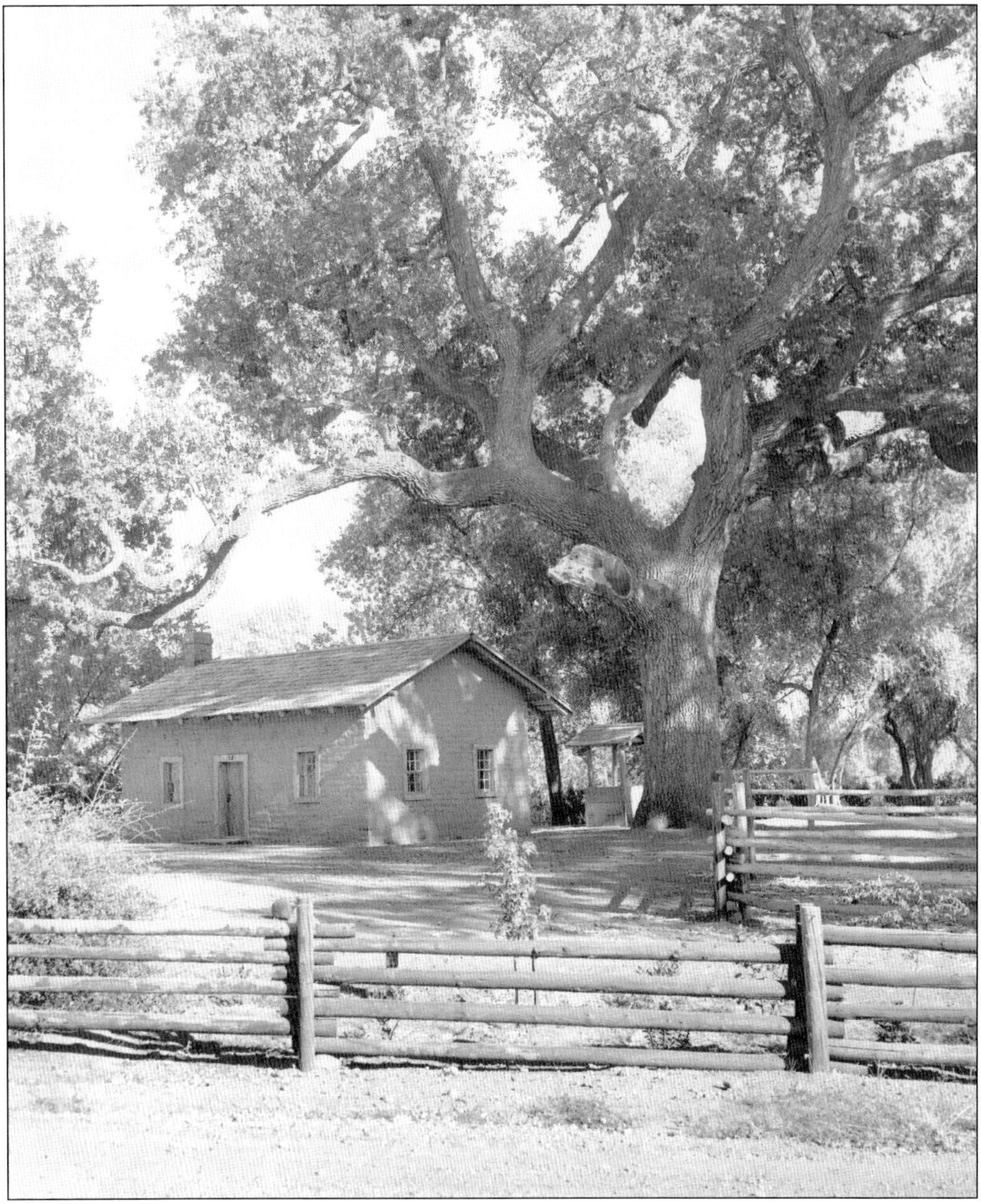

This adobe is part of the William B. Ide Adobe State Historic Park, although Ide never lived in it (he lived farther downriver). It was built in 1852 by Abraham Dibble. It was first mistakenly called Ide's Adobe by K.V. Bumpass. Judge Lewis continued the error in his 1880 *History of Tehama County*. It changed ownership at least 20 times before the State of California acquired the site in 1951, restored the adobe, and dedicated it as a park honoring Ide, an early pioneer and the only president of the short-lived Bear Flag Republic (which lasted from June 14 to July 9, 1846). Ide later settled in Monroeville (at that time, the seat of Colusa County), where he died of smallpox in 1852. Ide was virtually its one-man everything. A story recounts that he acted as prosecutor, defense attorney, and judge in the trial of a horse thief (found guilty). In 2014, several large limbs of the huge 350-plus-year-old Valley Oak that shaded the adobe fell and caused significant damage to it and nearby buildings. (Tehama County Library collection.)

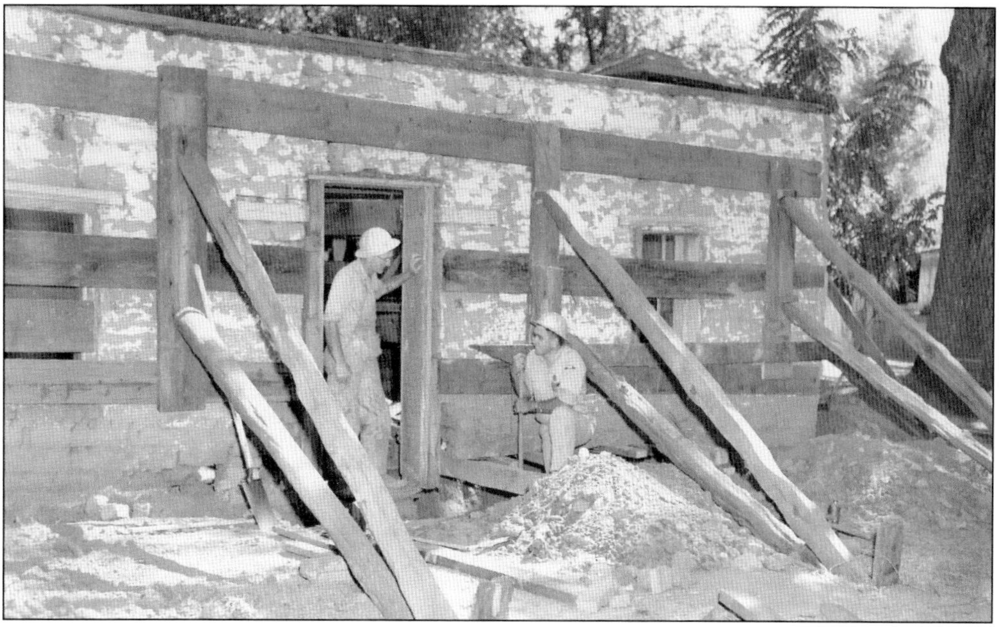

Archaeologists from California State University, San Francisco, aided in the restoration of the adobe at the William B. Ide Adobe State Historic Park. Adobe is mud mixed with straw, shaped, and dried in the sun to form large bricks that help dwellings stay cool in summer and warm in winter. This adobe departed from the typical Californio adobe by featuring Anglo innovations such as a fireplace, chimney, and plank floors. (Tehama County Library Collection.)

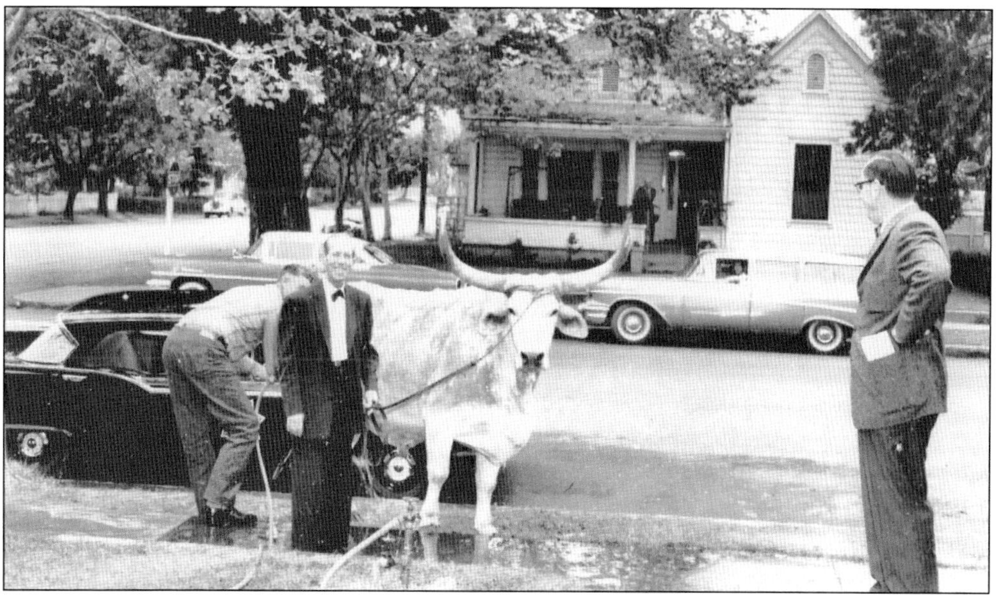

The dedication ceremony for the park was held April 30 to May 1, 1960. It began with a parade in Red Bluff and formal dedication ceremonies at the site. Preparing for the dedication on the corner of Oak and Jefferson Streets are, from left to right, Earl Davies, Fourth District supervisor (he rode the steer); E.C. Pryor, Second District supervisor; and Curtis E. Wetter, superior court judge for the County of Tehama. A barbecue attended by 4,000 people was held at the fairgrounds. (Maurice Ness collection.)

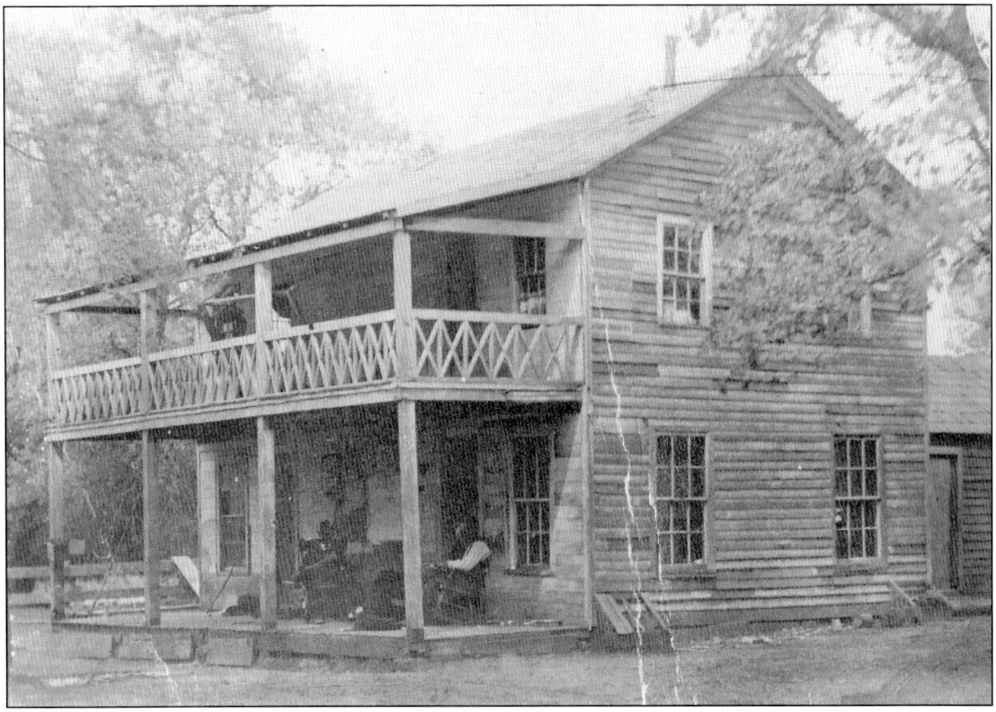

Dales Station was halfway between Manton and Red Bluff. In 1863, William and Mary DeHaven offered hot meals and a place to stay for teamsters and travelers on the Tehama County Wagon Road. Creath and Anna Dale arrived there in 1908. In 1936, Creath imported Louisiana bullfrogs with dreams of making a fortune on frog legs, but a flood in 1937 washed the frogs and his dreams away. (Tehama County Library collection.)

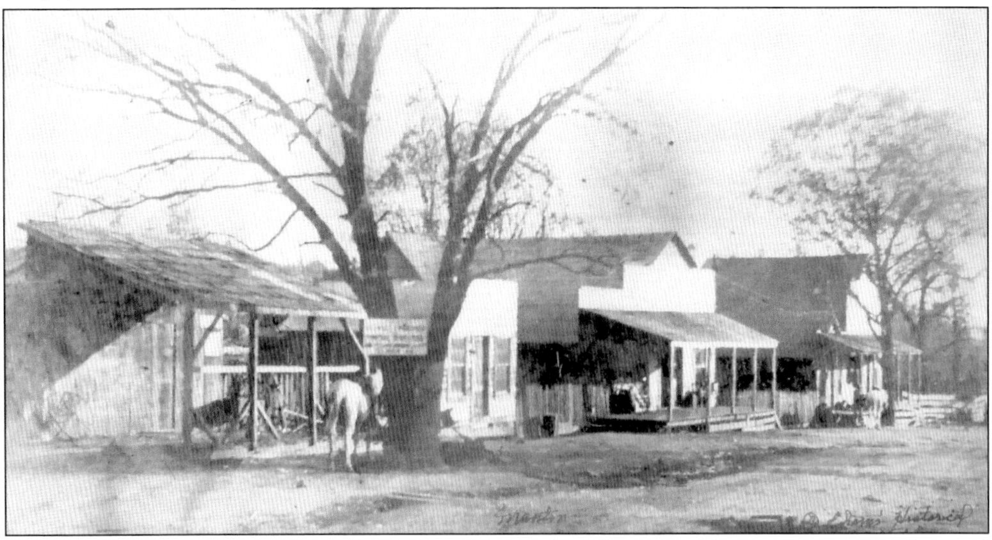

It is uncertain how Manton got its name. One story is that the name of Man's Town was submitted to postal authorities who changed it to Manton in 1889. Another is that an early settler, J.M. Meeder, named it after his hometown of Manton, Rhode Island. The area attracted settlers in the 1850s with its productive soil, virgin timber, and creeks supplying water for irrigation and hydropower. (Pamela Wilson/Manton Store collection.)

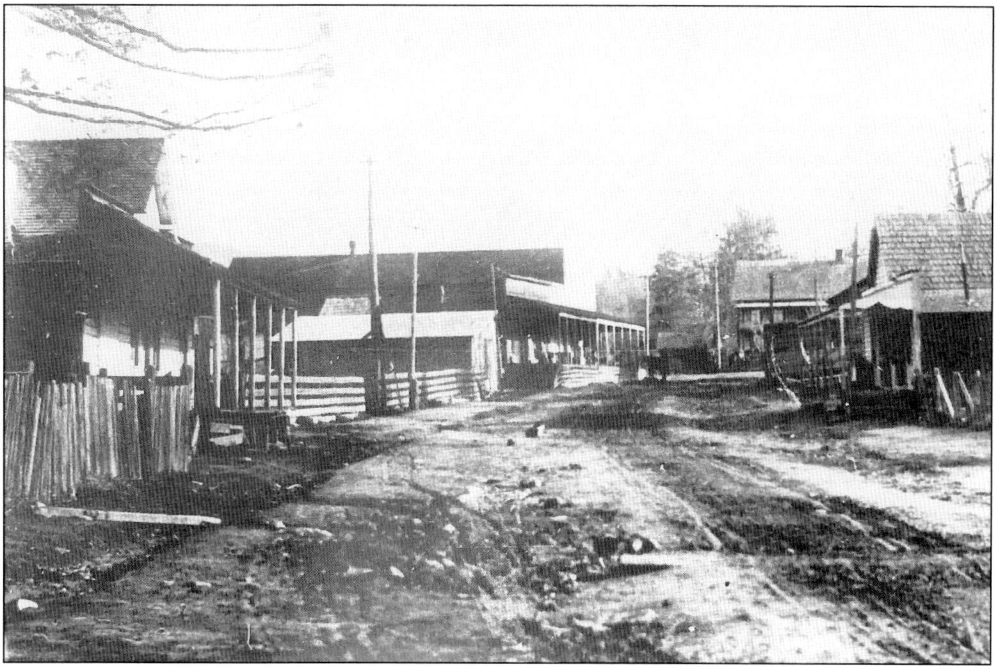

This c. 1900 view looks east along the Red Bluff–Manton Road. On the left, from front to back, is a saloon, blacksmith shop, store, and the Manton Hotel. Marion McGeehee was a Civil War veteran who sported seven-and-a-half-foot-long whiskers that he kept braided. He would ride his horse, Peacock, into town for provisions ("chawin' tobaccee") then make a beeline to the saloons. Once out of money, he would ride home or sleep it off in a nearby field. (Tehama County Library collection.)

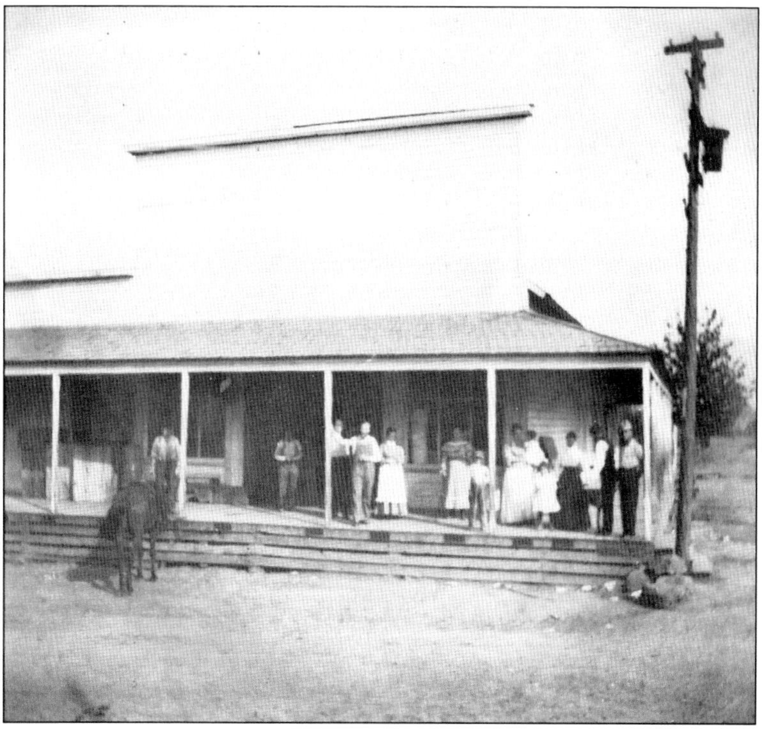

Manton's first store was built in the 1880s. It was later enlarged and established as the post office in 1889. The Manton General Store was built in 1904 by James L. Barham (at center with hand on post). Next door to it were two saloons, and across the street was the Manton Hotel, jail, and Woodmen of the World Hall, which was later dynamited by unknown persons. (Tehama County Library collection.)

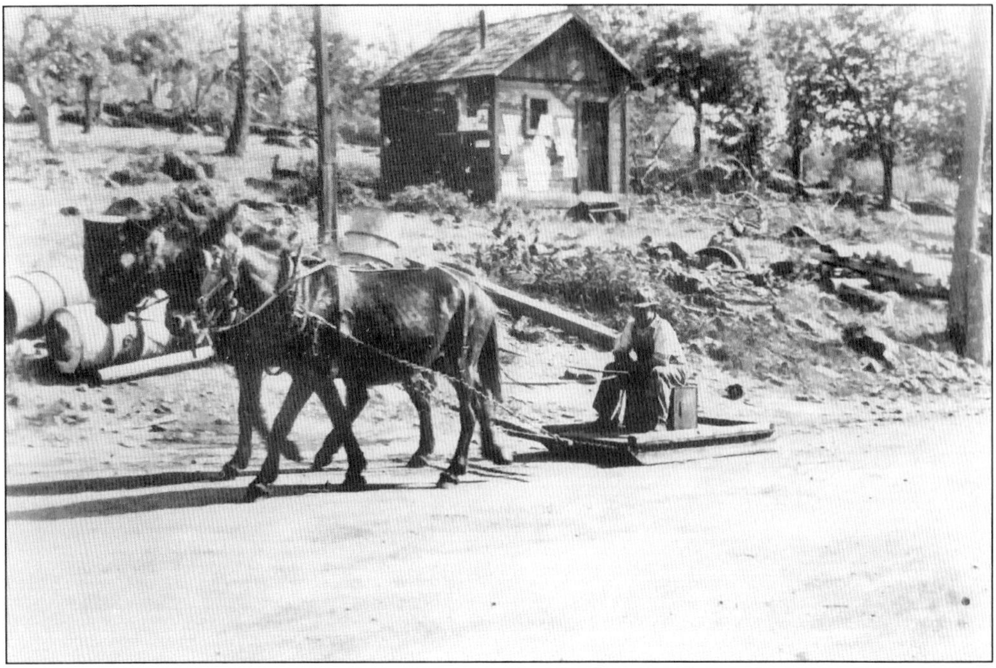

The Manton jail was built about 1902 from two-foot-by-four-foot fir. Its first inmate was a man jailed for stealing turkeys, Hugh Robertson. After that, it was called Robertson's Fort for a time. It was also used to store black powder. Here, Henry Myer is passing the jail on a sled pulled by mules around 1925. (Pamela Wilson/Manton Store collection.)

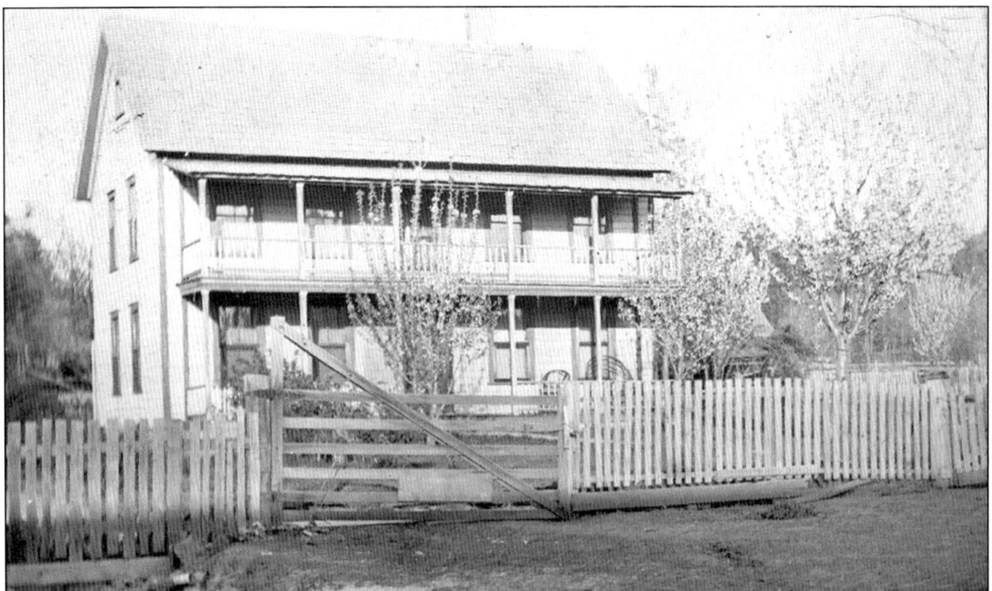

The Manton Hotel, pictured in 1890, sat at the wye east of the Manton Store. It was known for its excellent cuisine and comfortable accommodations. It had several different owners over the years. In the 1950s, Pacific Gas & Electric bought the property for its water rights and tore the building down. (Tehama County Library collection.)

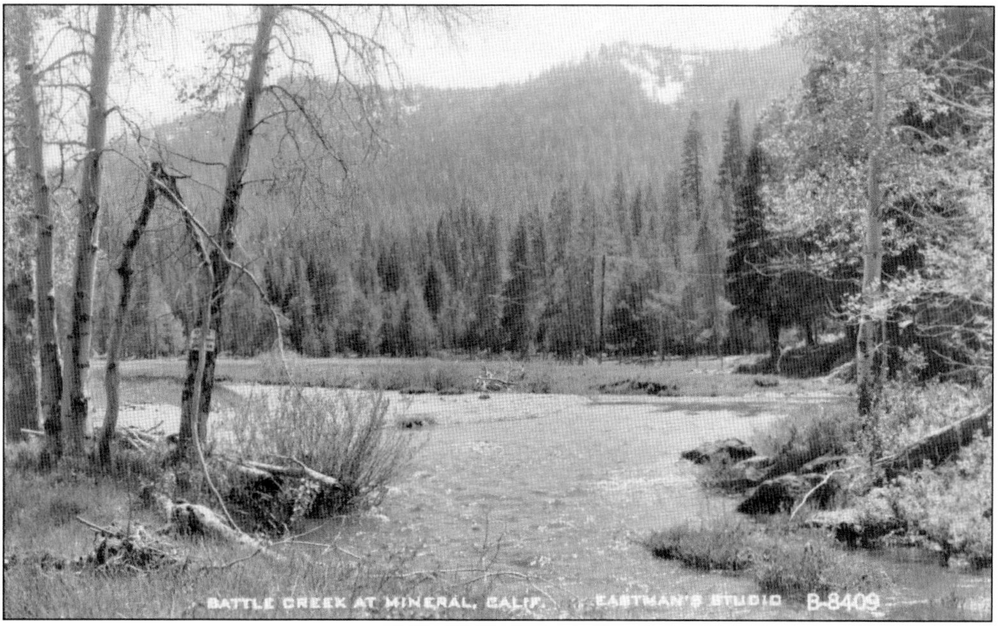


The first settlers in the Battle Creek Meadows area were G.W. Grayson and brothers Hi and C.B. Rawson, who grazed sheep there in 1860. The Rawsons gained title to the area in 1875 under the Swamp and Overflow Act, which required a perimeter survey by boat. The brothers reportedly put a boat on a wagon and drove the wagon around the meadows. (Tehama County Library collection.)

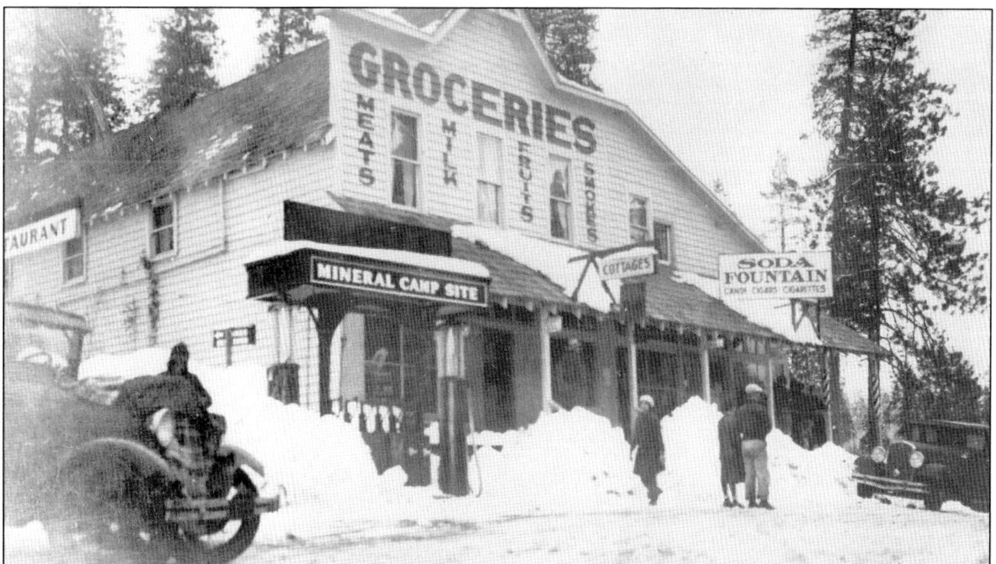


Mineral received its name when the Mineral Springs post office was moved from Morgan Springs and the name shortened to Mineral. Former names for Mineral have included Rawson's, Hampton's, and Mineral Camp Site. Bert Hampton built the store before 1920. It was torn down and replaced in 1934 by the Mineral Lodge. Hampton's sons Elbert and Olen guided tourists to nearby Lassen Peak. (Tehama County Library collection.)

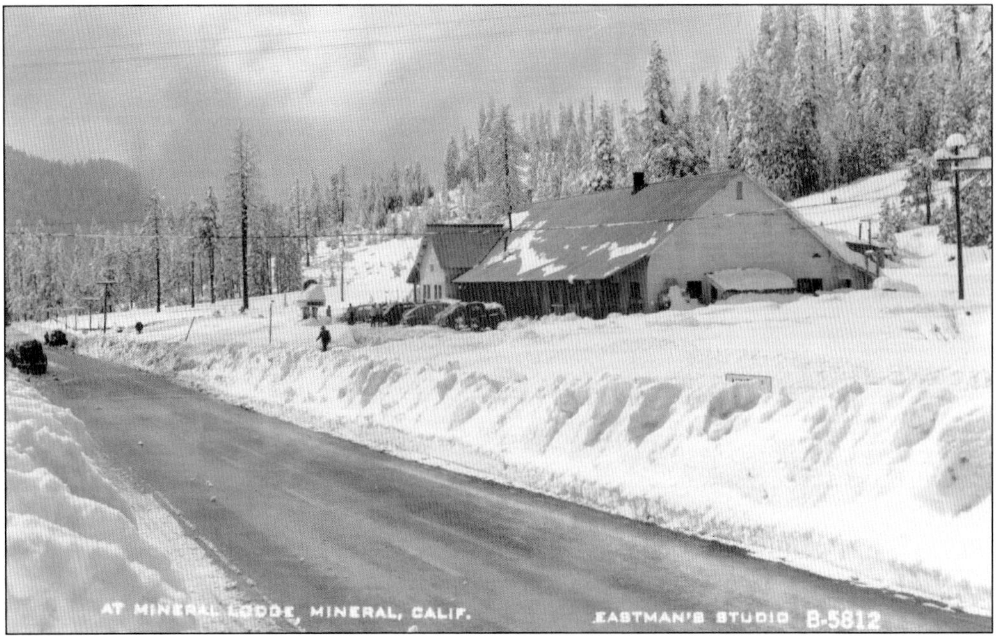


The second Mineral Lodge was built by Husky Beresford in 1940 after the first one burned down in 1939. To raise money to rebuild it, he cut trees from behind the lodge and sold the lumber. This lodge burned down in 1949 and was replaced by the current concrete block lodge later that same year. (Dan Bayles collection.)

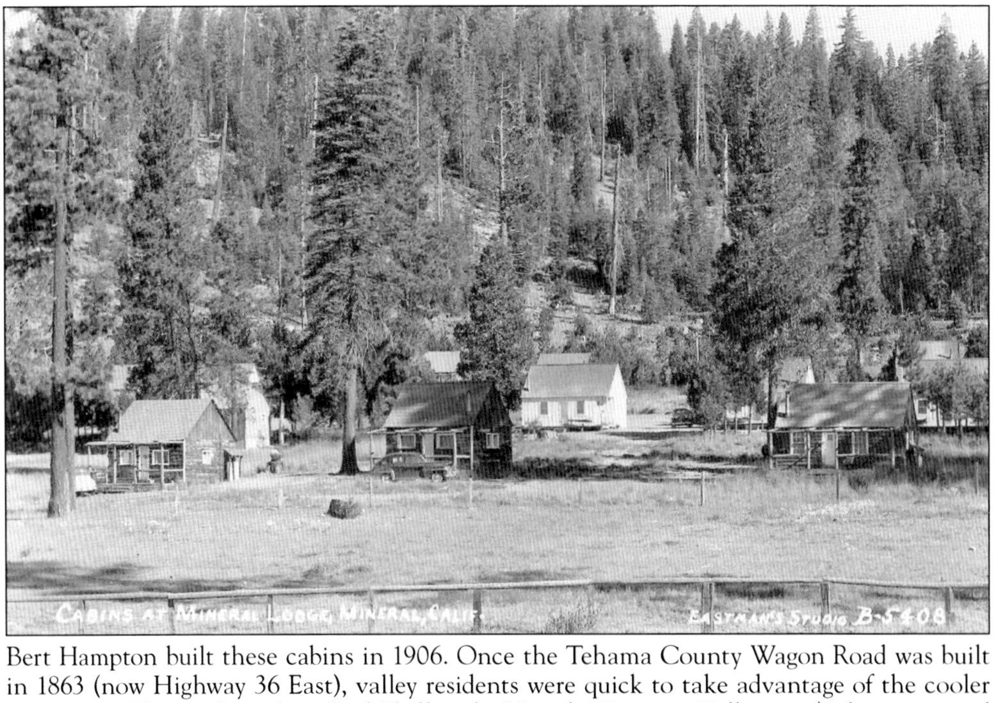


Bert Hampton built these cabins in 1906. Once the Tehama County Wagon Road was built in 1863 (now Highway 36 East), valley residents were quick to take advantage of the cooler mountains. The road ran from Red Bluff to the Nevada Territory. Tolls were $1 for a man and horse, $10 for an eight-horse team, 18¢ per head of cattle, and 10¢ per head of hogs and sheep. (Tehama County Library collection.)

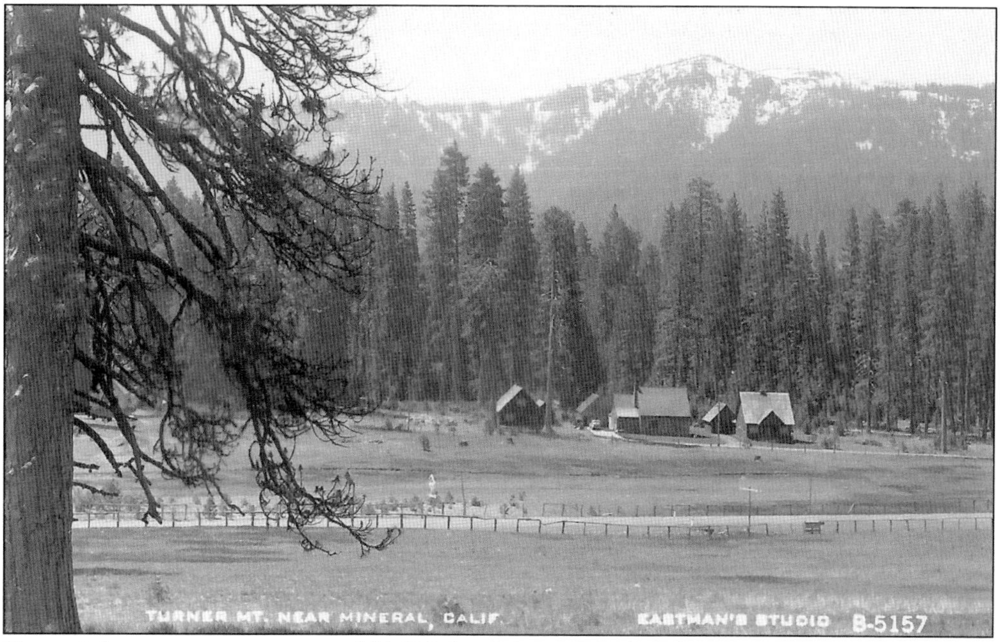


Turner Mountain is a remnant of 14,000-foot Mount Maidu. This stratovolcano stood where Mineral now sits (1.4 to 2.4 million years ago). Southeast loomed Mount Yana (2.4 to 3.4 million years ago), one source for the Tuscan Formation (3- to 4-million-year-old volcanic lahars or mudflows). The numerous rocks that dot the landscape in the eastern foothills are from these mudflows, not from Hollywood-style eruptions of Lassen Peak or Mount Tehama. (Tehama County Library collection.)

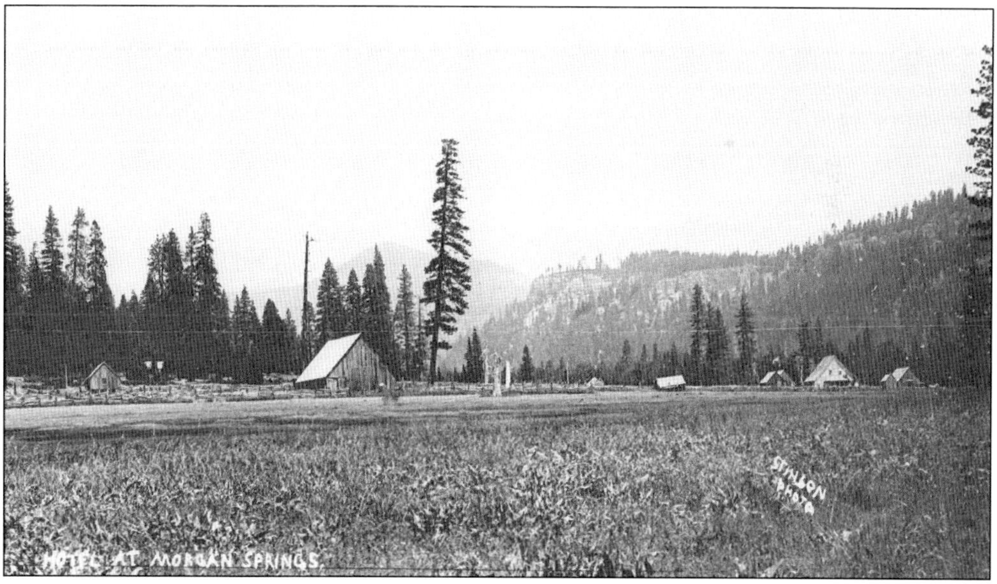


Morgan Springs was a small community a mile west of present-day Childs Meadow Resort. In 1865, John Morgan built the Mountain Home Hotel to promote the benefits of the hot springs there. In 1926, Richard W. Hanna of Standard Oil bought the property and made it into a family retreat. His friend Pres. Herbert Hoover loved to fly fish in nearby Mill Creek. (Tehama County Library collection.)

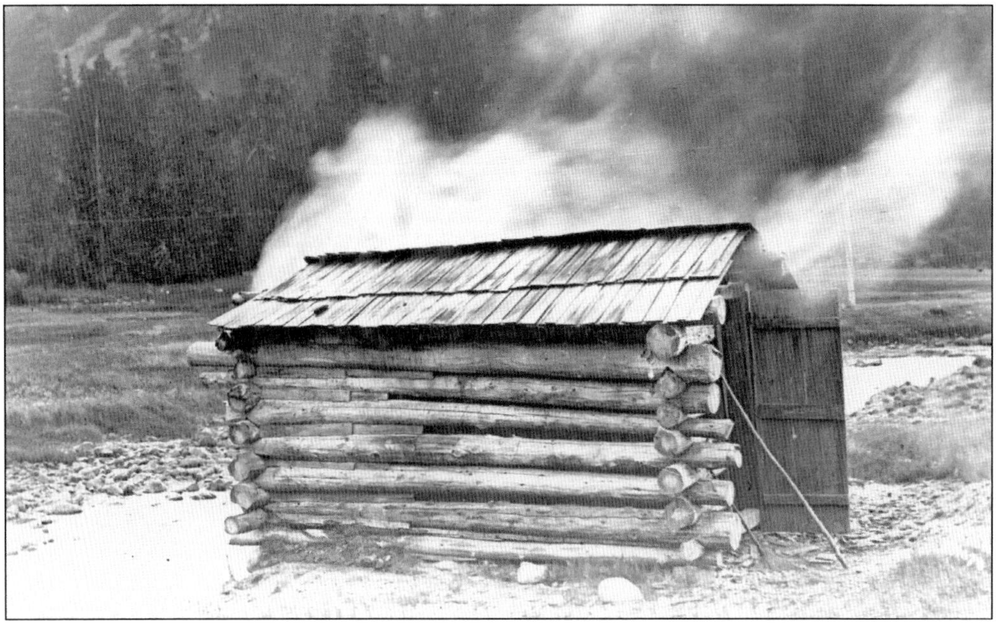

Pictured is a steam bath at Morgan Springs, named for Richard Morgan, who settled the area in the 1850s. John Morgan and his family joined Richard after crossing the plains in 1854 by wagon. They left Missouri in March and arrived at Morgan Springs in November with three wagons, one ox-team, two horse teams, and 15¢ in their pockets. (Tehama County Library collection.)

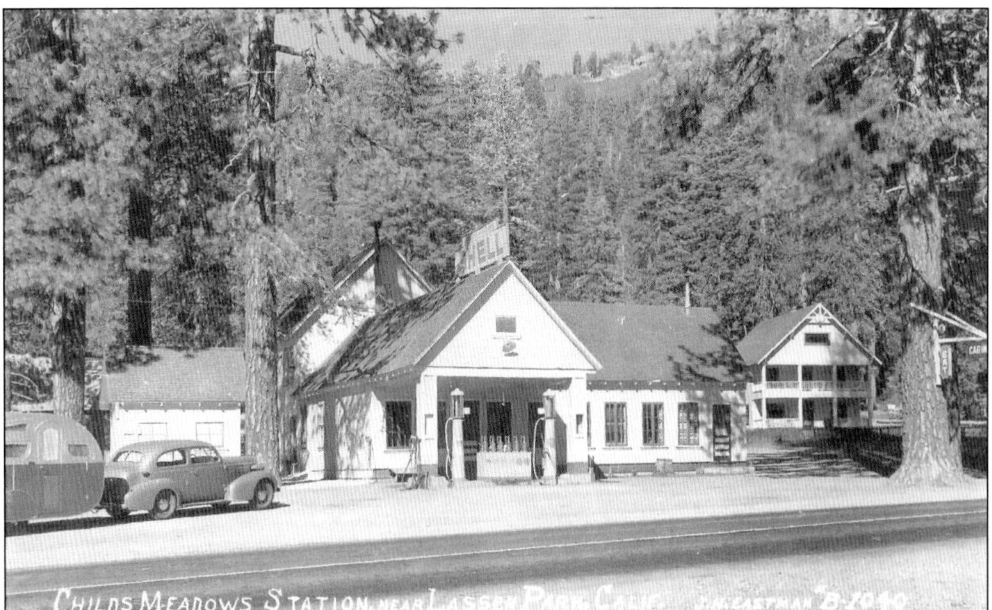


Childs Meadow is located along the old Tehama County Wagon Road. Once known as Tyler Meadows, Frank and Olive (Nanney) Childs made the meadow their summer cattle-grazing ranch in 1900. It was a snowbound homestead each winter until 1930, when the state started plowing the road to make it an all-year highway. (Tehama County Library collection.)

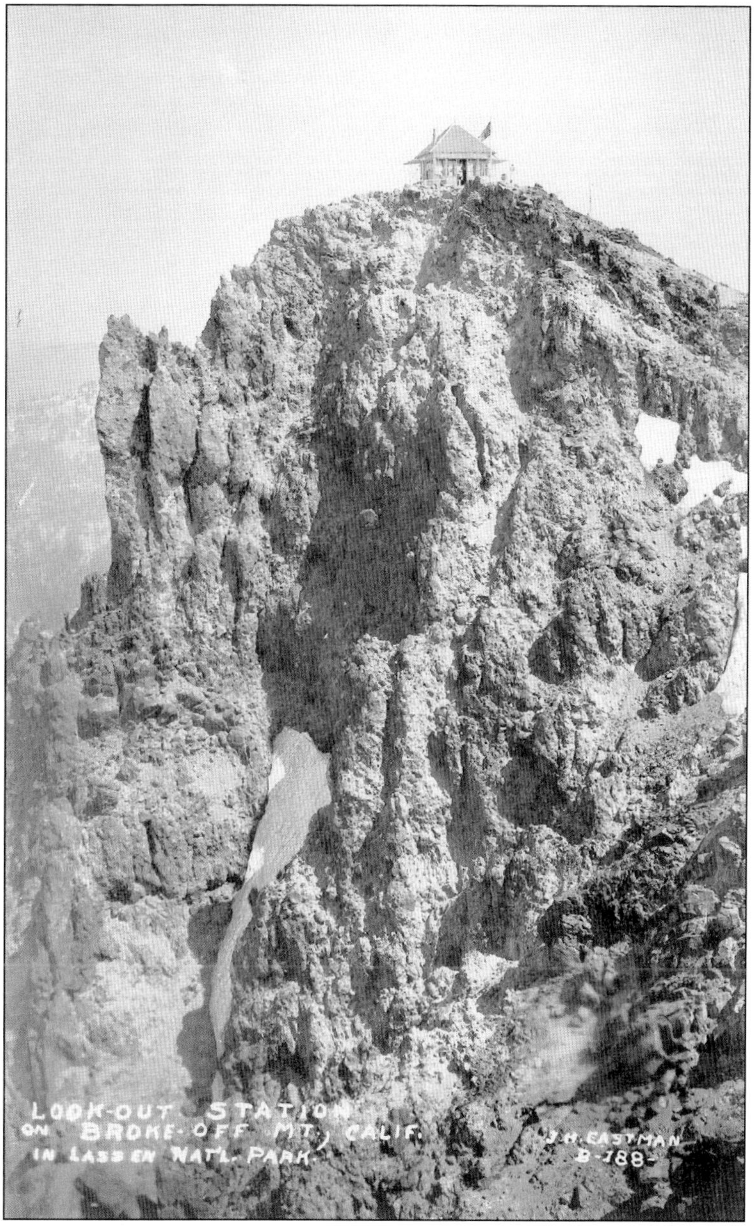


Brokeoff Mountain is the highest point in Tehama County at 9,235 feet. It is located in Lassen Volcanic National Park and is a remnant of ancient Mount Tehama (active 550,000 years ago), which towered 11,500 feet before becoming inactive and eroding away. Two Southern Pacific railroad carpenters who were temporarily laid off constructed this lookout in 1921. There were three fire lookouts in the area in 1923: Turner Mountain, Brokeoff Mountain, and Prospect Peak. There had been one on Lassen Peak, but volcanic eruptions in 1914–1915 destroyed it. The east face of Brokeoff is a cliff 1,000 feet high, the highest in Lassen Park that can be climbed, though it is not advised. But that did not stop 19-year-old Robert Stryker, who manned this lookout and climbed the cliff one August day in 1923: "I took my rope and went over the cliff this afternoon. Roped the noose over a boulder, swung down, flipped the rope off, hitched it to another, and went on down. Coming back, I cast up at the same boulder until I could come on back." (Author's collection.)

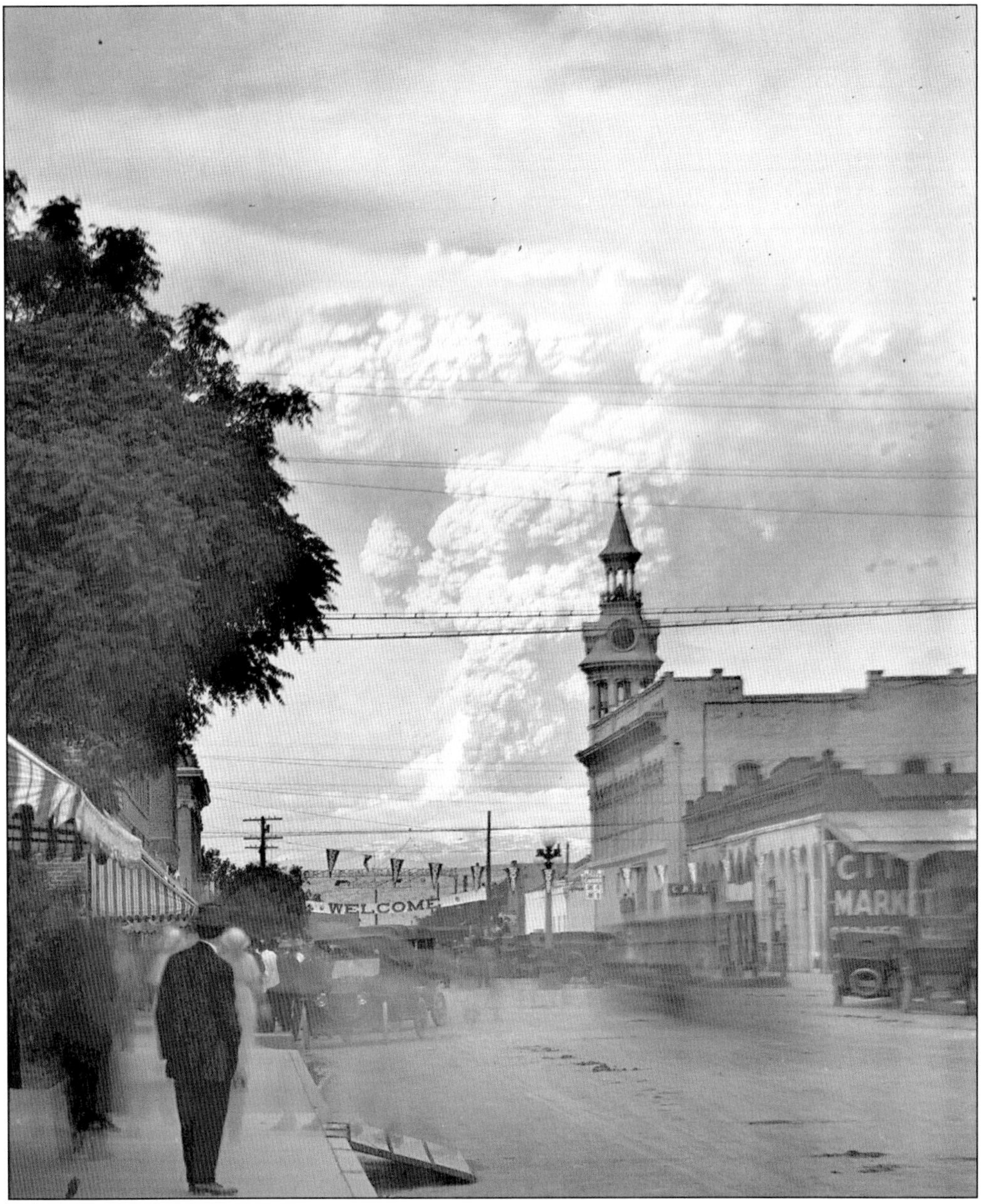


The great 1915 blast of Lassen Peak on Saturday, May 22, is pictured here as seen from Walnut Street in Red Bluff 37 miles away. The "Welcome" sign over the street was for the celebrations being held when Main Street was finally paved. The front page of the *Red Bluff Daily News* on May 23, 1915, proclaimed, "The column of smoke, dust, and debris rose to a height estimated at between 30,000 and 40,000 feet. The eruption was visible in Sacramento and seen there by thousands." The column began drifting to the east. At Eagle Lake, 50 miles east, John Spalding was rowing his boat when the skies suddenly darkened and he was showered with a fine sprinkling of volcanic ash that became so dense he could not see. An engineer on a Western Pacific freight train approaching Winnemucca, Nevada, 200 miles east, noticed a hazy reflection in his locomotive's headlight. By the time the train reached Gerlach, Nevada, 100 miles from Lassen, visibility was reduced to 50 feet. Ash drifted as far as Elko, Nevada, 445 miles to the east. (National Park Service collection.)

On June 14, 1914, while climbing Lassen Peak, Lance Graham and some friends were caught in an eruption. He was struck by a rock and badly wounded. His companions tried dragging their unconscious and bleeding friend to safety. Deciding he was mortally wounded, they left him since his "body" was slowing their retreat. Other hikers brought him down. Graham's collarbone and several ribs were broken, and he suffered serious internal injuries along with a deep gash in his shoulder. Graham recounted, "We went up there to see what it was doing. I wasn't scared a bit: I just thought we were all killed. I'll never climb that peak again." (Graham family collection.)

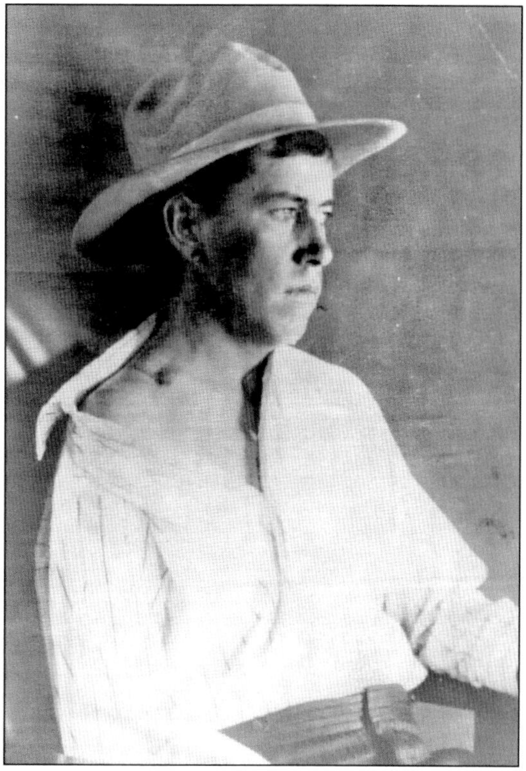

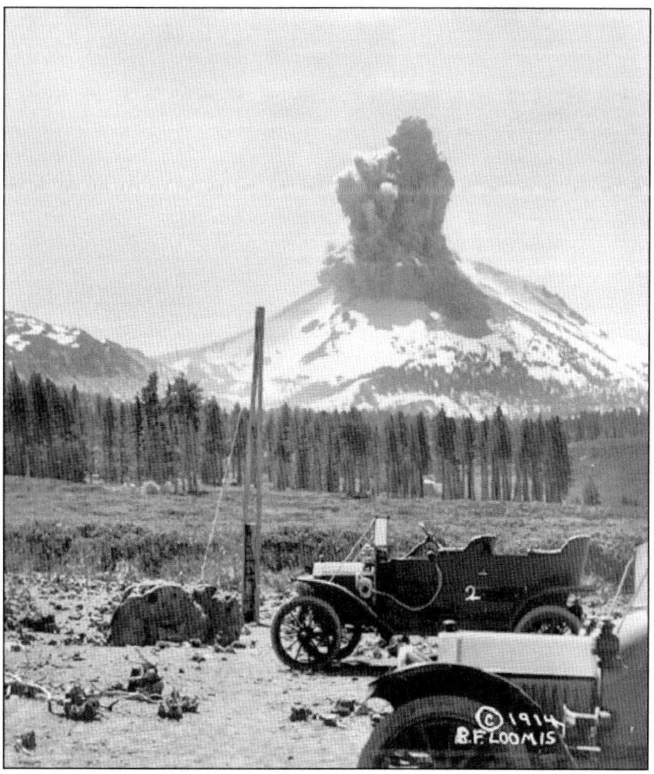


This is the beginning of the eruption Lance Graham and his friends were caught in while on the summit. Photographer B.F. Loomis was 10 miles away and took this picture of the eruption that almost killed Graham. Loomis described the sight as "fearfully grand." (National Park Service collection.)

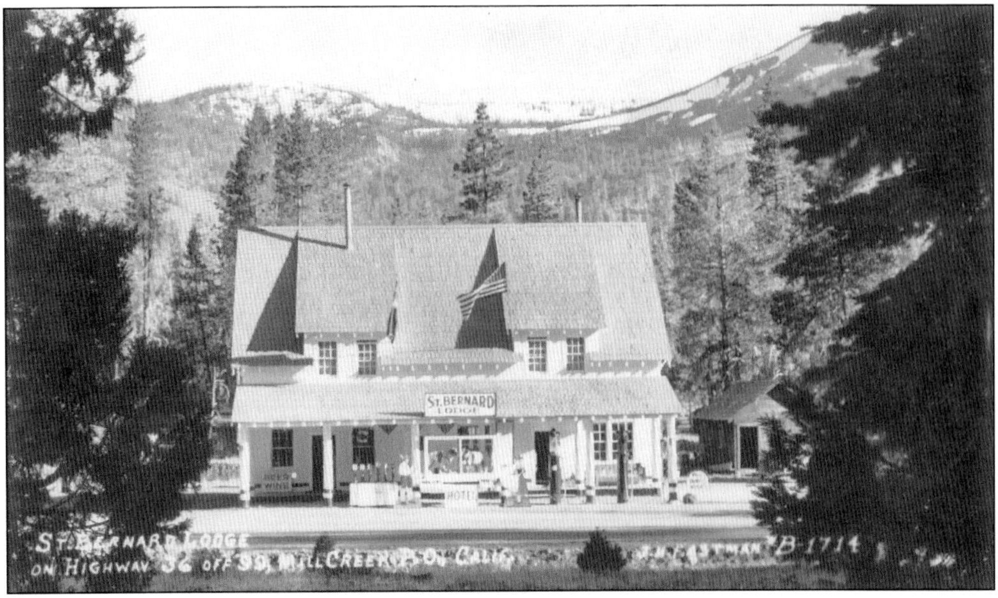


Carl Fink, a German immigrant, came to Tehama County and fell in love with the Mill Creek area. He bought land and built the Deer Creek Coffee Shop. His brother Mike joined him years later. Cabins were built, and the coffee shop became the Deer Creek Lodge. The brothers had a falling out. Mike bought out Carl's interest, added a second story, and renamed it the St. Bernard Lodge, because he loved the dog breed so much. (Tehama County Library collection.)

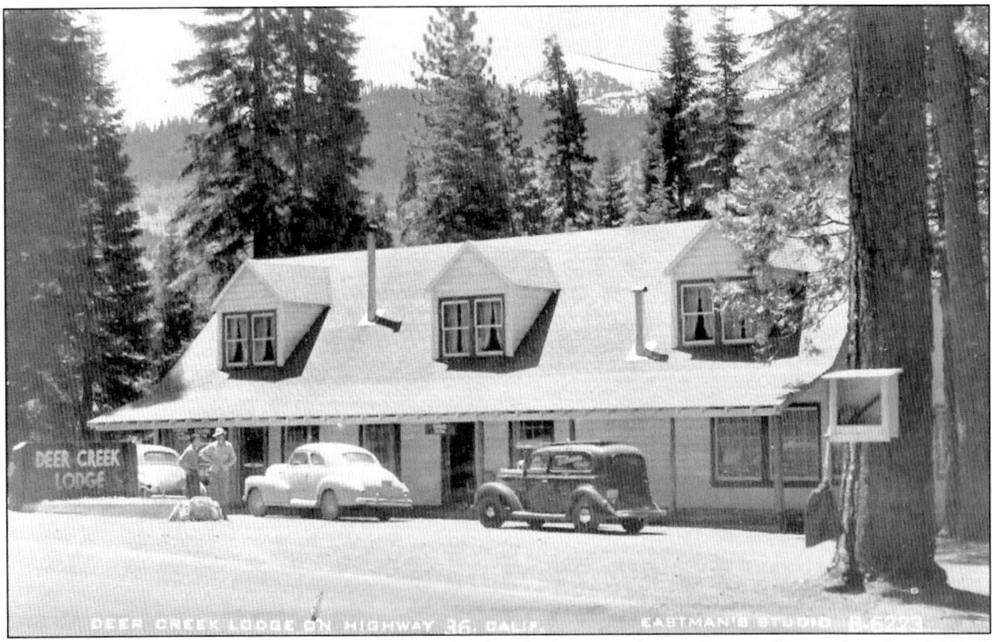


In the 1930s, another brother, Ernest Fink, built a lodge just down the road from brother Mike's that he called the Deer Creek Lodge after the original one Carl Fink had built. (Tehama County Library collection.)

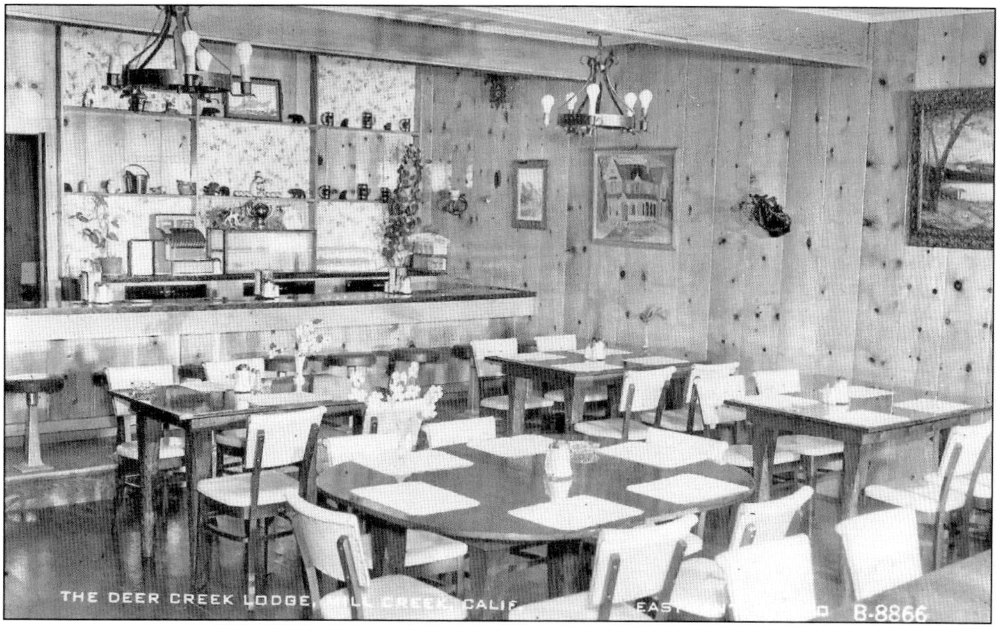


Pictured here are the dining area (above) and the bar (below) of the Deer Creek Lodge. In 1952, sister Ada joined Ernest Fink to be his cook. Ernest would get upset with her because she prepared food for only so many people and would get overwhelmed when more people showed up, which happened when Mike Fink at the St. Bernard Lodge got upset with someone, kicked out his customers, and locked the doors. Ada quit and built the Black Forest Lodge down the road from the St. Bernard. Because of the bickering and falling outs, none of the siblings would set foot inside the others' lodges. Meanwhile, the first brother, Carl Fink, began building fish hatcheries. The Mt. Lassen Trout Farm became the second-largest private producer of trout eggs in the United States in the 1950s. (Both, Tehama County Library collection.)

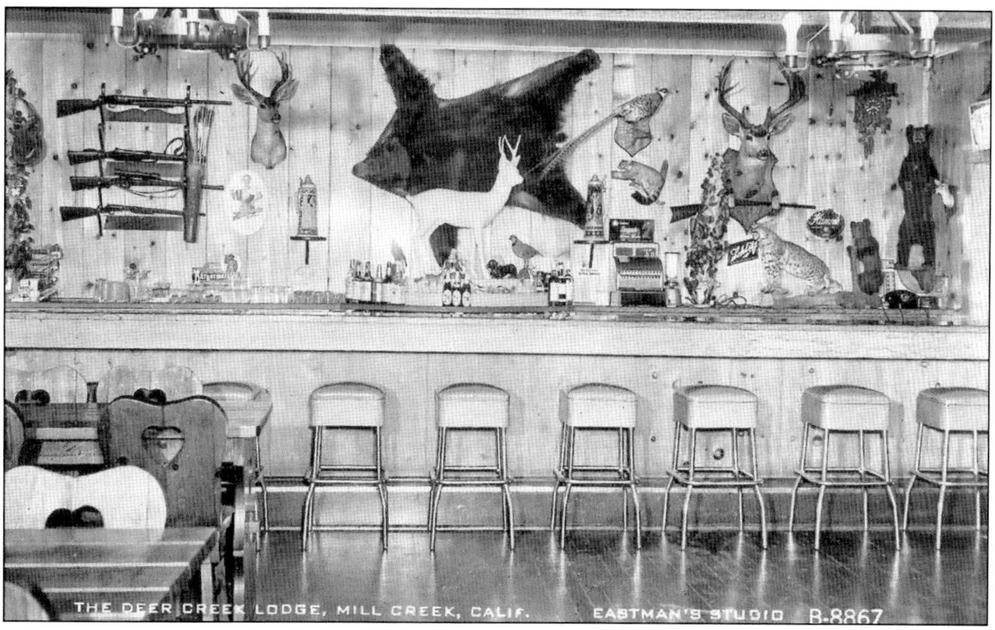

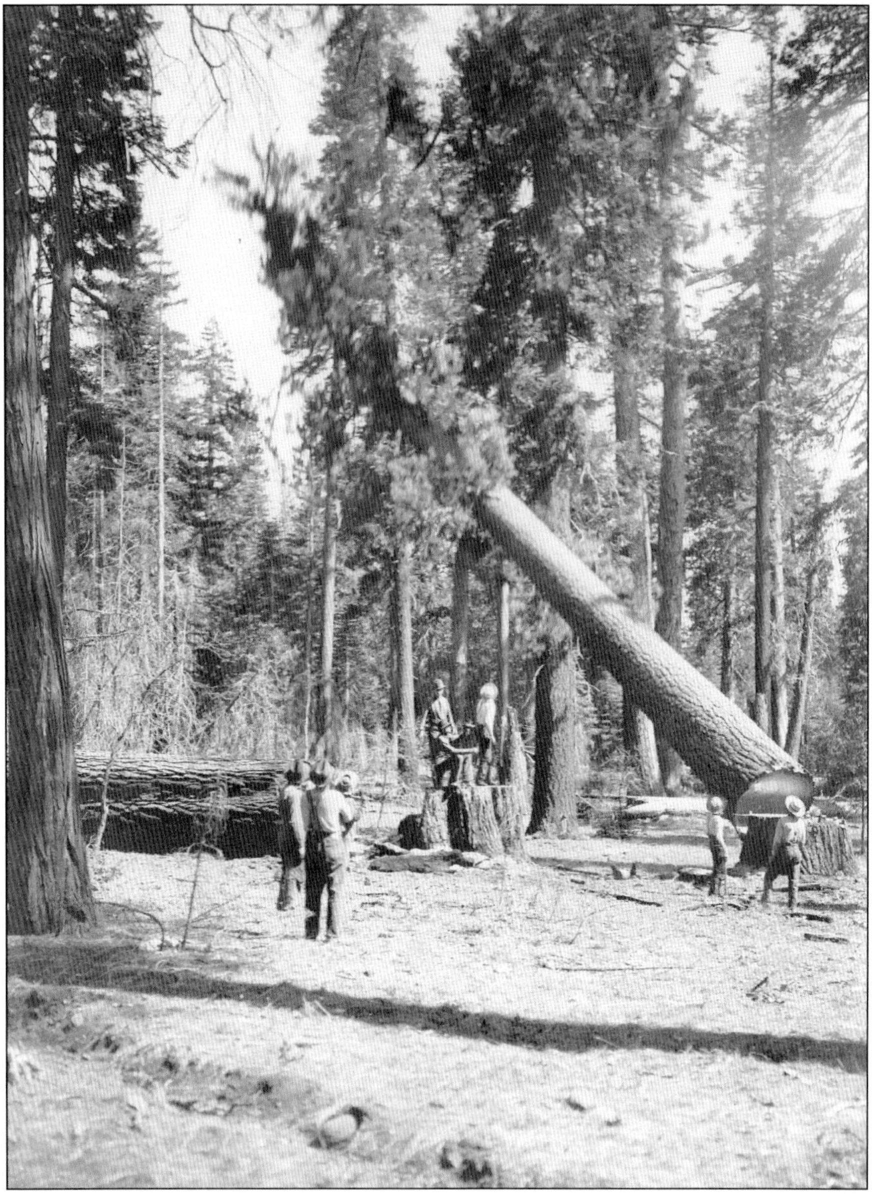

From the first small mills operated by a few individuals to the corporations that eventually moved in, lumber has been a major industry in Tehama County. The gold mines in California and Idaho and the North's need for turpentine and resin during the Civil War created tremendous growth in the industry. Transporting the lumber from the mountains was accomplished with the building of V-shaped wooden flumes, which helped keep lumber from jamming (water pressure "lifted" the boards so they floated smoothly). Built in 1871–1873, the Empire Flume ran from Lyonsville to mills by the Sacramento River 35 miles away until 1914. It varied from ground level to as high as 96 feet. Charles F. Ellsworth designed and built this flume, which was called "Ellsworth's Folly." Expensive to build ($1,000 to $2,000 per mile), flumes reduced transportation costs—80¢ per thousand feet of lumber versus $10 per thousand feet by wagon. Ellsworth never saw the success of his flume. While on an inspection, he fell 20 feet and died of his injuries. (Tehama County Library collection.)

Lumberjacks saw a sugar pine into sections near Lyonsville around 1896. Pitch is running down the cut surface of the tree. Trees would be felled by hand, then sectioned into various lengths with a crosscut saw. Steam-powered chain saws were experimented with in the 1890s, but they were awkward and hard to handle. The first gas-powered chainsaws became available in the 1930s. (Tehama County Library collection.)

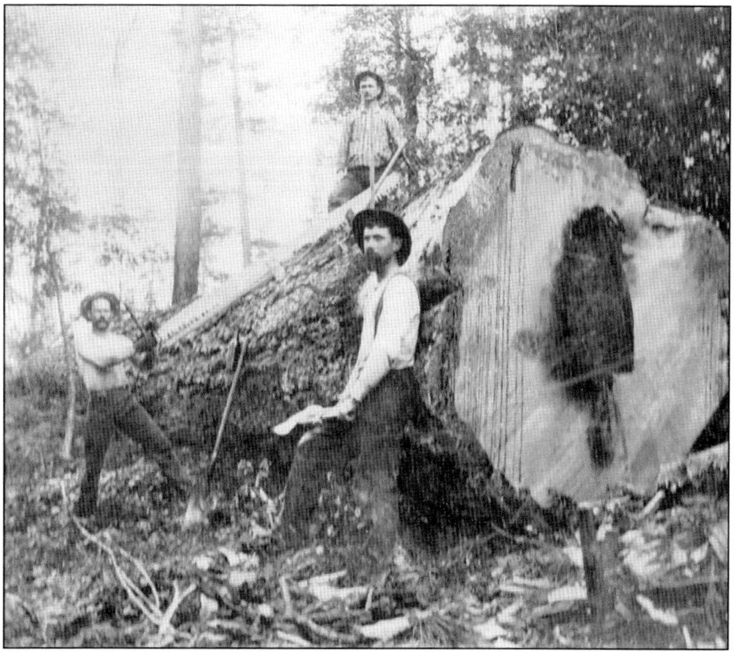

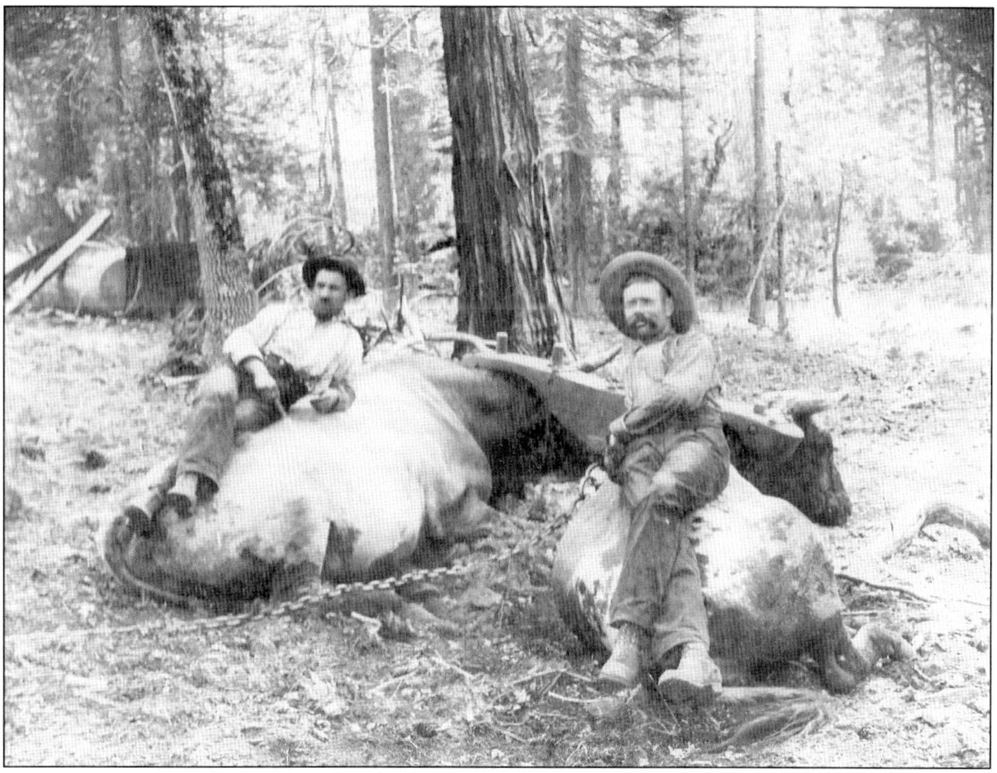

Not all lumbering occurred in the eastern forests of the county. The western mountains were also harvested for lumber. As early as 1858, ranchers were hauling lumber using oxen, horses, and mules until the 1920s, when they started using trucks with solid rubber tires. Oxen were usually used to pull logs to the mill using tramways, chutes, or wagons. (Tehama County Library collection.)

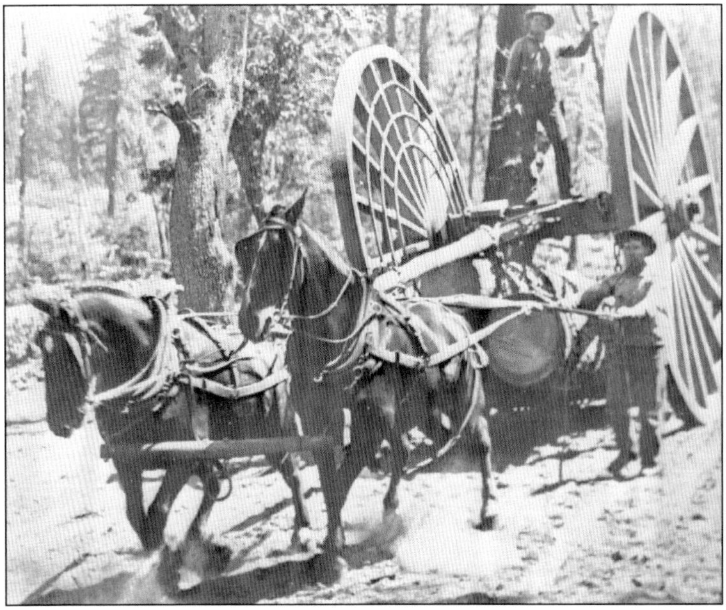

Michigan Logging Wheels ("Big Wheels") were invented in 1875 by Silas Overpak. They were skidders designed to carry logs up to 100 feet in length, several at a time. The load was carried under the axle, which made it easier on horses and oxen. These wheels were used where land was flat. Big Wheels did not work well in hilly areas because they did not have brakes. Billy Glines is standing on the axle and Cal Chase is driving this team around 1906. (Dan Bayles collection.)

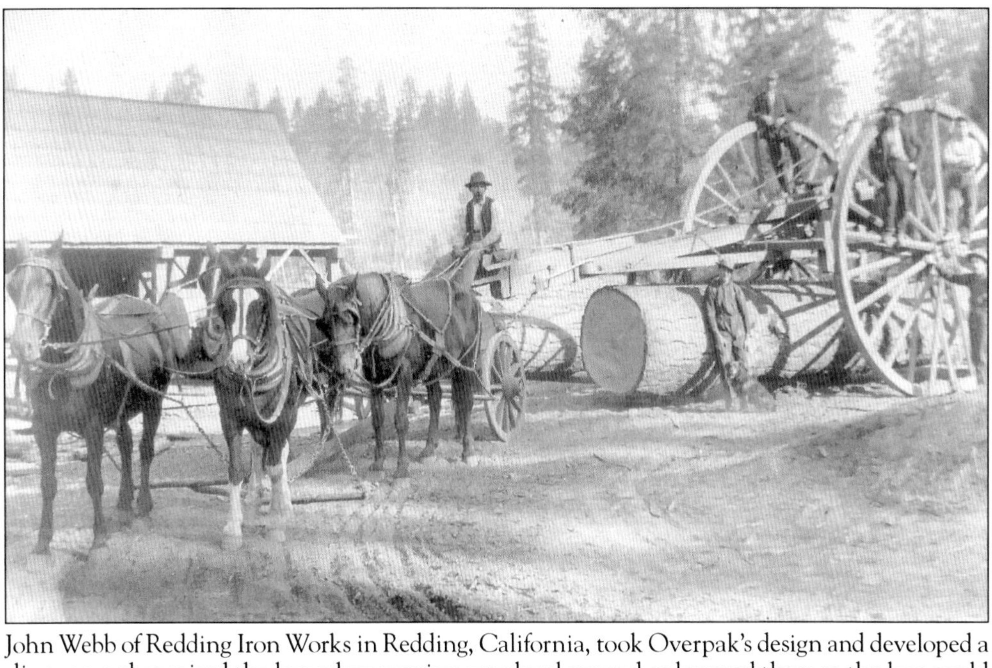

John Webb of Redding Iron Works in Redding, California, took Overpak's design and developed a slip tongue that raised the logs when moving over level ground or lowered them so the logs could be used as brakes when going down a slope, which allowed these wheels to be used in more hilly areas. They became known as Redding High Wheels. (Dan Bayles collection.)

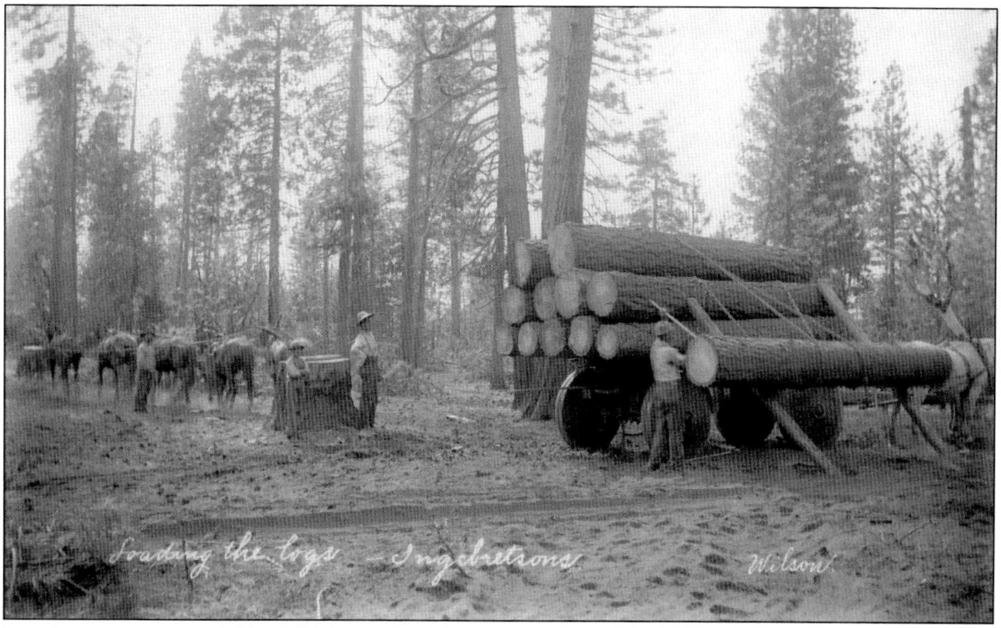


Lumber cut near a mill could be easily dragged to it. But lumber cut farther away had to be transported by wagons or, sometimes, small logging trains. Oxen were used for their strength and endurance, while horses were used for their speed. Here, a team of horses pulls logs onto a wagon to be hauled to the Engebretson Mill around 1895. (Chris Hafley collection.)

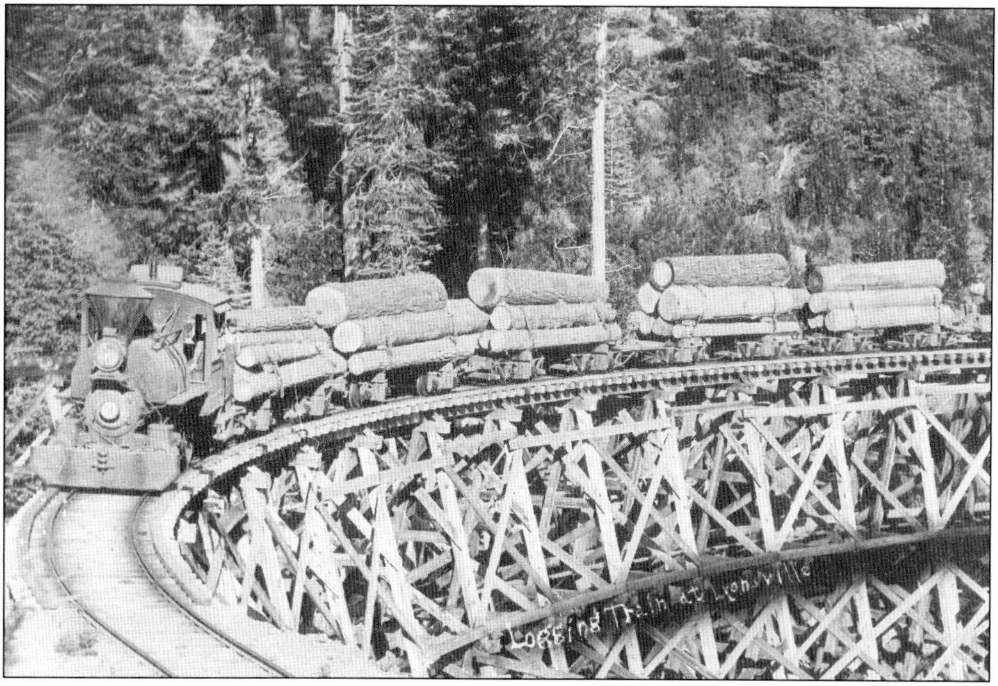


Here is a No. 3 H.K. Porter steam engine narrow-gauge logging train at Lyonsville. To escape taxes levied against standard American gauge, tracks with a narrower European gauge were built. Even after this loophole was closed, these tracks continued to be used because they were cheaper to build and better suited for the terrain. (Tehama County Library collection.)

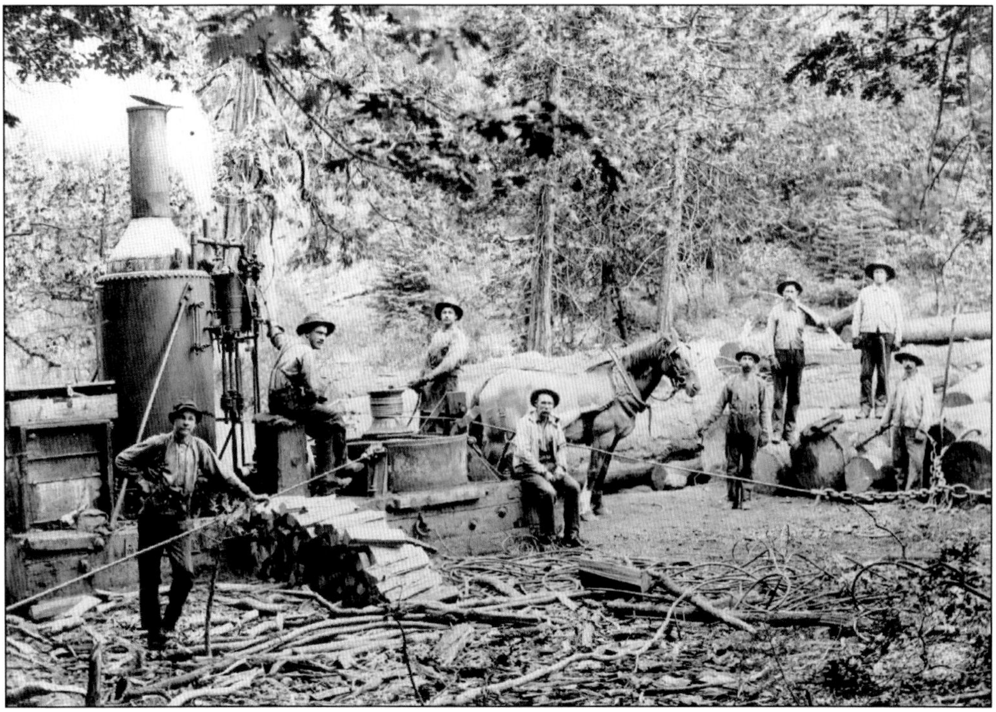

In 1882, the Dolbeer Steam Donkey Winch revolutionized logging. It could move logs faster than horses or oxen—30 minutes versus half a day for oxen. Logs attached to a cable, brought out by a horse from the winch, were quickly dragged (or skidded) back. Fired by wood, they often threw sparks, burning the crew or causing small fires. From left to right around 1900 are Carl Clark, Gene Stevens, Henry Schafer, Larry Patterson, George Trabue, Alec Anderson, Jim Cotton, and Jess Wilson. (Chris Hafley collection.)

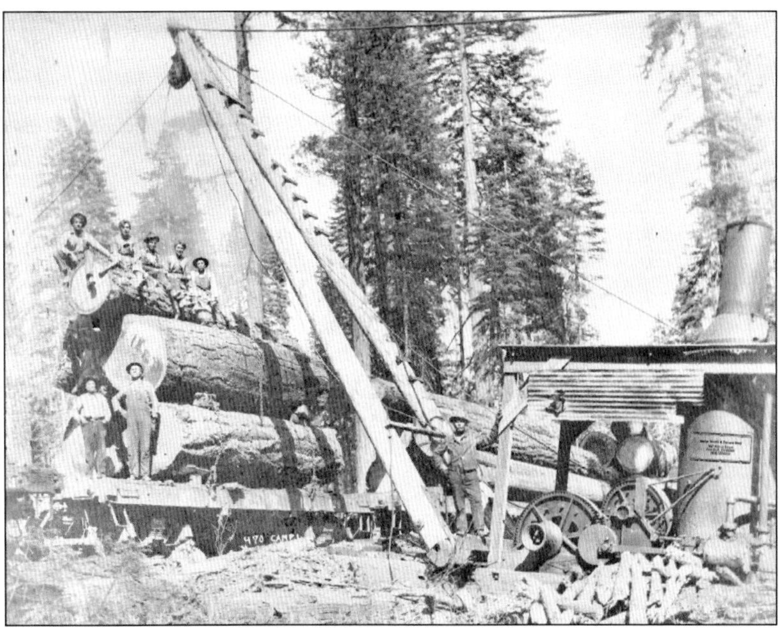

Steam donkeys powered slide-back loaders (or cranes) used to load logs onto flatbed railroad cars. Steam Donkeys were small, tough, and strong. To move to a new location, one of its cables would be attached to a tree or stump so the machine could drag itself to the next location on its skids. (Dan Bayles collection.)

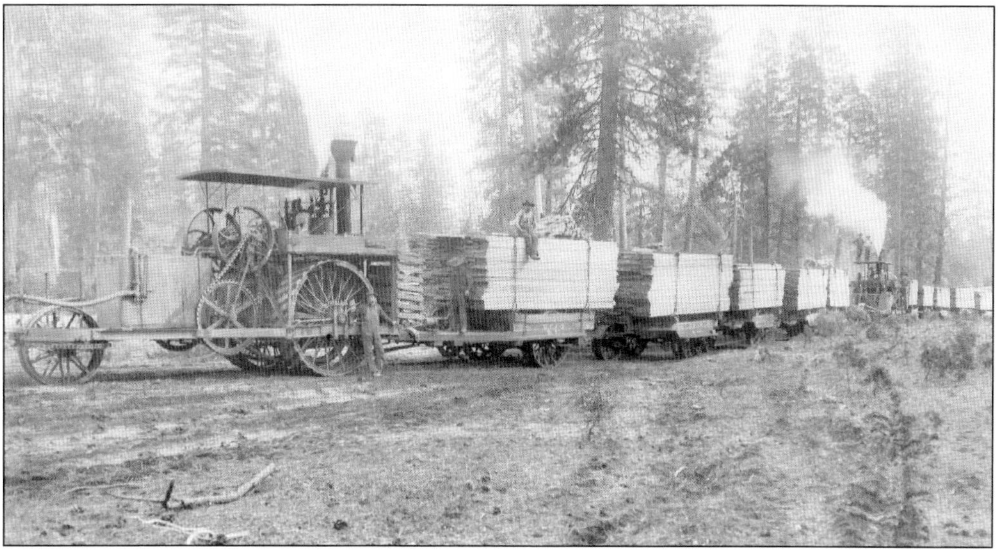

A hauling train of two steam-powered Holt engines is transporting rough finished lumber. The Holt Manufacturing Company enlarged this picture and sent it to the 1905 World's Fair at Portland, Oregon, for display. The company later merged with its largest competitor, Best Manufacturing Company, to form the Caterpillar Tractor Company. (Tehama County Library collection.)

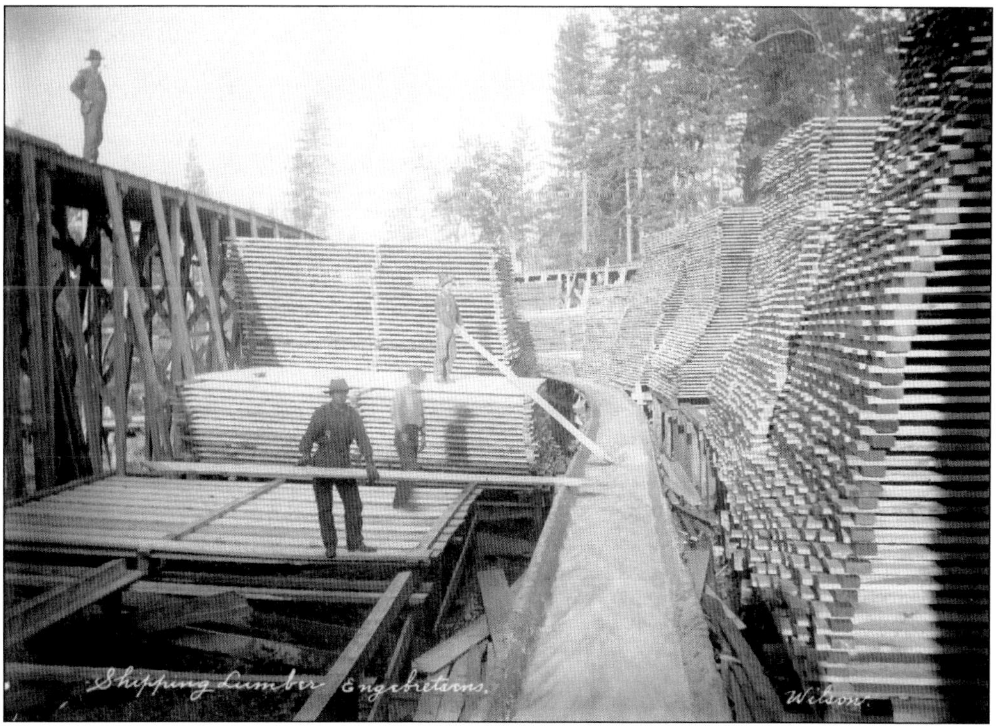


The Empire Flume floated rough-sawn lumber from Lyonsville to Red Bluff mills. At the Engebretsen Mill, Billy Glines has a board in the water, and Tony Michelson readies another one around 1900. Flume tenders lived along the flume to make sure lumber moved smoothly. A five-gallon can would be hung from a rope across the flume to rattle when boards passed against it. If the rattling stopped, something was wrong. (Chris Hafley collection.)

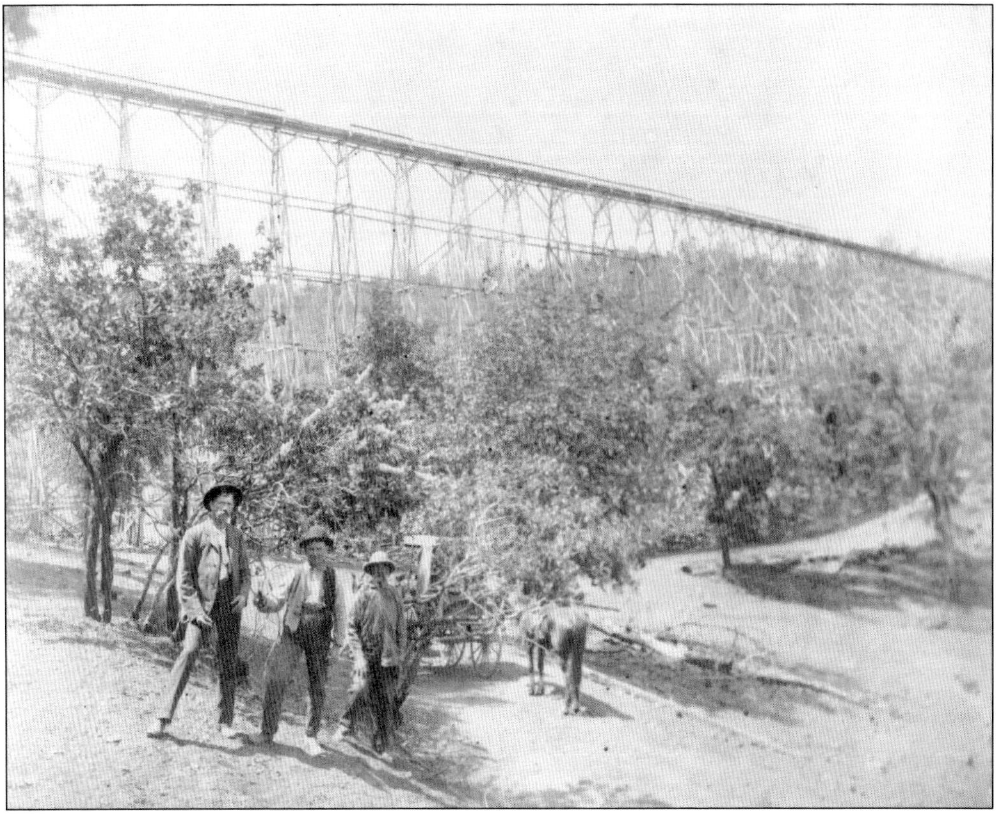

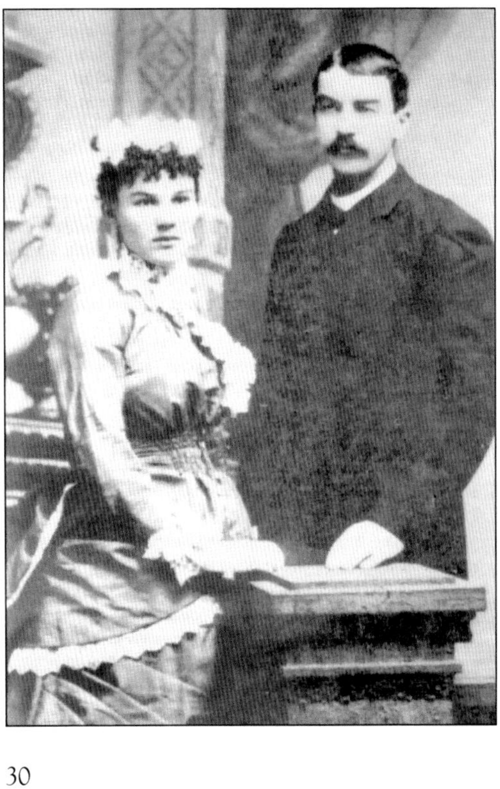

The flume at "High Trestle" was 96 feet high and 2,000 feet long. Flume boats often floated people to Red Bluff. One day, a Chinese mill worker was pronounced dead. Lumberman Pearl Edwards agreed to float with the body to Red Bluff at night. He reported: "In the moonlight, [as] the raft floated silently on the High Trestle, the 'corpse' came to life." Startled, Edwards could not jump out. He had to stay with the semi-conscious man all the way to Red Bluff. (Tehama County Library collection.)

Jim Payne, an eccentric character in the Lyonsville area, married Minnie in 1885, as shown here. They lived in a cave, and she died at age 20. Jim then married Jennie Shelton. It was a tumultuous marriage. Jennie loved to play her organ, which Jim hated. One day, he dragged it out of their cabin and threw it over a cliff. Jennie retaliated by throwing his rifles over the cliff. They later divorced. (Tehama County Library collection.)

# *Two*

# Transportation

One of the first "roads" in Tehama County was the Old Emigrant Trail (1851). It branched off the Lassen Trail at Deer Creek Meadows, went north through Childs Meadow, over Morgan Summit, and through Battle Creek Meadows before descending to the valley. The first good road was the Tehama County Wagon Road, built in 1863 to compete against John Bidwell's Humboldt Wagon Road. Highway 36 was constructed in 1933–1937. The construction of State Highway 99 in 1910–1915 and Interstate 5 in the mid-1960s brought the modern highway system to Tehama County.

Another "road" runs north/south in the eastern mountains of Tehama County. The unmaintained Ponderosa Way was built as part of a 700-mile (from Shasta County to Kern County) firebreak and truck trail to protect the pine and fir forests of the higher elevations from brush fires in the lower elevations. The Civilian Conservation Corps built it in 1933–1936.

The Sacramento River could be considered Tehama County's first highway because it was a major artery of transportation that dominated commerce during the early years. Many towns sprang up along its banks to take advantage of riverboat traffic. In 1854, riverboat companies combined to form the California Steam Navigation Company, which monopolized the freight and passenger trade until the Central Pacific Railroad arrived in 1871.

The Iron Horse brought tremendous change to Tehama County's economy and way of life. There would be no more delays caused by impassible roads or fluctuating river levels. Traveling became faster. The coming of the railroad even changed how time was kept. Before the Transcontinental Railroad was built in 1863–1869, localities used solar time, which reckons time based on the sun's position in the sky (and kept by the town clock). This worked well for local stagecoaches, riverboats, and small railroads, but not for the larger railroads. Trains shared the same track and passengers needed to make connections. Safety and reliable timetables required an accurate standard time that all regions would follow. In 1883, the major railroads took it upon themselves to develop their own time zones that standardized time across the nation. Congress finally made it law by passing the Standard Time Act of March 19, 1918.

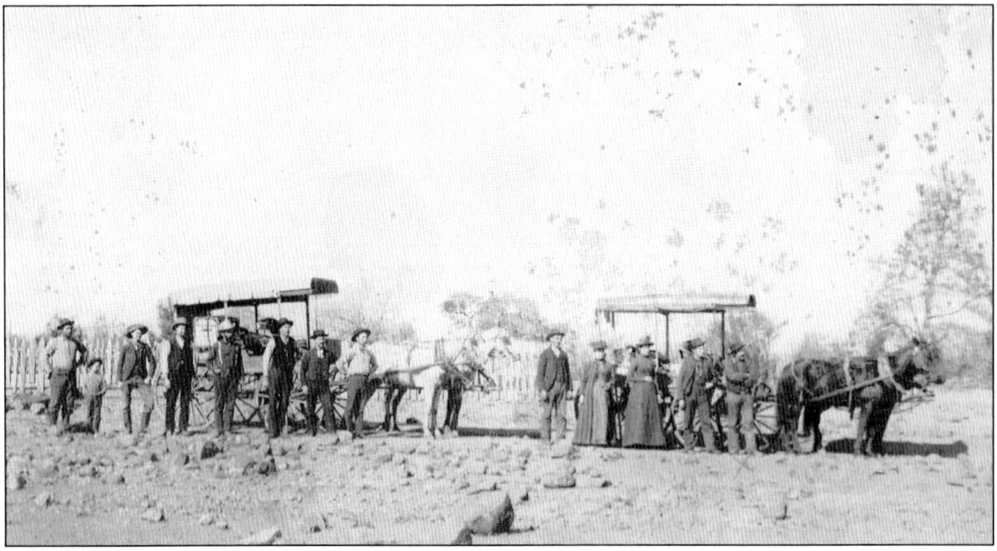

Pictured here in 1892, stages on the Belle Mill Road left Red Bluff at 6:30 a.m. and arrived at Lyonsville, 35 miles away, by 6:00 p.m. It took two days for teamsters. The road followed the flume, which was the only water supply for homesteads there. Water could be used when lumber was not being floated to mills. Once the flume was abandoned in 1914, all settlements vanished. Today, it is the notorious Hogsback Road. (Tehama County Library collection.)

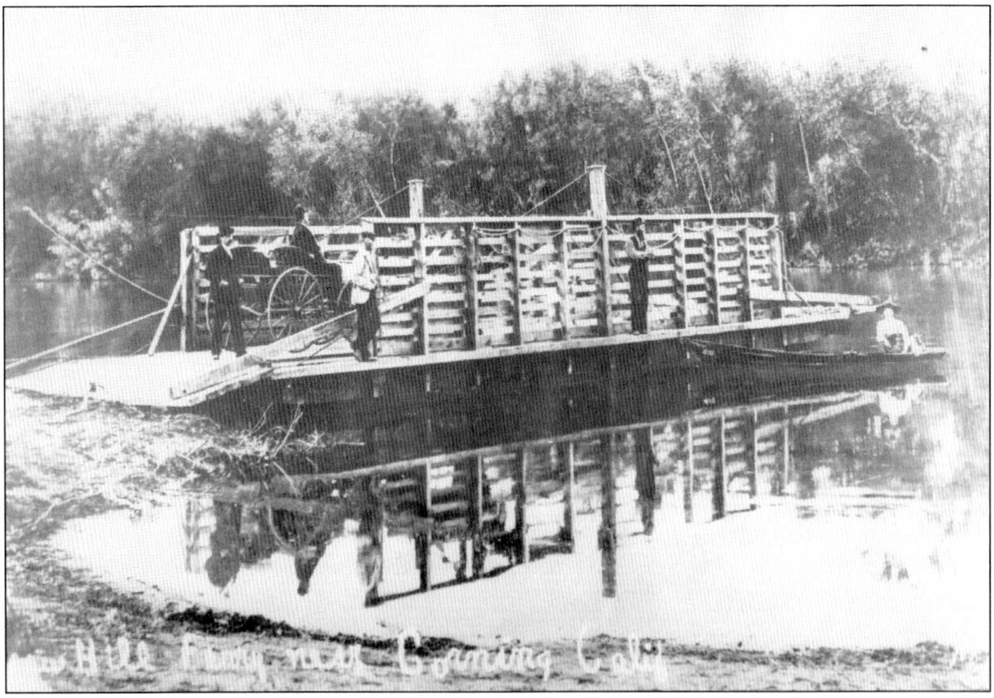


Too frail to follow their families, two elderly Indian women lived on the west bank of the Sacramento River and waved to passing riverboats. The captains began calling this area Squaw Hill, which also became the name of the ferry seen in this c. 1890 photograph. When riverboats approached, the ferry cables were lowered into the water so they could pass. Service stopped in 1922 when the first Woodson Bridge (replaced in 1974) was built. (Tehama County Museum collection.)

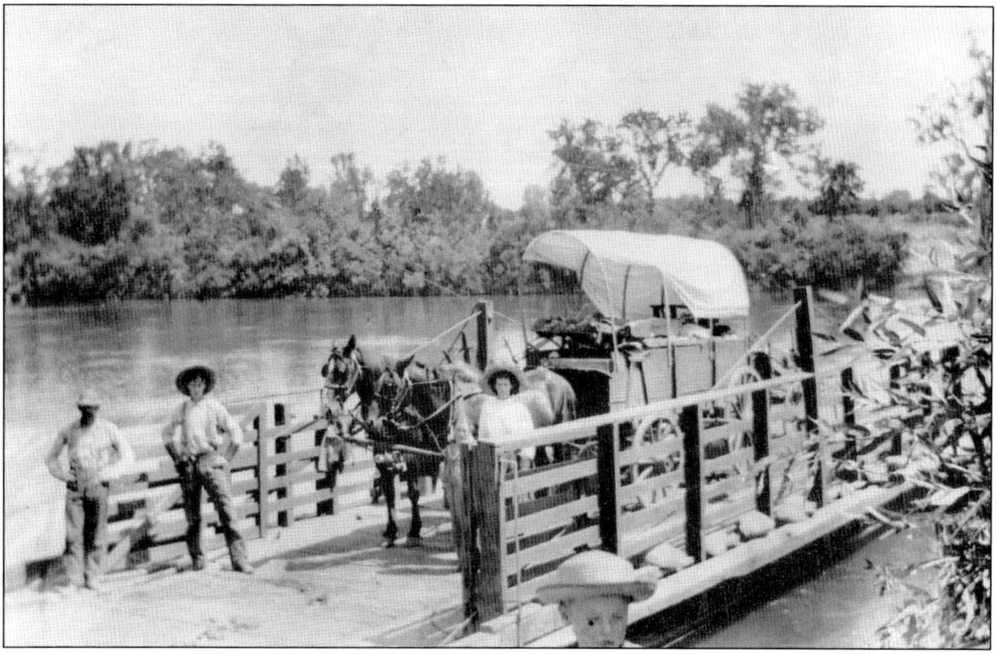

People would ferry themselves at Bend, where there was a small rowboat and ferry. Courtesy dictated leaving a boat on each side. This meant ferrying the team across (or rowing first to get the ferry), offloading them above the landing, tying them up, going back, tying the rowboat to the ferry, crossing, securing the ferry, rowing back, securing the rowboat, walking to the team, untying them, and going on one's way. (Tehama County Library collection.)

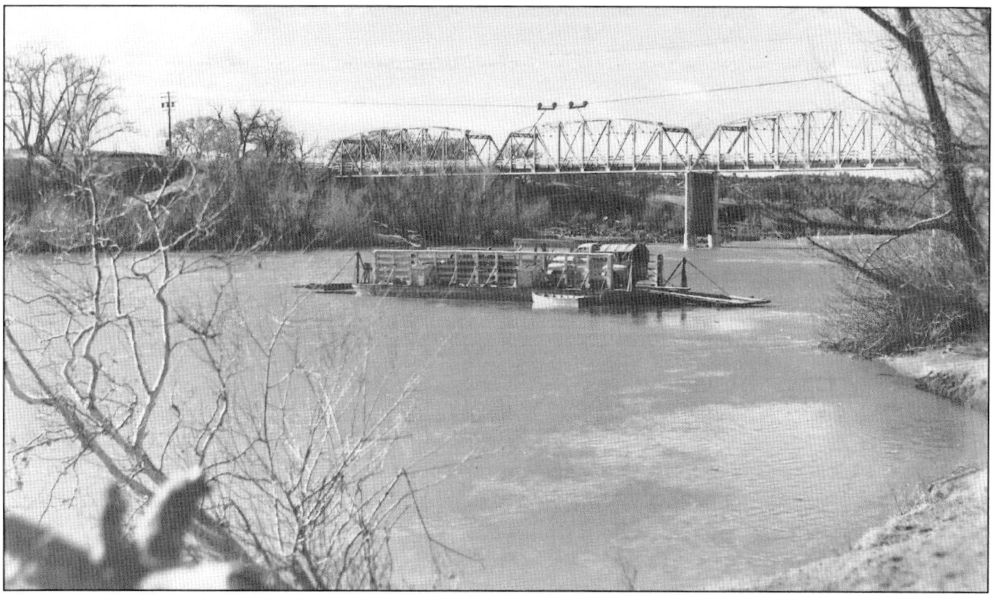

Jelly's Ferry operated until replaced in 1950 by a steel bridge, which partially collapsed in July 2016. Andrew Jelly built the ferry in 1857. Early ferry boats were propelled across the river by the current. Operators slanted the hull slightly into the current. Water sliding along the upstream side would propel it across the river along a trolley cable. Overhead cables kept it from drifting downstream. The trip took three and a half minutes. (Tehama County Library collection.)

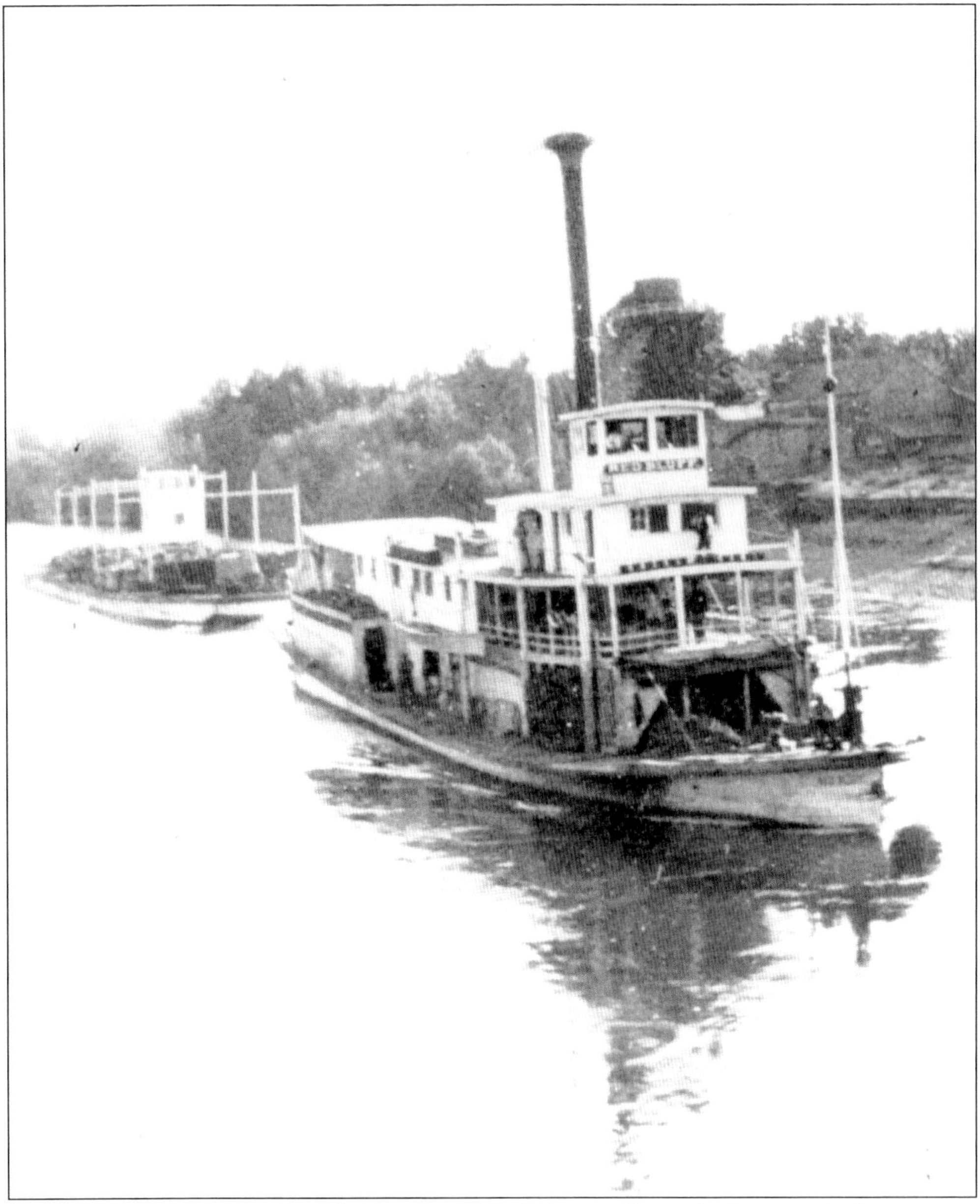

The most famous riverboat in Tehama County, and the one that rode the river the longest, was the 150-foot *Red Bluff No. 3*, built at West Sacramento in 1894 and dismantled in 1936. The *Red Bluff* could run in less than three feet of water. (According to Jerry MacMullen's *Paddle-wheel Days in California*, "she could run wherever the ground was a bit damp.") To keep the river channel clear, specialized riverboats called snag boats would remove trees and snags that had been washed in by floods during the winter. Despite fierce competition from the railroad, riverboat schedules were maintained until 1916. By the 1930s, no more colorful paddle wheelers plied the Sacramento River. The final blow came in 1932 when a large fire in Sacramento destroyed most of the docked riverboats. In 1936, the last riverboat, *Josie Lane*, attempted to come up the Sacramento River but only got as far as the town of Tehama. When it blew its whistle, everyone stopped what they were doing to go see it. (Tehama County Library collection.)

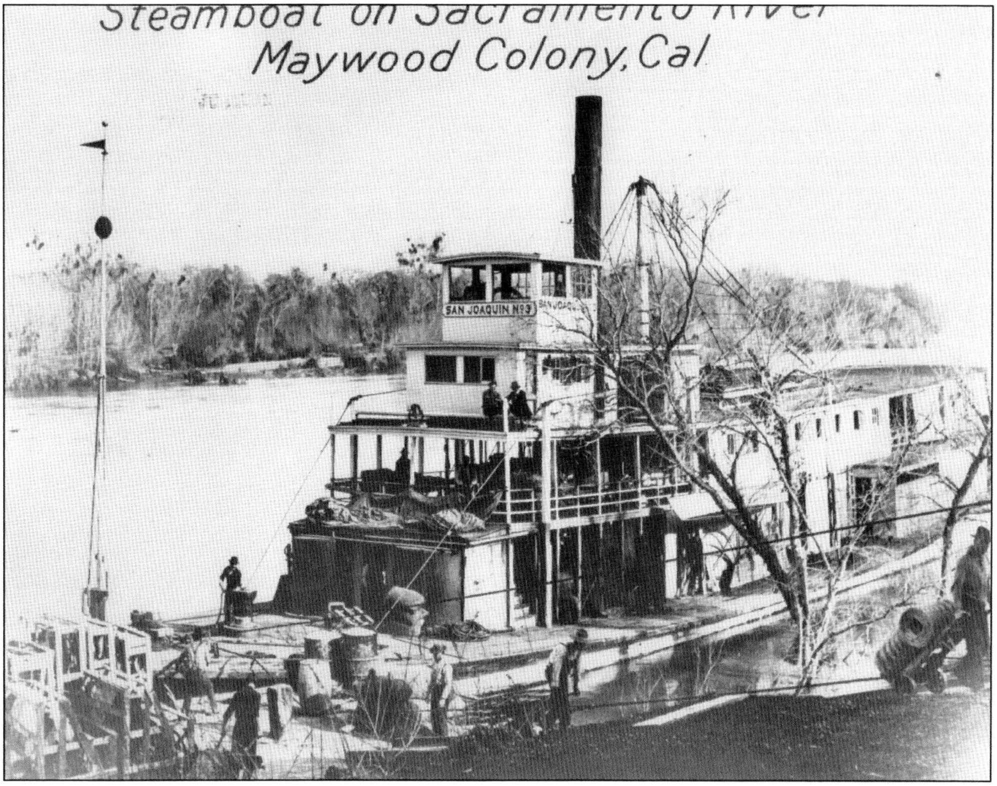


The 148-foot riverboat *San Joaquin No. 3*, built in 1877, is docked at Squaw Hill, four miles east of Corning. Many landings along the river were brush landings, where masses of brush and tree prunings were dumped along the riverbank. Boats would carefully nose up to these landings, swing out their gangplanks, lay boards across the brush, and load or unload cargo. (Tehama County Library collection.)

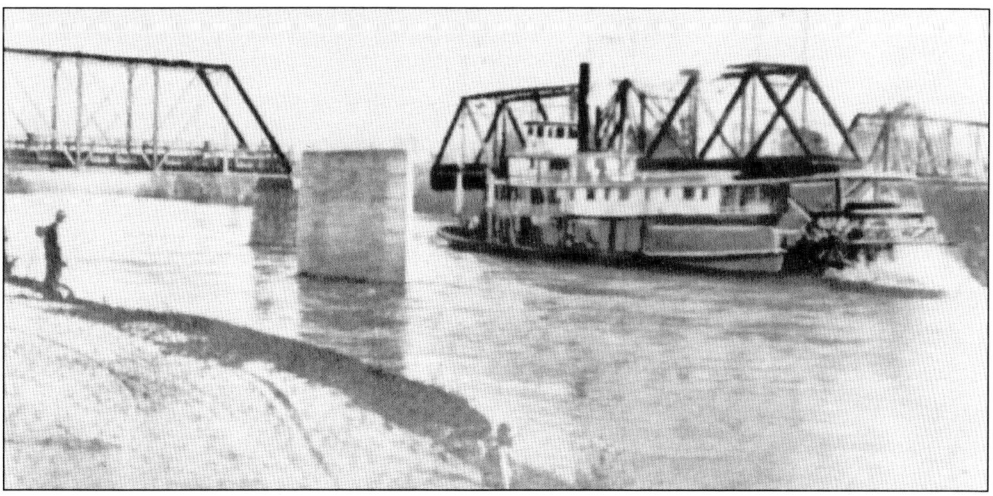

Sternwheelers were the most suitable boats for traffic on the northern reaches of the Sacramento River. Sidewheelers were more suited for the larger delta and San Francisco Bay areas of the Sacramento River drainage. Sternwheelers were smaller, narrower, more maneuverable, and had a more shallow draft for the upriver trade. (Tehama County Library collection.)

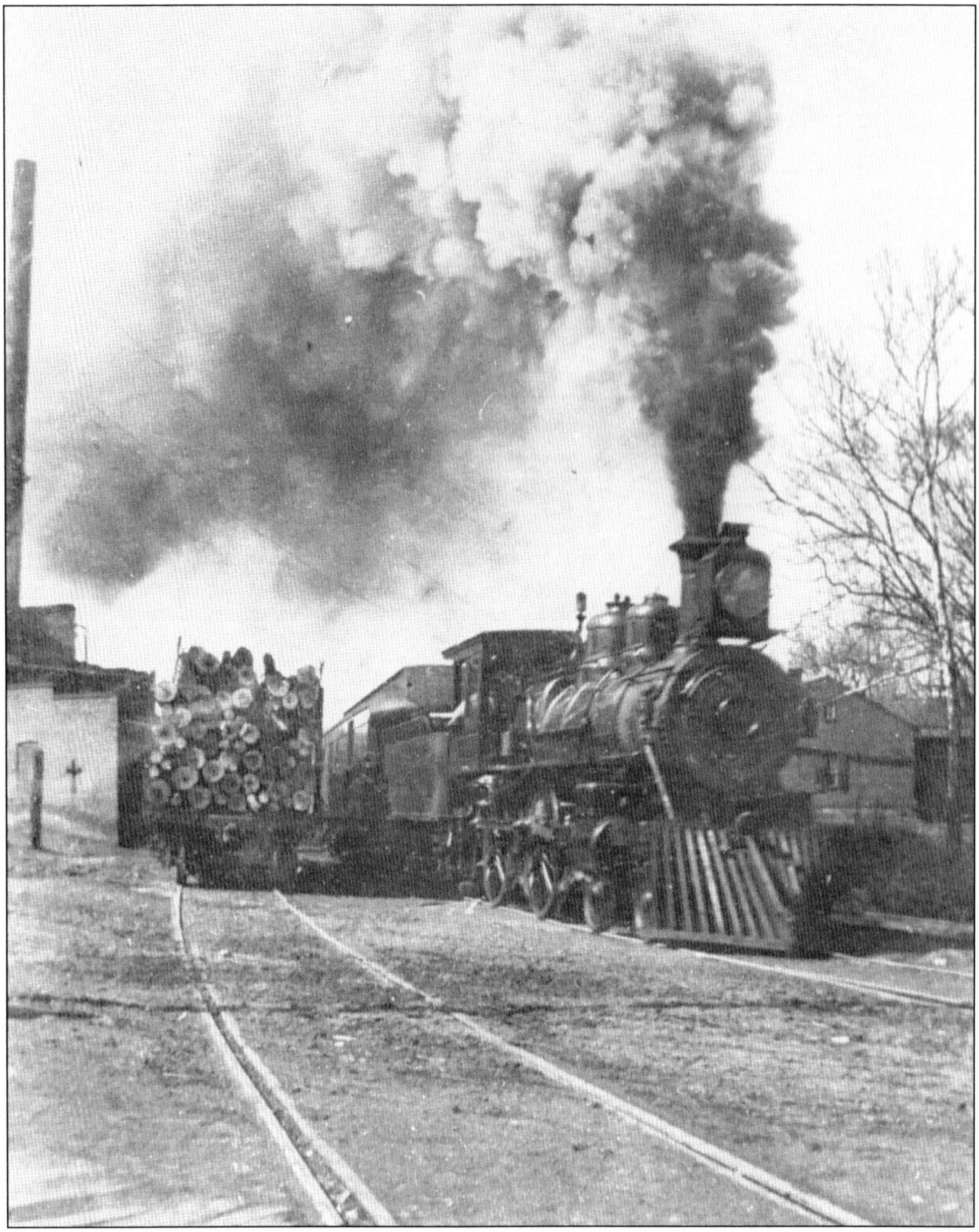

The Central Pacific Railroad reached the town of Tehama in August 1871 and Red Bluff in December 1871, then pushed north to Shasta County in 1872. The owners of the Central Pacific (Leland Stanford, Collis Potter Huntington, Mark Hopkins, and Charles Crocker) founded the Northern Railway Company in 1871 to build a line through the west side of the Sacramento Valley. In July 1876, building began at Woodland. The road was dug by horse-drawn plows. Gangs of Chinese laborers with picks and shovels loaded the dirt into wheelbarrows or one-horse dump carts. By 1882, work began to connect the branch at Orland with the Tehama County lines. The Northern Railway was consolidated into the Southern Pacific Company in 1888. The Central Pacific officially became part of the Southern Pacific in 1959. The Southern Pacific was taken over by Union Pacific in 1996. (California State University, Chico, Special Collections.)

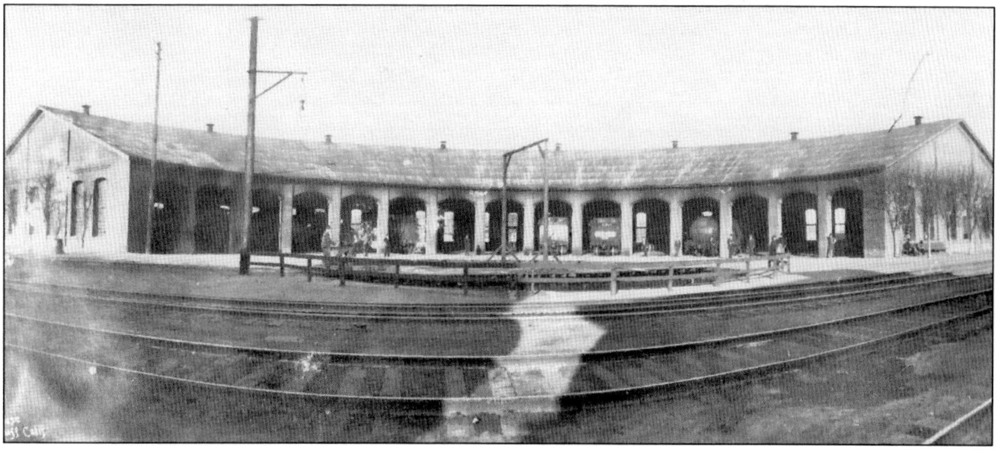

The Red Bluff Roundhouse at Hickory and Madison Streets, seen here in 1910, serviced, stored, and turned steam locomotives around on its adjacent turntable. In 1916, the Southern Pacific moved its division from Red Bluff to Gerber. Once engines changed from steam to diesel (which could travel greater distances), operations were gradually phased out and shut down in 1965. (Tehama County Library collection.)

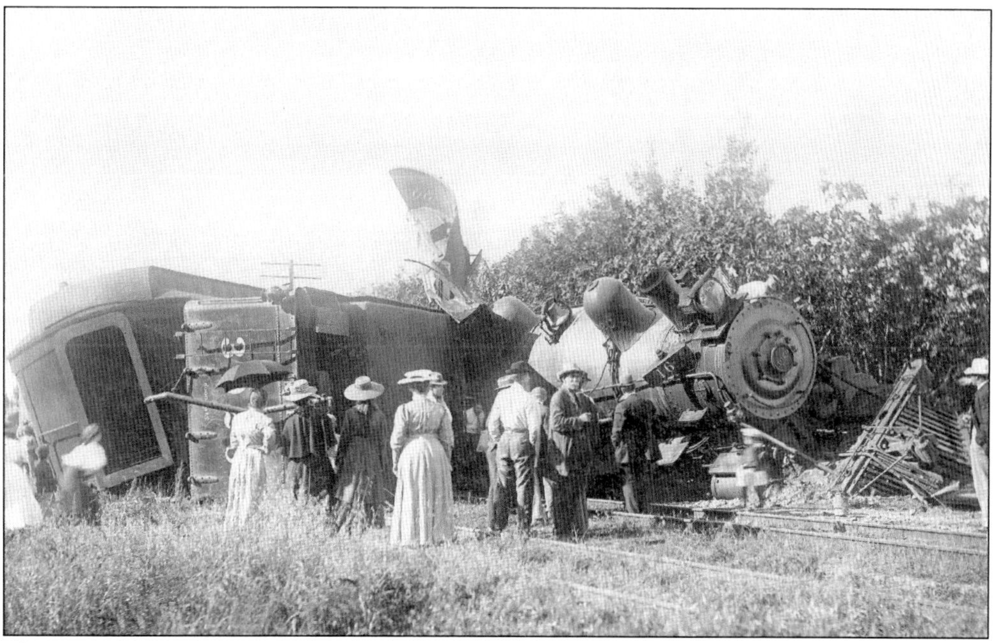

The wreck of train No. 16 at Corning on April 19, 1900, at 3:30 a.m. was caused when ties were placed on the track. One tie was picked up by the engine and carried several hundred feet before jamming on a switch and derailing the engine. Engineer Gardiner and his fireman escaped with slight injuries. (Sacramento Valley Museum collection.)

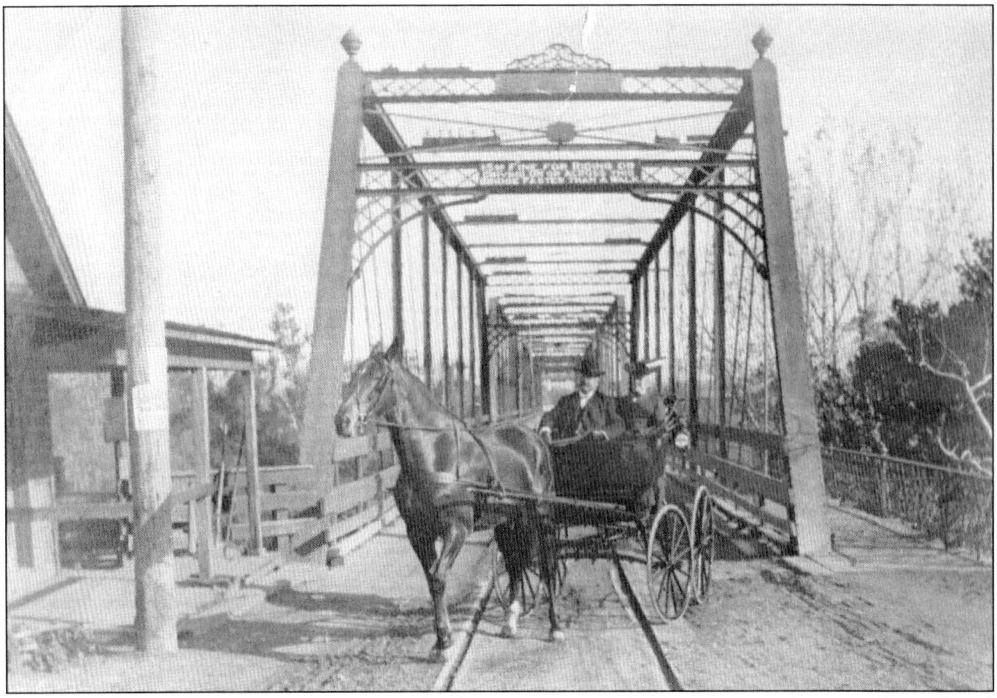

Red Bluff's Centennial Free Bridge was built in 1876 over the Sacramento River. The railroad tracks were for the Sierra Lumber Company's little "dummy" engine (called that because they were not considered "real" engines). The engine hauled lumber to the mill located between Oak and Pine Streets. The sign on the bridge reads, "$5.00 fine for riding or driving on or across the bridge faster than a walk." (Tehama County Library collection.)

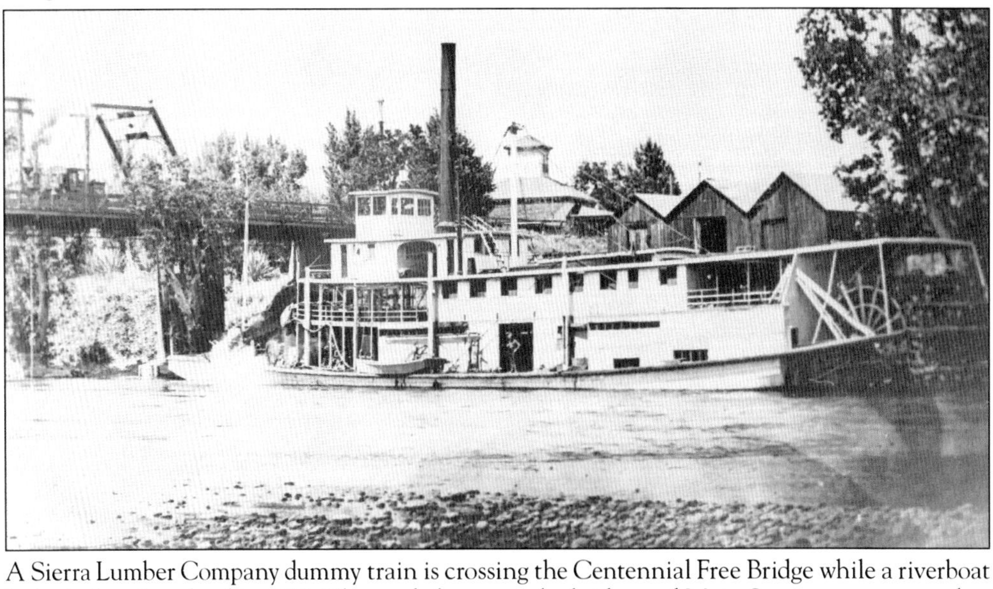

A Sierra Lumber Company dummy train is crossing the Centennial Free Bridge while a riverboat is docked at the wharf in 1890. The grade between the bridge and Main Street was so steep that the small locomotive could only haul two car loads of wood. All traffic would be stopped so it could cross without incident. The buildings in the background belonged to the Sierra Lumber Company. (Tehama County Library collection.)

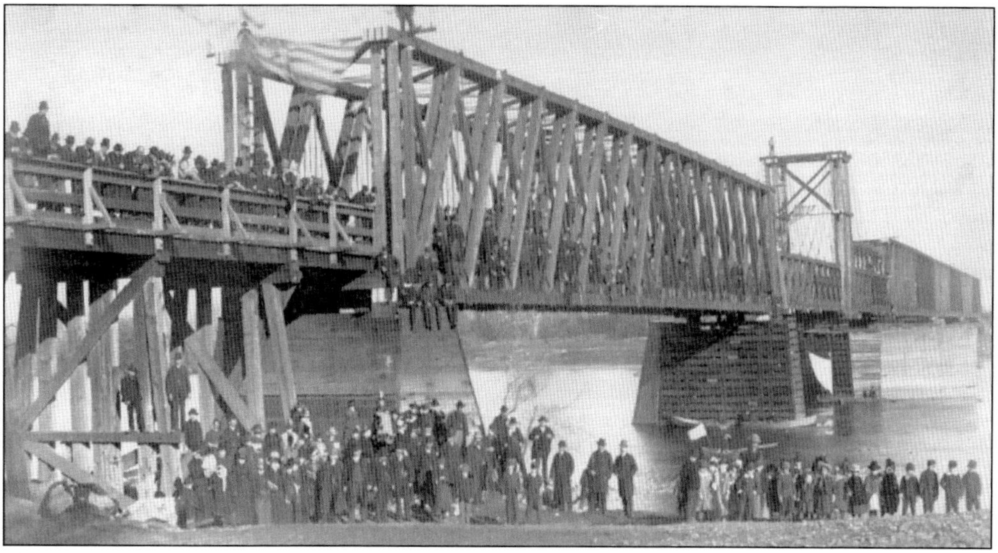

The first Tehama Railroad Bridge was board planked to allow teamsters to use it. A more modern bridge replaced it in 1881. The railroad caused a sharp decline in riverboat trade, which caused hostilities. In 1892, the riverboat *Jacinto* could not pass because the bridge was spiked shut. The steamship company gave the railroad a choice: fix it or dynamite would. It was fixed within three hours. (Tehama County Museum collection.)

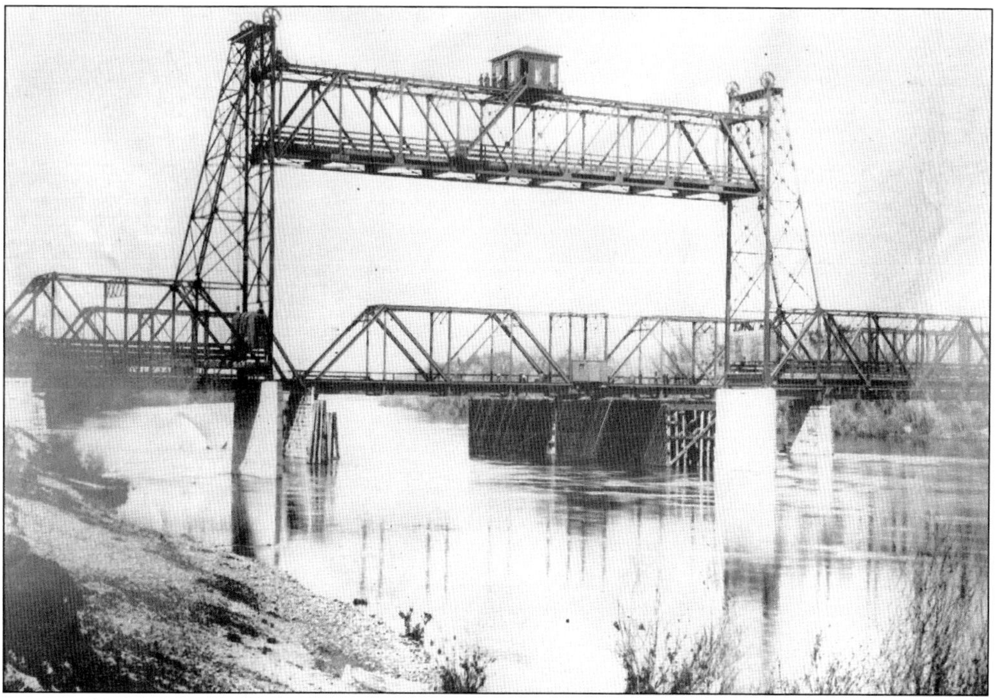

Designed by Tehama County surveyor and engineer William F. Luning, the Tehama–Los Molinos Lift Bridge was the second bridge of its type in the United States (the first was in Chicago, which Luning studied) and the first one on the West Coast. On the day of its dedication in September 1911, it failed to lift but was quickly fixed. Directly behind it, a "turn-span" railroad bridge can be seen. (Tehama County Library collection.)

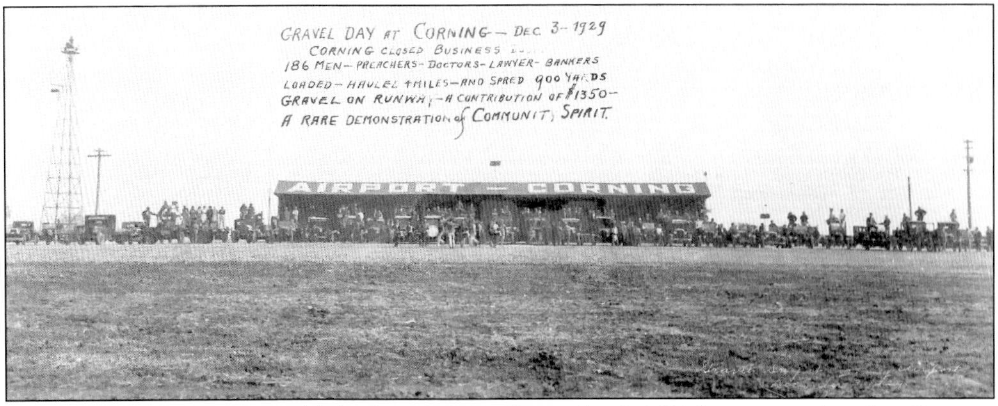


The Corning airport was established in 1919. On December 3, 1929, businesses closed in Corning so 186 men could load, haul, and spread 426 truckloads (900 yards) of gravel on the runway. In 1924, the first public hangar was built, making it the only airport north of Los Angeles to have one. In 1933, field lights were installed, making it the largest lighted airport north of San Francisco. (Corning Museum collection.)

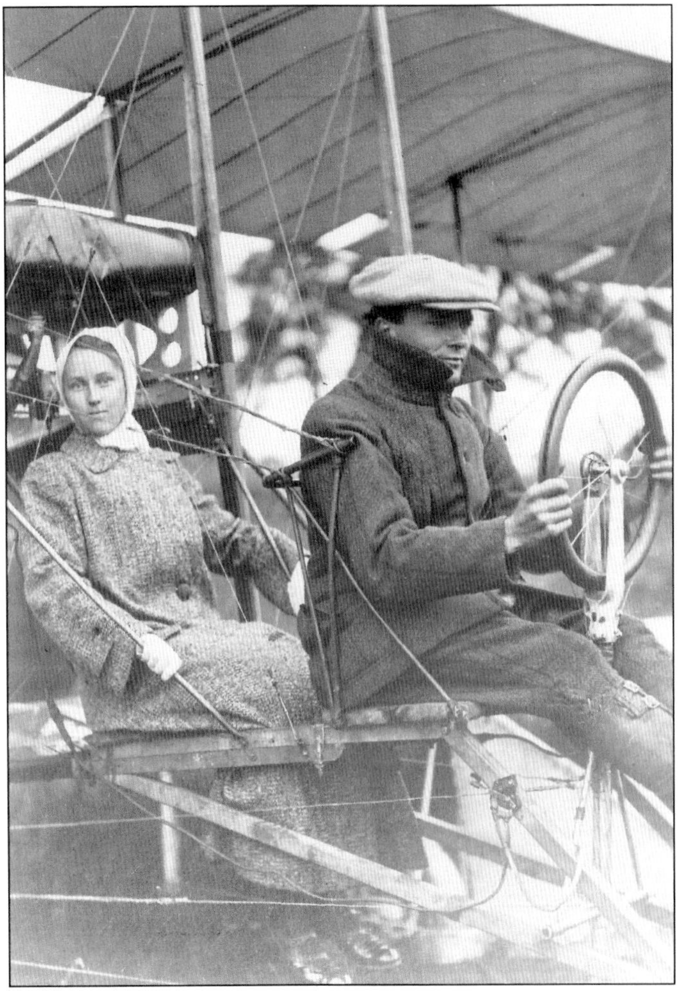

On April 13, 1912, Red Bluff High School student Henrietta Lee ran home to get her mother's permission to go on the first airplane ride in Tehama County. The pilot was Frenchman Didier "Bird Man" Masson, who later flew in World War I. The plane, a Curtiss "Pusher," had been shipped by flatbed to Red Bluff for an air meet at what is today the Tehama County Fairgrounds. (Tehama County Library collection.)

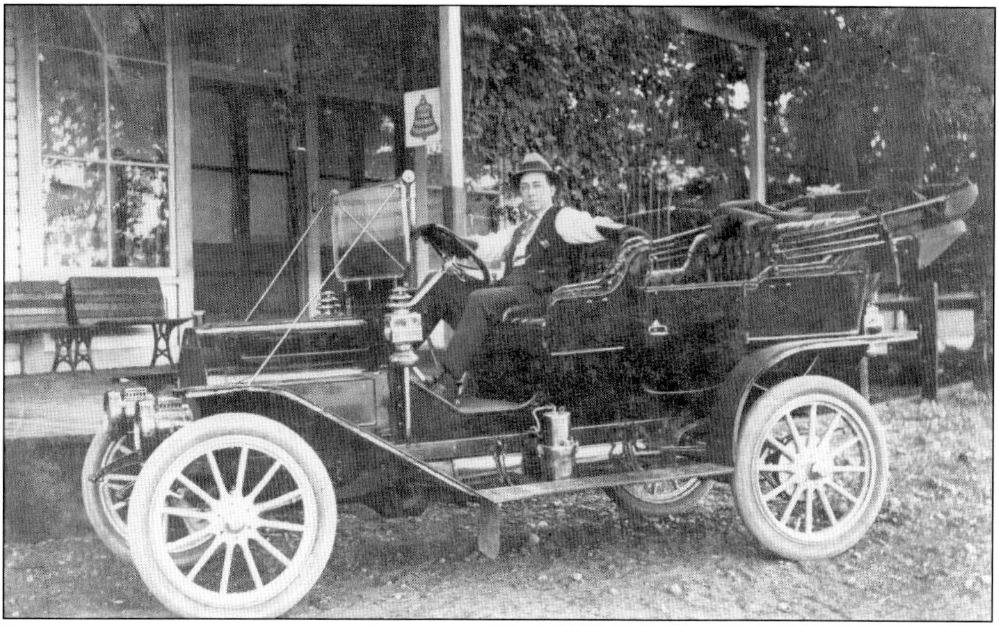

Roy Smith is pictured in one of the few cars in Tehama County in Vina around 1910. Many early cars were steam or electric powered. Learning to drive cars could be a challenge for people used to horses. Forgetting how to brake, some early drivers would pull on the steering wheel and yell "Whoa!" Broken gates and fences bore the brunt of the learning curve. (Frances Leininger collection.)

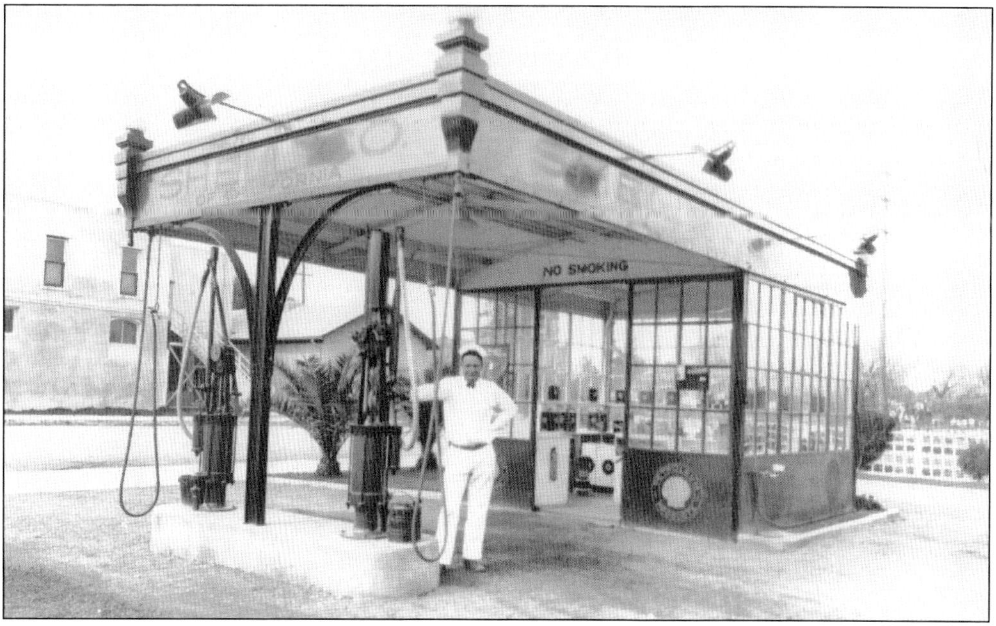


Gas stations offered well-known brands of gas, excellent service, personable and competent employees, and convenient locations. Attendants dressed in crisp uniforms would meet cars with welcoming smiles and friendly greetings. Tires were checked, windshields washed, batteries inspected, radiator water levels topped off, hoses and belts checked, and gas pumped. Some stations sold tires and batteries, did auto repair, and had free road maps for the asking. (Corning Museum collection.)

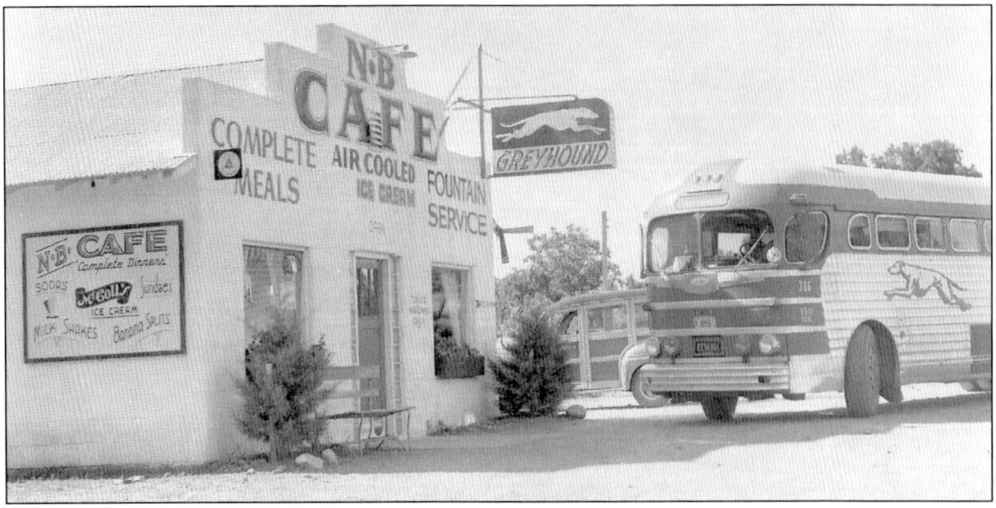


The N•B Café in Los Molinos belonged to Gus and Victoria Nago, who came from Detroit in 1947. It also served as the Greyhound bus depot. Greyhound started in 1914 in Minnesota as a shuttle service for miners and their families. It became Greyhound when a driver noticed that the reflection of his bus in a window looked like a greyhound, which the company later adopted. (Tehama County Library collection.)

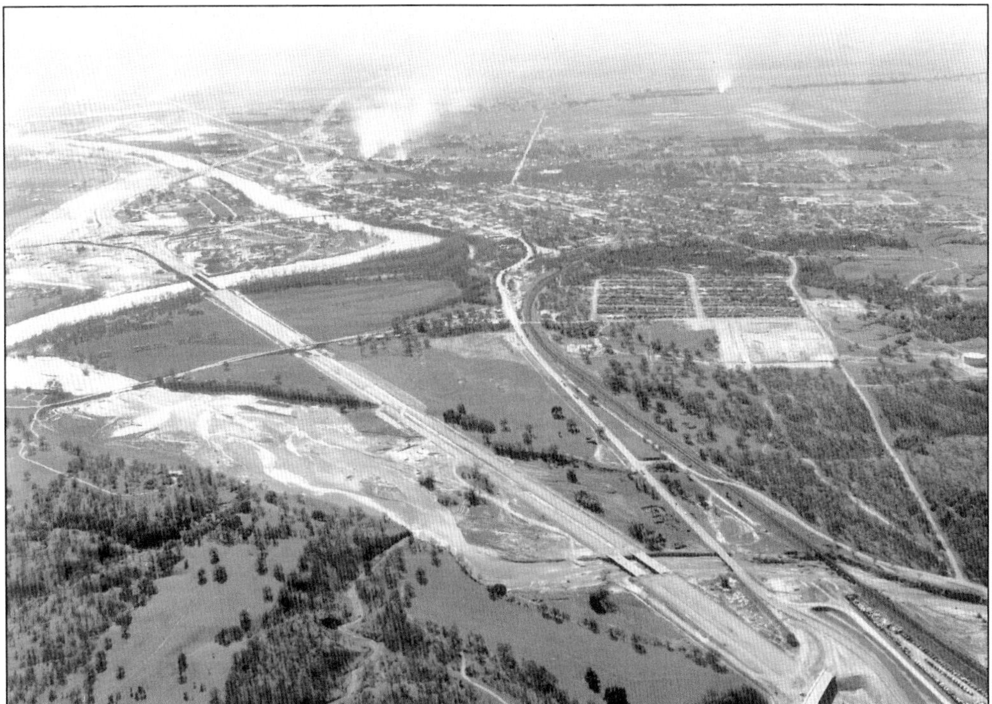

Interstate 5 was built through Tehama County in the 1960s. North of Red Bluff, after Jelly's Ferry Road near the northbound lanes of Interstate 5, grows a lone tree. Local resident Carrie Bogue asked to save it from Interstate 5's construction; officials said no. Later, the tree died, and Bogue died in 1969 at age 93. One day, leaves reappeared. Convinced Bogue came back to her little tree, "Carrie's Tree" is decorated every Christmas. (Tehama County Library collection.)

# *Three*

# Southeast

Most towns here are near the river. The town of Tehama, mapped in 1850, was the county seat until a vote in 1857 moved it to Red Bluff, a point that rankled for many years.

When the railroad refused to come through Riceville in 1882, the town picked up and rolled itself by mule team one mile east to the new railroad station named for Central Pacific Railroad assistant superintendent John Corning. (Corning, New York, home of Corning Glass, was named after John's uncle Erastus, a railroad man and industrialist.)

Kirkwood built a Methodist church in 1888 on donated land. When the landowner claimed the church was his because there was no deed for it, residents moved it while he was out of town.

Many towns were started as planned communities, or colonies, by land development companies: Richfield; Gerber; Proberta, which was the site of a horrific accident one foggy day in November 1921 when a train struck a school bus killing 14 children (this accident prompted the state law that mandates buses to stop at all railroad crossings); Dairyville, named for its dairies that never recovered from bovine tuberculosis and state regulations regarding the transport of fresh milk to market; and Los Molinos, developed to replicate the achievements of the Maywood Colony. (Ulysses S. Grant invested in Los Molinos but never lived there.)

The Maywood Colony's success was due to the marketing genius of Warren Woodson. He sold a dream—affordable land ownership in the land of milk and honey. Lured by his vision and easy payments, people flocked there. It grew from 3,100 acres in 1891 to 40,000 acres surrounding Corning. Woodson, known as the "Daddy of Corning," once remarked that Corning was the child of advertising.

Vina supported the Gerke Ranch and the Stanford Vina Ranch. In 1955, Trappist-Cistercian monks founded the Abbey of New Clairvaux on a portion of the old Stanford Ranch. They are slowly rebuilding a chapter house with carved stones from a 12th-century Spanish Cistercian abbey. William Randolph Hearst bought the ruined abbey in the 1930s. He gave the stones to San Francisco when he did not want them anymore. They languished until the monks received the stones in the 1990s.

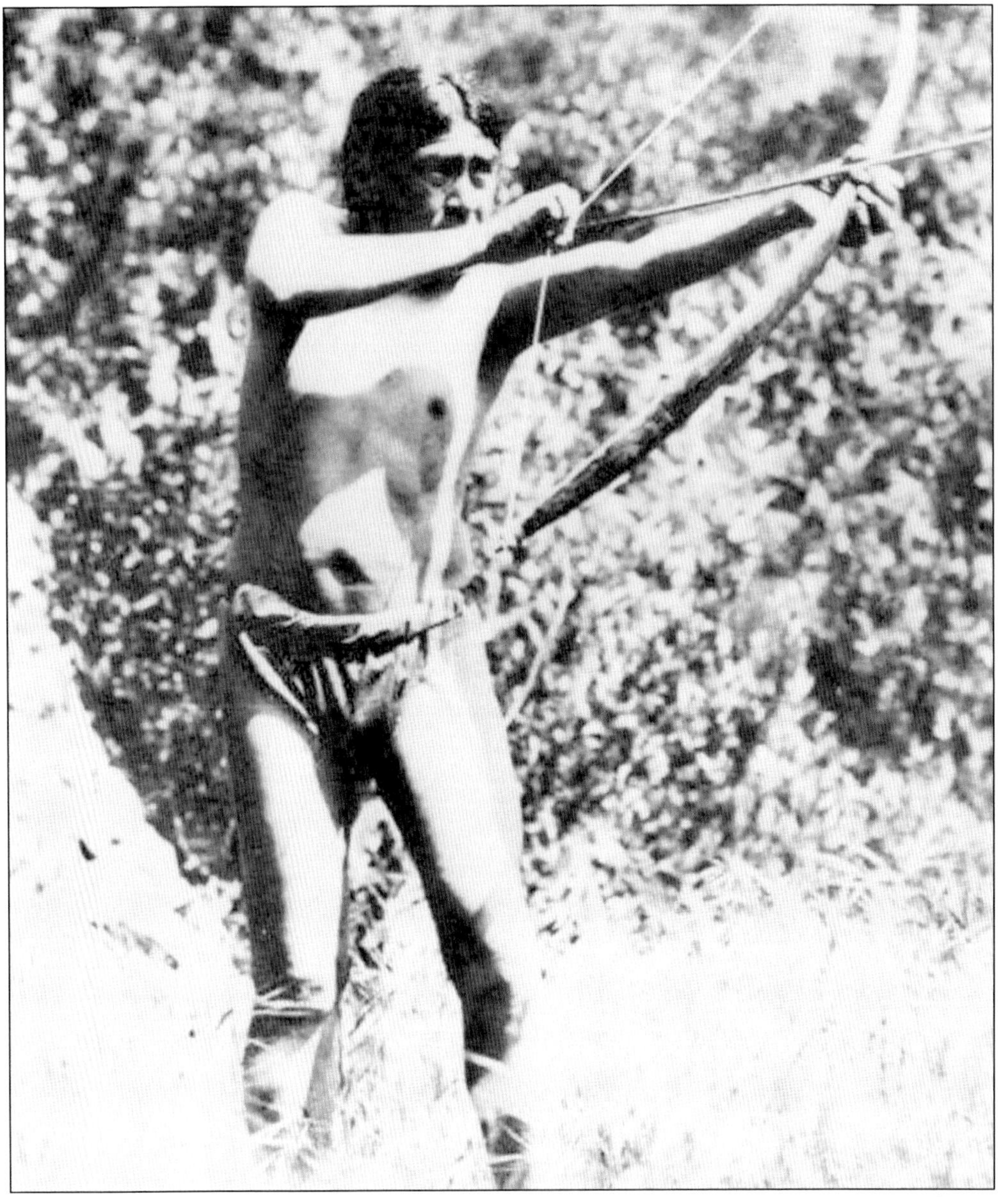

Over 40 years after the Yahi tribe was thought to be extinct, a "wild Indian" was found near Oroville in 1911, emaciated and starving. Alfred Kroeber and Thomas T. Waterman, professors at the University of California, brought him to Berkeley. He was named "Ishi," meaning "man" in the Yahi language. In 1914, he was brought back to eastern Tehama County to show the anthropologists his old haunts and record his Yahi names for them. He died March 25, 1916, of tuberculosis. His friends at the museum buried him near San Francisco in the traditional Yahi way by cremating him with some of his belongings. His brain was sent to the Smithsonian Institution. Ishi's remains were finally reburied in his native country in 2000. According to Saxton Pope, a physician who knew him, "Ishi looked upon us as sophisticated children—smart, but not wise. He was kind; he had courage and self-restraint, and though all had been taken from him, there was no bitterness in his heart. . . . His were the qualities of character that last forever." (California State University, Chico, Special Collections.)

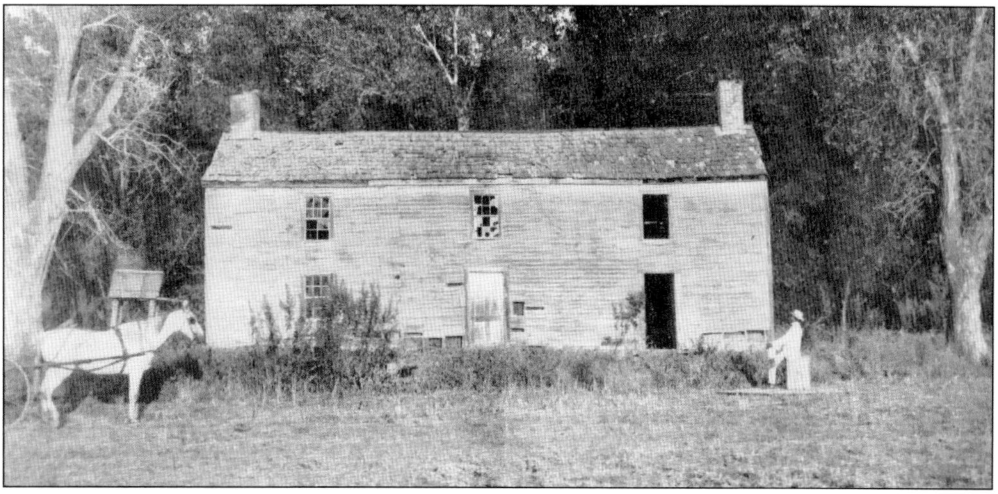

Probably the first timber house built in Tehama County was constructed in 1847–1849 by William Moon on land two miles south of Squaw Hill not included in any Mexican land grant. The wood came from a sawmill in Weaverville. In 1851, a stage line ran right past his home, making it an important place for travelers. It was torn down in 1910. Warren Woodson sits opposite his gray mare in about 1898. (Frances Leininger collection.)

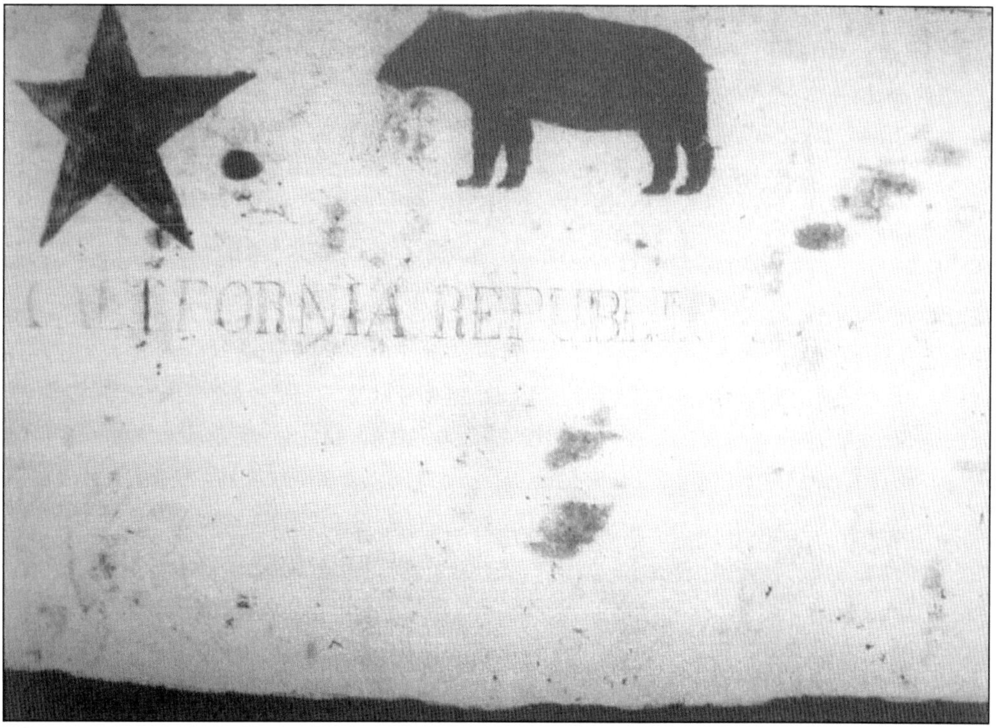

This is a c. 1890 photograph of the Bear Flag that flew over Sonoma in June 1846 proclaiming a California Republic free from Mexican rule. William Levi Todd (nephew to Abraham Lincoln) designed this flag with a California grizzly depicting strength and resistance. (The last grizzly was killed in Central California in 1922.) This flag was given to the Society of California Pioneers in 1855 but was destroyed in the 1906 San Francisco earthquake and fires. (Tehama County Library collection.)

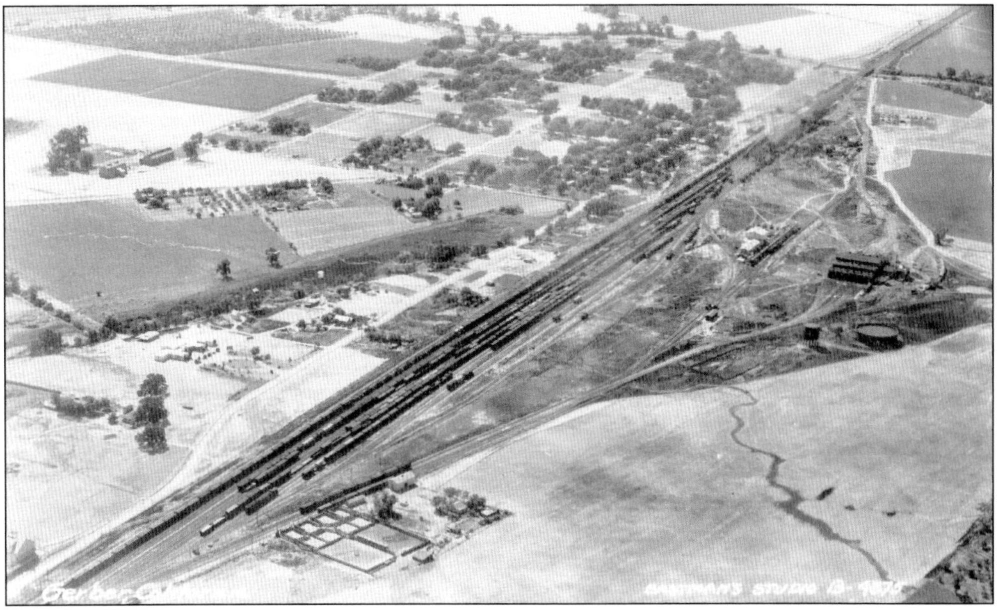

Gerber has known many names: Los Flores, the Mexican land grant; Logan's Field, for Pleasant Logan (he and Alvin Coffey helped establish the Oat Creek School in 1866, the first nonsegregated school in Tehama County); Tyler's Switch, because Jonathan Tyler donated land to the railroad (seen here); Alfalfa, when W.E. Gerber built an alfalfa mill; and Gerber, when the Gerber family surveyed the town. (California State University, Chico, Special Collections.)

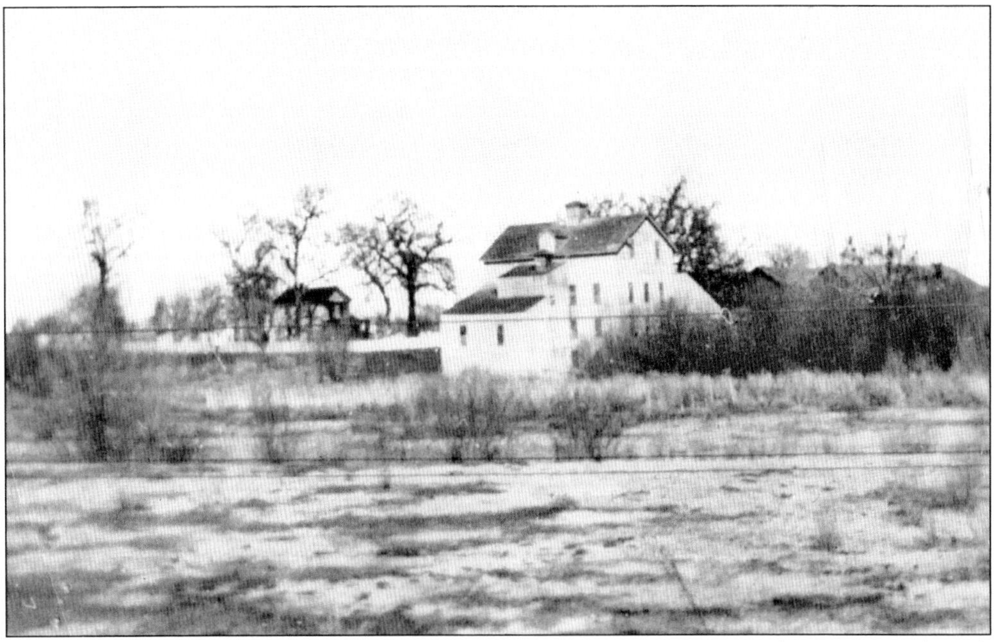

The first flouring mill was built in 1854 in Sesma, near Los Molinos. It was four stories high with four sets of grinding stones and was powered by water from Mill Creek. In the 1880s, the mill made the famous Hungarian Process flour, in which wheat is crushed with metal rollers rather than ground with flat milling stones. This flour was shipped to markets worldwide. (Tehama County Library collection.)

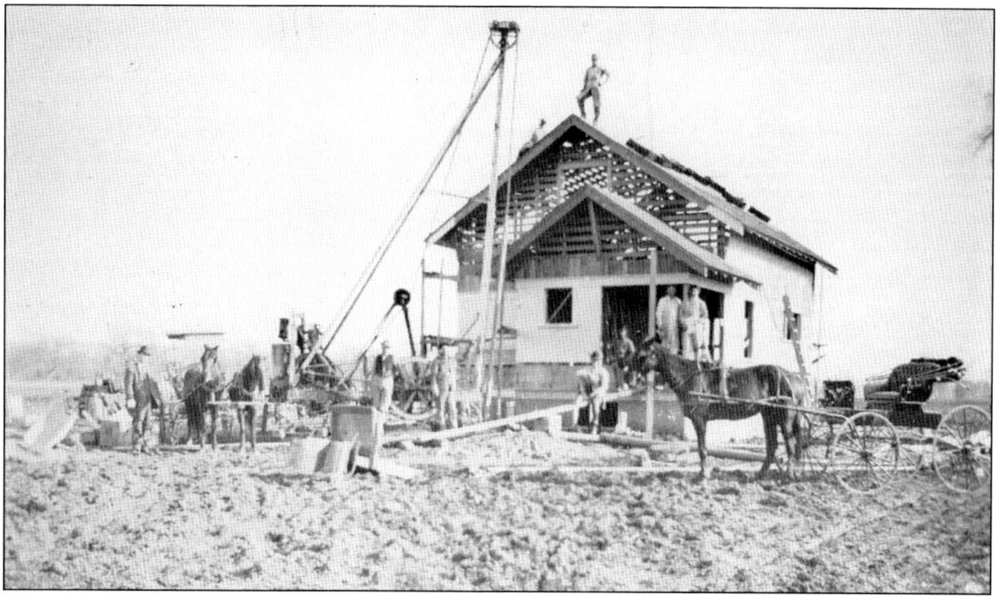

Pictured is a home being built at Los Molinos. Joseph Cone arrived in California in 1850 with a pony and a mule but died a wealthy man. His ranch was divided between his heirs. Daughter Josephine was married to land developer J.D. Sherwood, who started the Los Molinos Land Company in 1905 to sell the subdivided land. By 1913, there were 400 families and 21 businesses in Los Molinos. (Tehama County Library collection.)

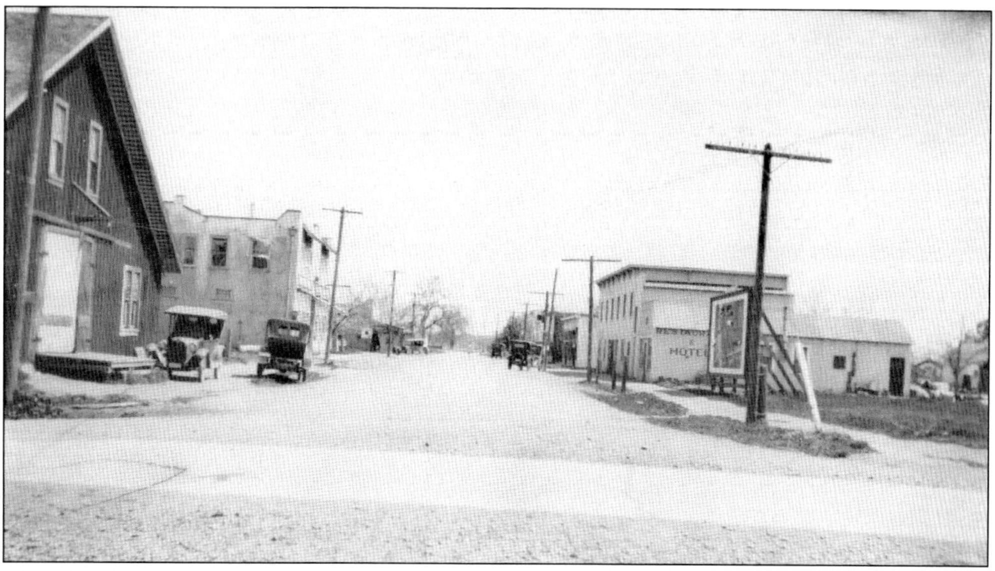

This view looks east down Main Street (today's Josephine Street) in Los Molinos. On the right, the billboard stands in a lot where Vic Hardy built an ice-cream parlor and pool hall in 1923. The hotel is Dray's Boarding House, with rooms upstairs and businesses on the ground floor. On the left is the livery stable, and next to it down the road is the land office. (Tehama County Library collection.)

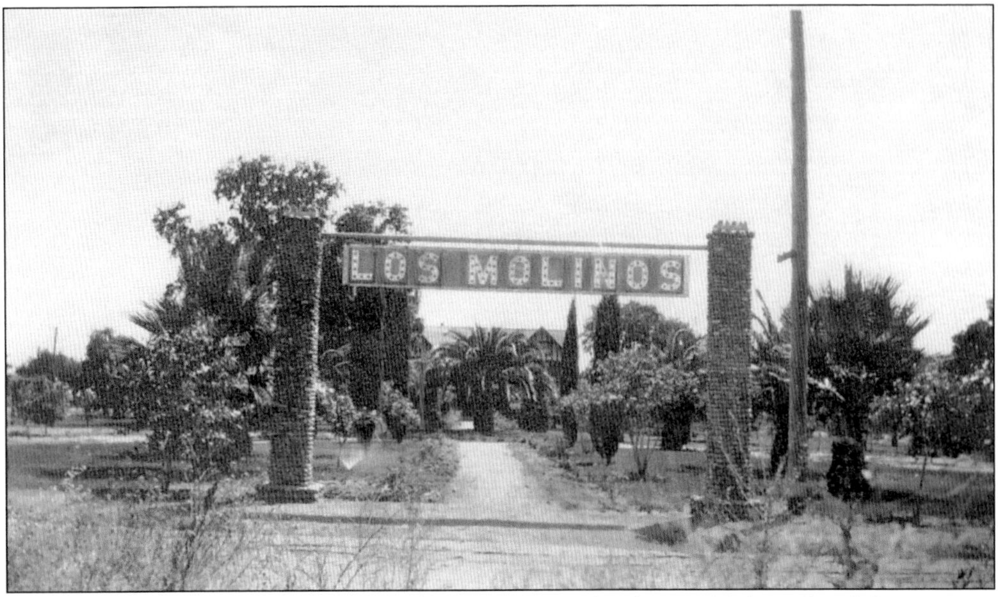


The two-story Los Molinos Inn was built in 1906–1908 by the Los Molinos Land Company as a hotel to accommodate potential land buyers. The dirt road in front of it is Railroad Avenue, which later became Highway 99 East. The first telephone switchboard in the county was installed in the inn's lobby. (Tehama County Library collection.)

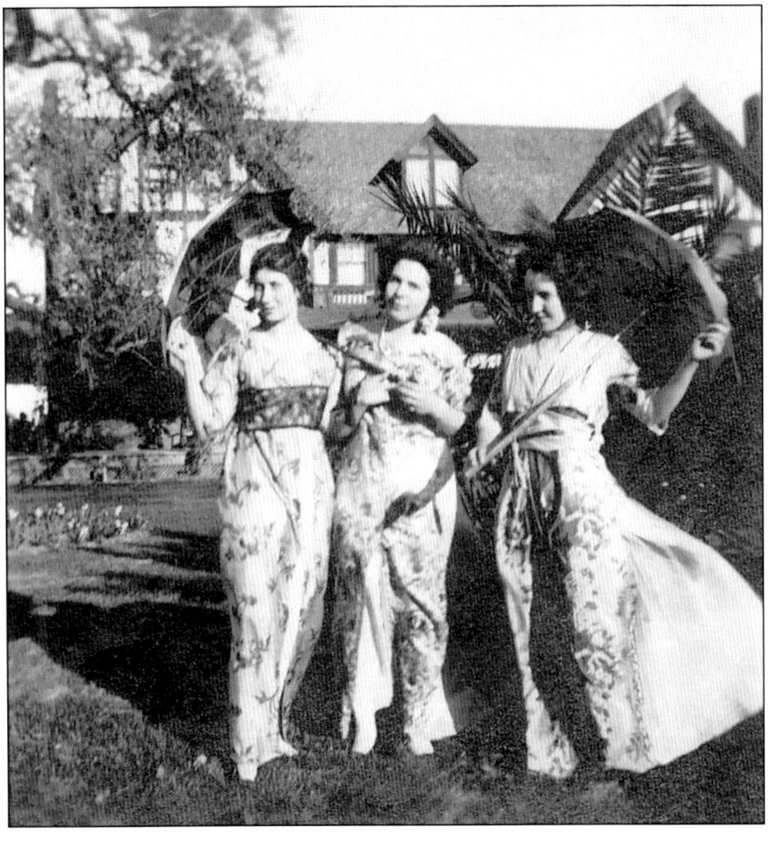

The Los Molinos Inn became a very popular social spot for dinners and parties. Its grounds showcased plants that would grow in the valley. Japanese gardener Mr. Katayama cared for its abundant roses and other lush foliage. Large flower shows were regularly held on its grounds. (Tehama County Library collection.)

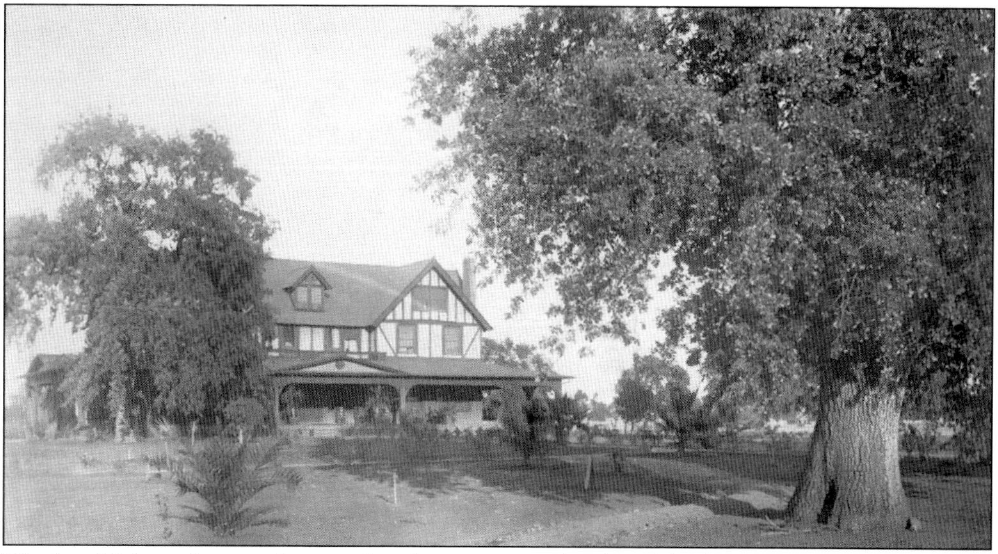

The Los Molinos Inn, gardens, and park encompassed a three-block area of town. The inn was piped for gas, electricity, and running water. Behind it was a livery stable, blacksmith shop, saloon, and cottages. The inn burned down in 1955. Some palm trees still remain, as well as the cobblestone gate posts. (Tehama County Library collection.)

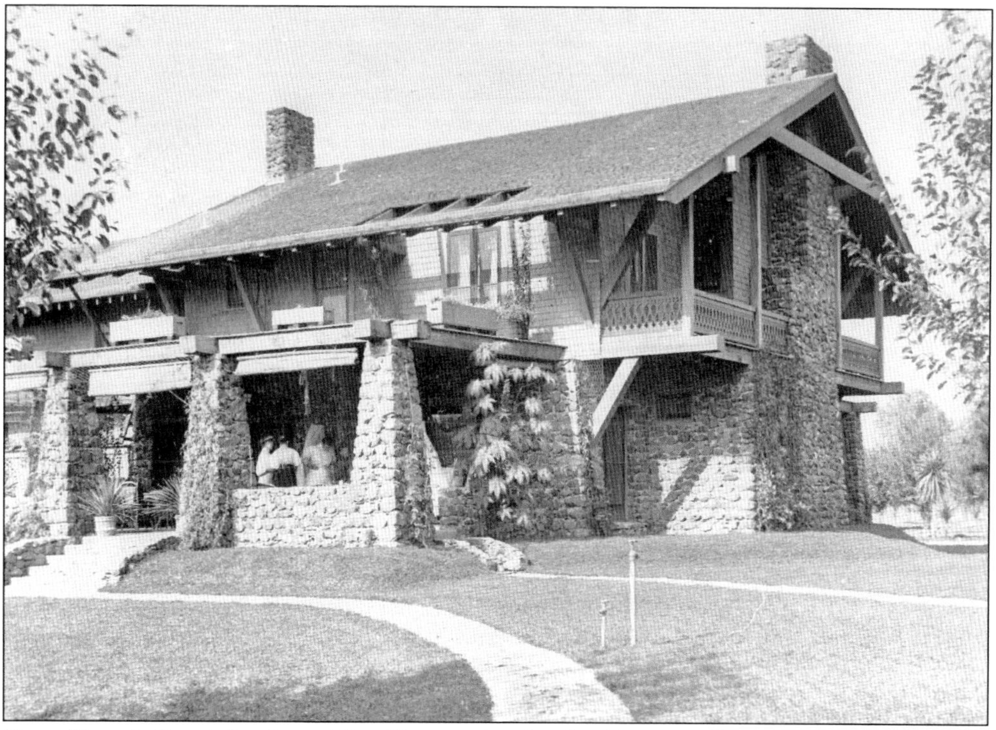

One of Joseph Cone's daughters, Mary Runyon, lived in San Francisco during the 1906 earthquake and fire. Returning to Los Molinos, she built an earthquake-proof, fireproof house. The concrete foundation was 11 inches thick. Large water mains were plumbed at each corner of the house, and a 500-gallon water tank was installed in the attic with an attached fire hose in case of fire. (California State University, Chico, Special Collections.)

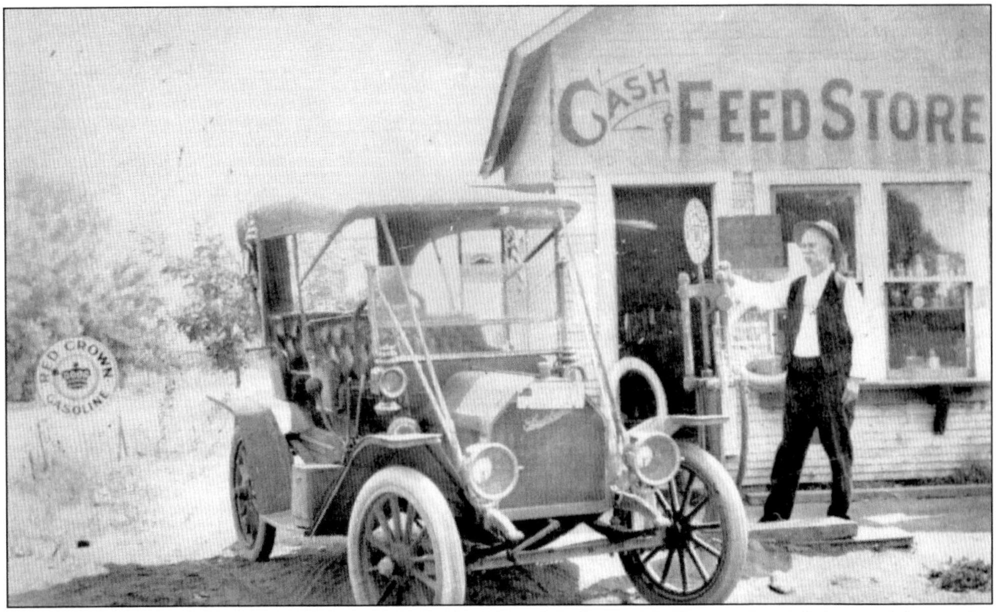


On the southeast corner of Grant Street and today's Highway 99 East in Los Molinos, Alexander Cruikshank built his feed store, pictured here in 1915. West of it, across the highway by the railroad tracks, stood the Airplane Factory. In 1928, Charles Stryker built a monoplane designed by Frank Gordon. The *Miss Tehama* cost $6,000 to build and had a flying speed of 130 miles per hour. Government regulations grounded it. (Dan Bayles collection.)

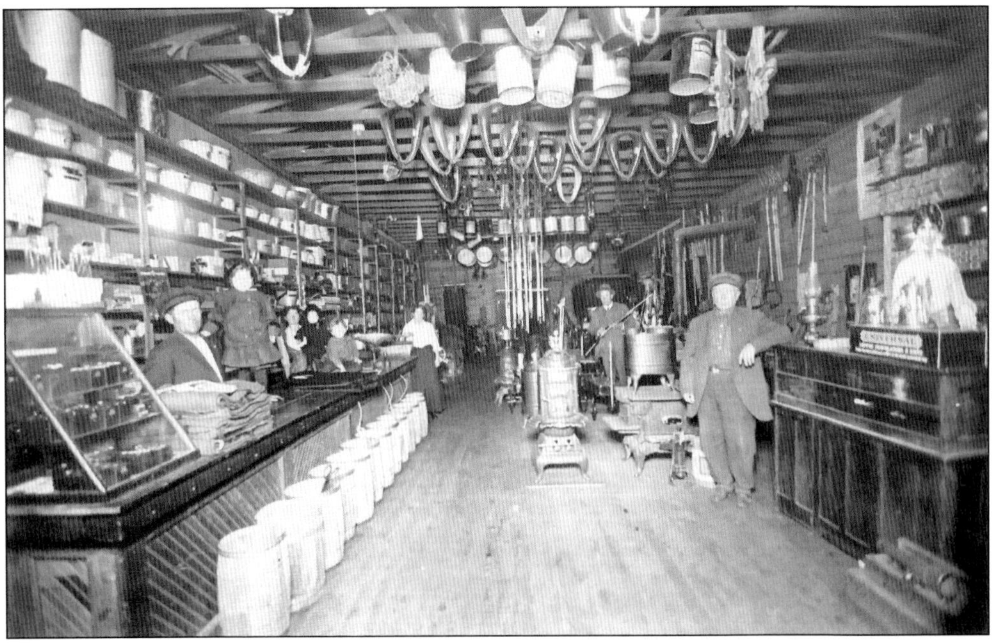

The first hardware store in Los Molinos was operated by Grow and Fitgerald on Josephine Street. In the 1920s, they sold it to Isidore Riffle, who later relocated the business along Highway 99 East. A 1941 advertisement for the store showed it carried radios, electric refrigerators, paints, furniture, stoves and ranges, sporting goods, hardware and implements, and electrical supplies. (Tehama County Library collection.)

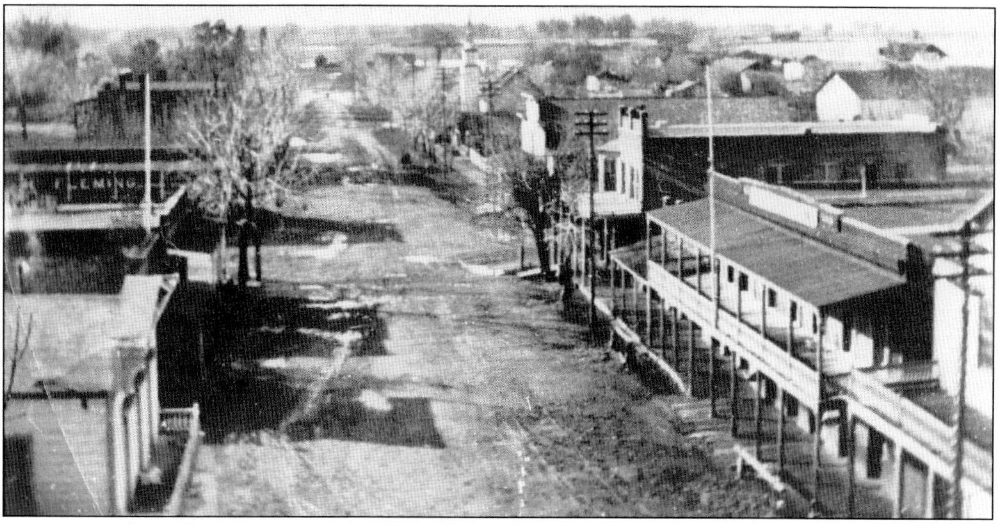

Tehama is the oldest town in the county (it even predates the county) and one of the earliest settlements north of Sacramento. It had its beginnings when Albert G. Toomes constructed an adobe home there about 1845. By 1846, many homes had been built in the area, and the town was officially surveyed in 1850. It grew prosperous with riverboat traffic. (Tehama County Library collection.)

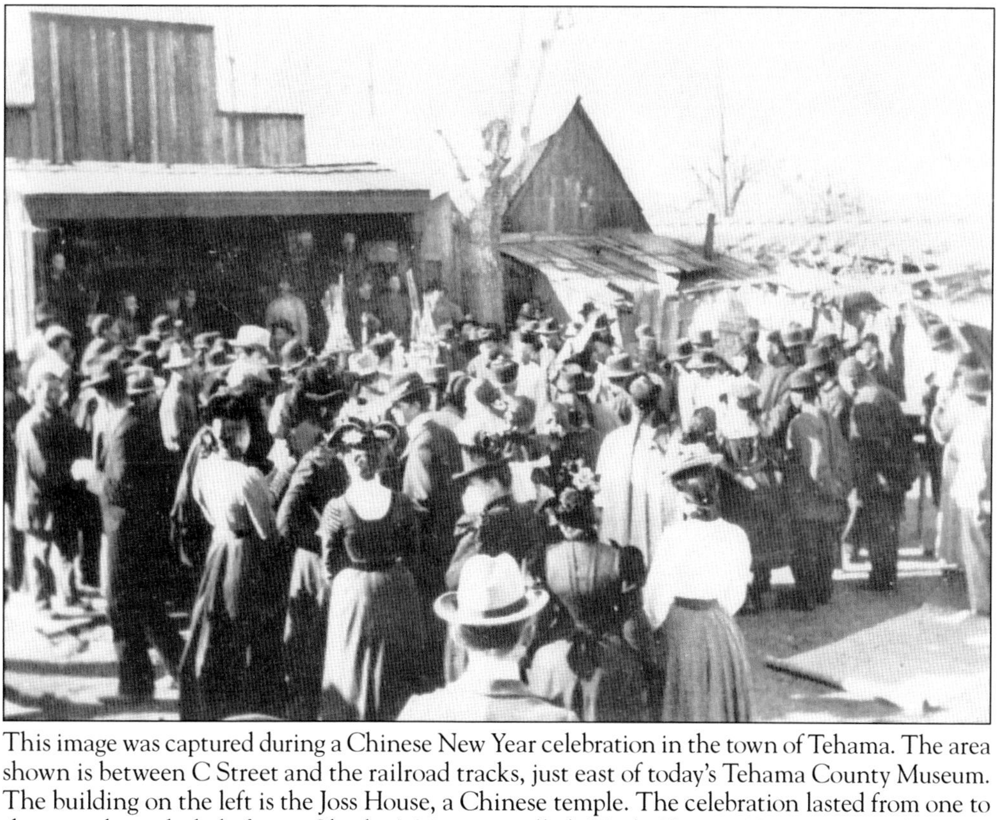

This image was captured during a Chinese New Year celebration in the town of Tehama. The area shown is between C Street and the railroad tracks, just east of today's Tehama County Museum. The building on the left is the Joss House, a Chinese temple. The celebration lasted from one to three weeks with daily feasts. Charles McLane recalled, "Each Chinese New Year's, we kids had the time of our lives." (Tehama County Library collection.)

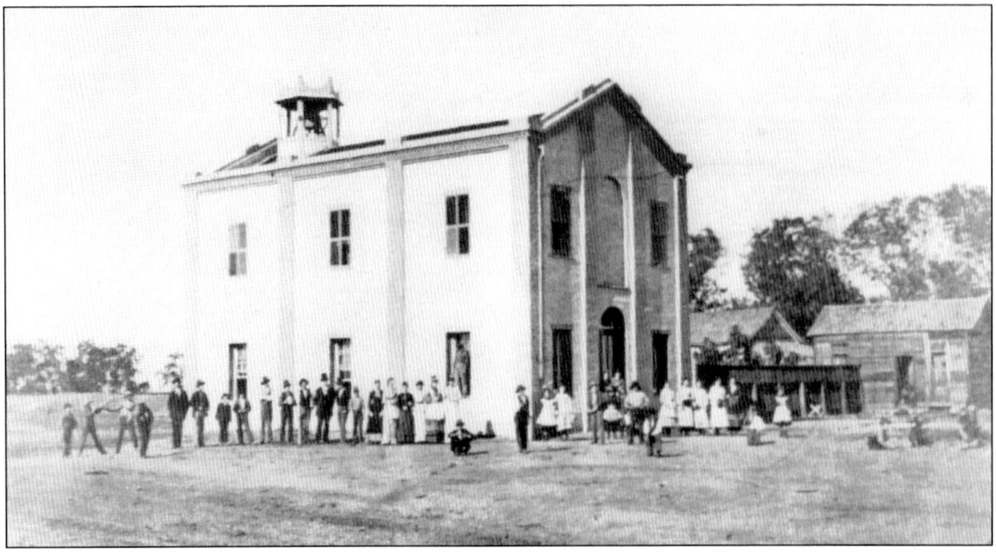

The Tehama Schoolhouse/Masonic Lodge was built in 1859 to meet the need for a school and a meeting place for the local Masonic order in the town of Tehama. A two-story brick building that served both purposes was built; the ground floor was the school, and the second floor was the Masonic Lodge. Now it is the Tehama County Museum, "where old fossils pose nude just to make people wonder." (Tehama County Library collection.)

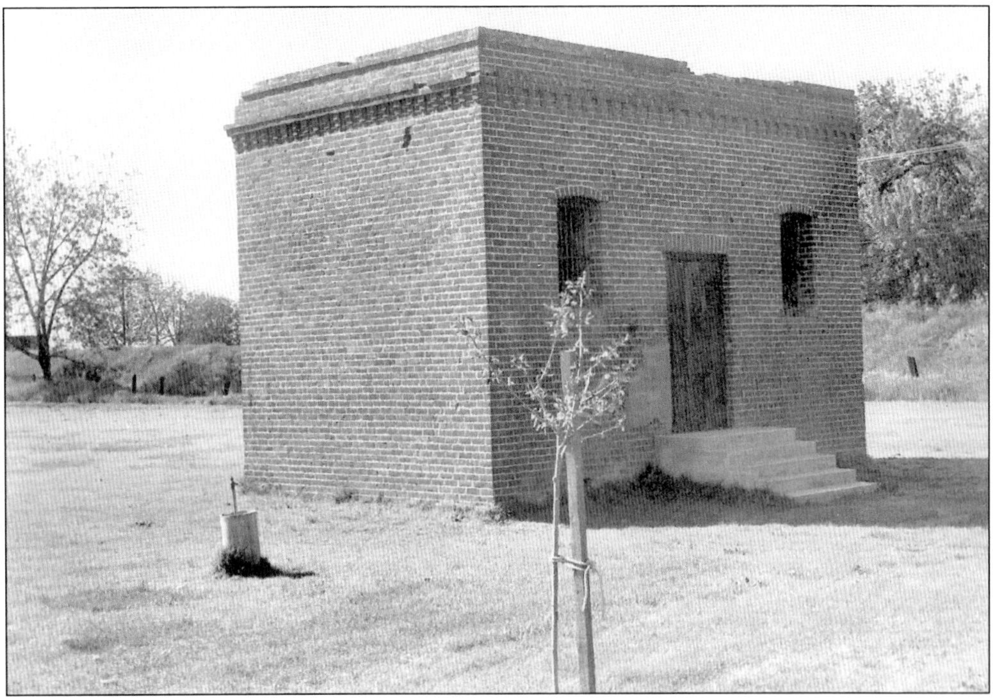

This small brick jail was built in one month in 1884 for $1,153. The first felon to occupy and escape from it was a cattle rustler. In 1885, it housed 17 to 20 Chinese for allegedly attacking a deputy sheriff. The last two people were jailed in September 1913 (for stealing a boat) before it closed in August 1914. It still stands in Tehama next to the Tehama County Museum. (Tehama County Library collection.)

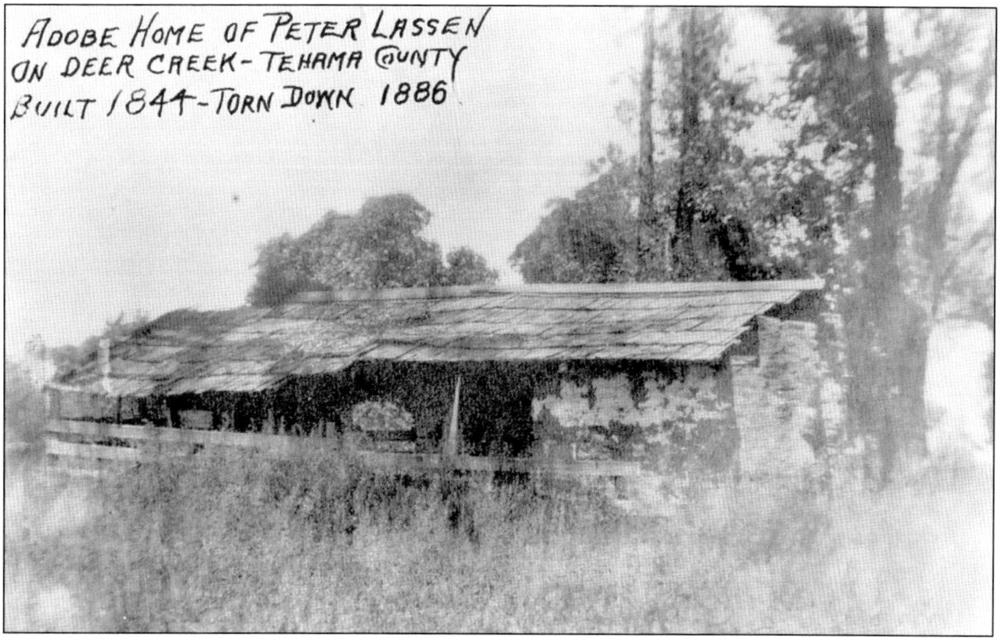


Peter Lassen's 1844 Mexican land grant is mistakenly called Rancho Bosquejo, which is supposed to mean "wooded ranch." In Spanish, *bosquejo* means "sketch" and *bosque* means "woodland" or "forest." Early deeds refer to it as Bosque. Written on John Bidwell's April 14, 1852, survey map is *Bosquejo del terreno solicilado por Pedro [Lassen]* (translated as "sketch of the terrain requested by Peter Lassen"). Subsequent mapmakers erroneously used "Bosquejo" as the name, and it stuck. (National Park Service collection.)

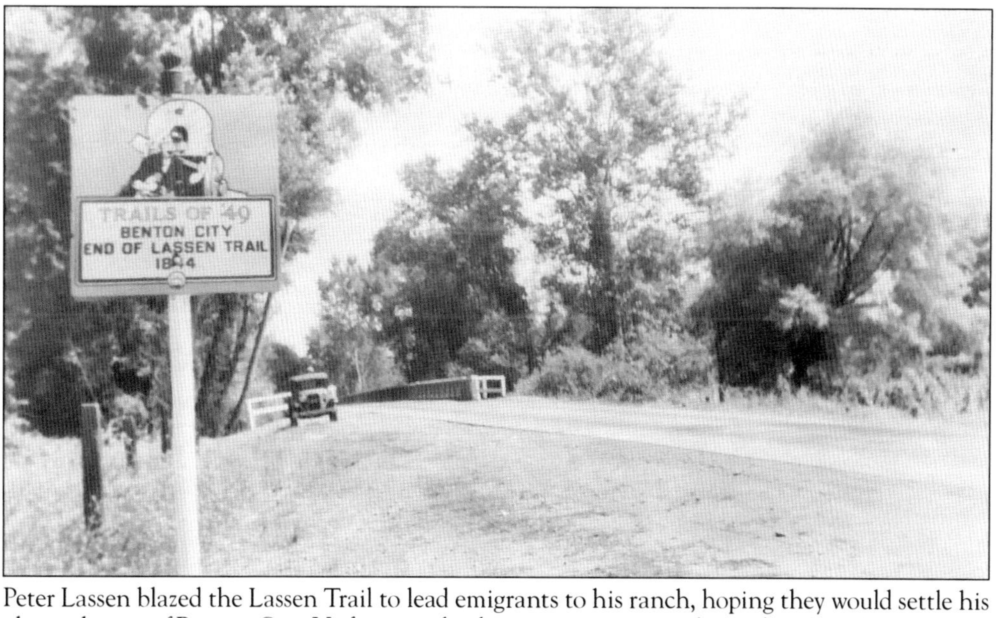


Peter Lassen blazed the Lassen Trail to lead emigrants to his ranch, hoping they would settle his planned town of Benton City. Unfortunately, the timing was not right, and nothing became of it. Lassen's dream of a thriving town could not compete with the Gold Rush stampede. Henry Gerke acquired what was left of his ranch in 1852. Lassen moved east into Plumas County. Unknown assailants later killed him in Nevada. (Tehama County Library collection.)

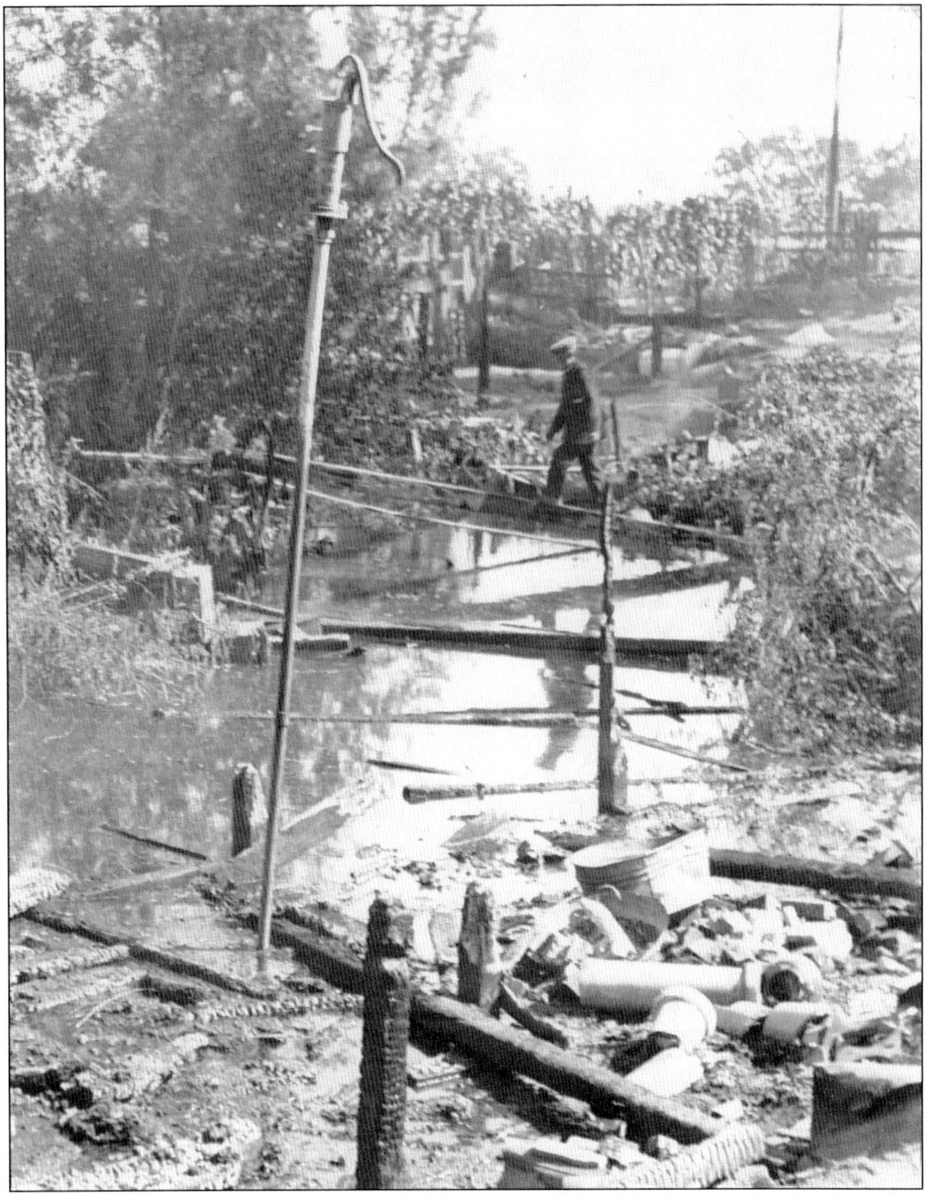

Vina's Chinatown was north of town along the railroad tracks. In 1915, a fire burned five buildings and caused one fatality. This fire, on July 11, 1920, burned down the remaining Chinese community. Most of the residents moved to Marysville. Chinatown mayor Fong Chong moved a section of the Stanford bunkhouse into Vina for the remaining Chinese residents (becoming the Lee Hotel). A cause for the fire was never officially determined, but in 2010, a local resident said his great uncle told him the fire was set as a diversion to rob the safe of a Chinese gambling den, but the fire raced out of control. The discovery of gold in California and the deterioration of the Manchu (or Qing) Dynasty led Chinese immigrants to California, the Mountain of Gold. Some were merchants, but the majority were peasants who borrowed money for their passage that had to be repaid from their earnings. The Chinese people worked at various occupations and opened businesses, and through their hard work, contributed much to the building of railroads, levees, and roads. (Frances Leininger collection.)

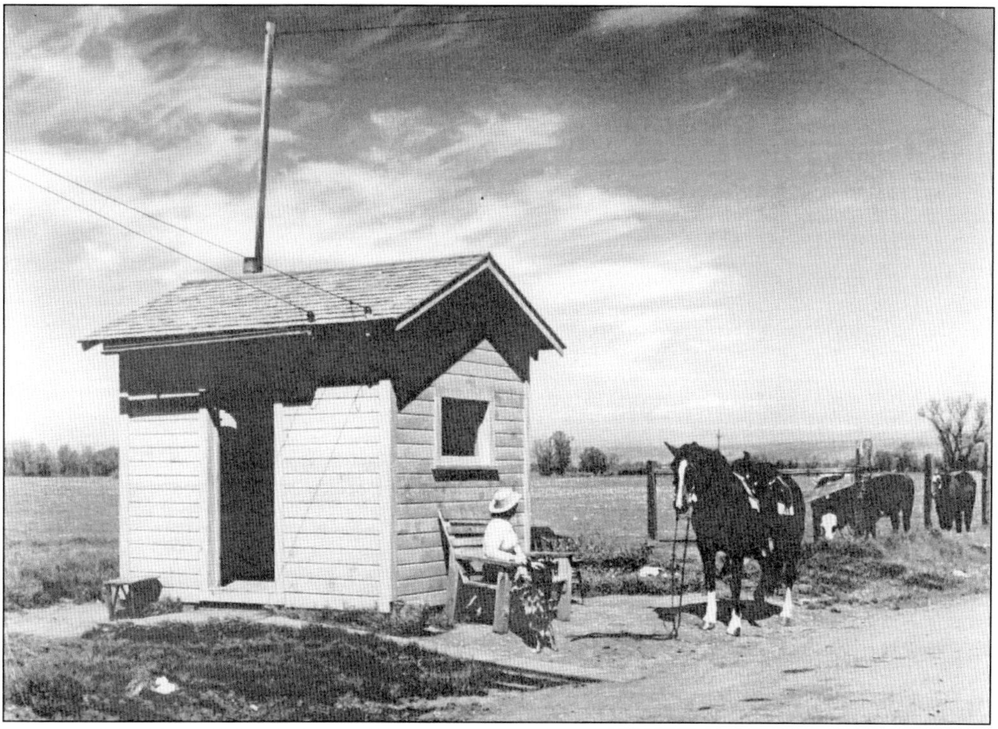

As part of the World War II Ground Observer Corps, local volunteers staffed aircraft observation posts 24 hours a day, seven days a week. This little building was located at the northeast corner of the intersection of Highway 99 East and East Vina Road. Observers watched and listened for aircraft overhead and reported the type of aircraft (if possible), height, and direction of travel to the Army Air Corps. (Frances Leininger collection.)

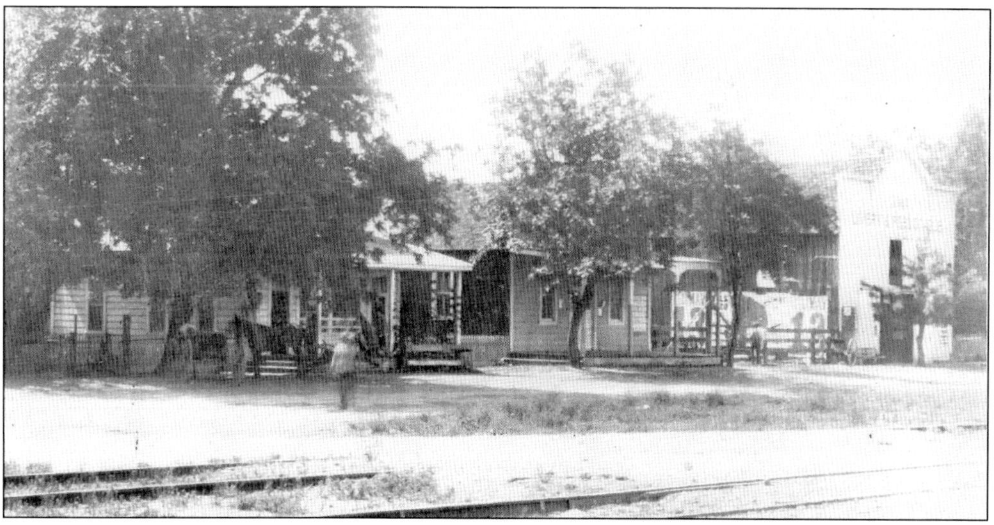

The first recorded mention of Vina comes from an 1865 advertisement for wines from the Gerke winery. Vina grew to support the Gerke Ranch and then Leland Stanford's Great Vina Ranch. This c. 1915 photograph of part of the town west of the railroad tracks shows, from left to right, the office of Dr. Andrew Lappeus, the Vina Hall (which held town meetings and dances and was owned by Buck McCollum), and the Vina Livery and Feed Stable. (Frances Leininger collection.)

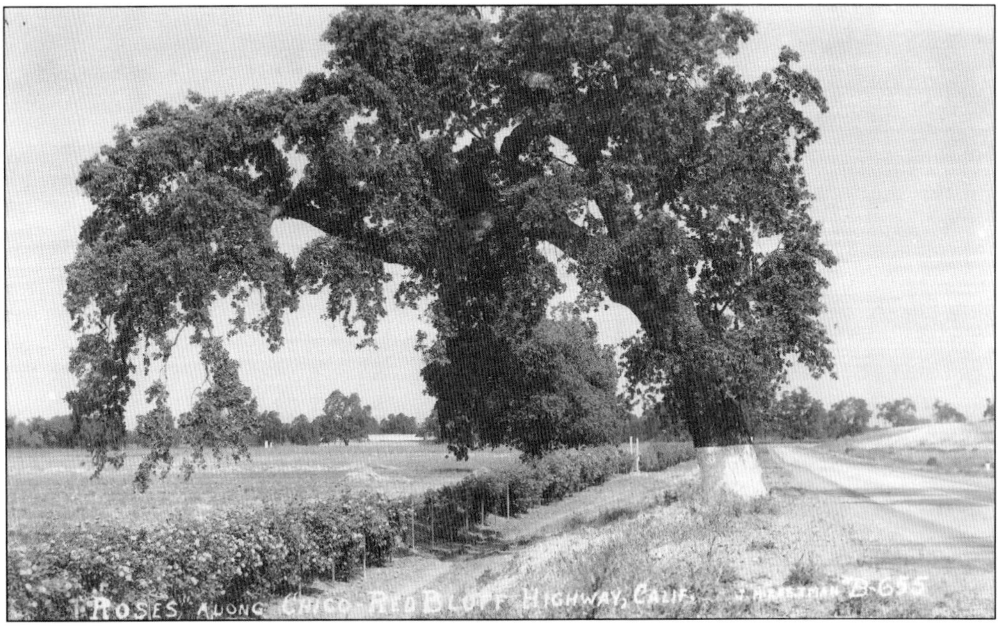


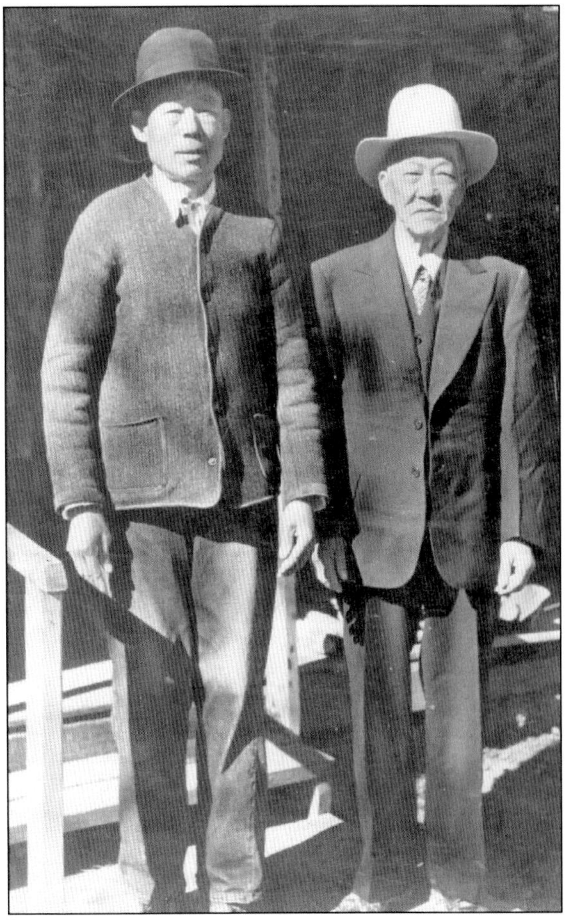

When Richard W. Hanna of Standard Oil bought a ranch, his wife said, "You can have your cows, orchards, crops, and oil, but I need roses." Stretching a mile along the west side of Highway 99 East north of Vina are remnants of her vivid Paul's Scarlet roses. Lee Sing helped plant them. China Sam, Jew Sing, Ah Mee, Ah Shook, and Joseph Valente cared for them. Long neglected, some stubbornly linger as flowering reminders of a once lovely landmark. (Author's collection.)

In this c. April 1939 photograph are Big Sam (left) and Jew Sing (right), who were bosses over the Chinese workers in the orchards near Deer Creek. The largest populations of Chinese lived in Red Bluff, Tehama, and Vina. In 1880, there were 31 Chinese market gardens employing up to 18 workers each in Tehama County. The Chinese owned or leased the gardens, which were very successful—one garden yielded $75,000 worth of dried fruit annually. (Frances Leininger collection.)

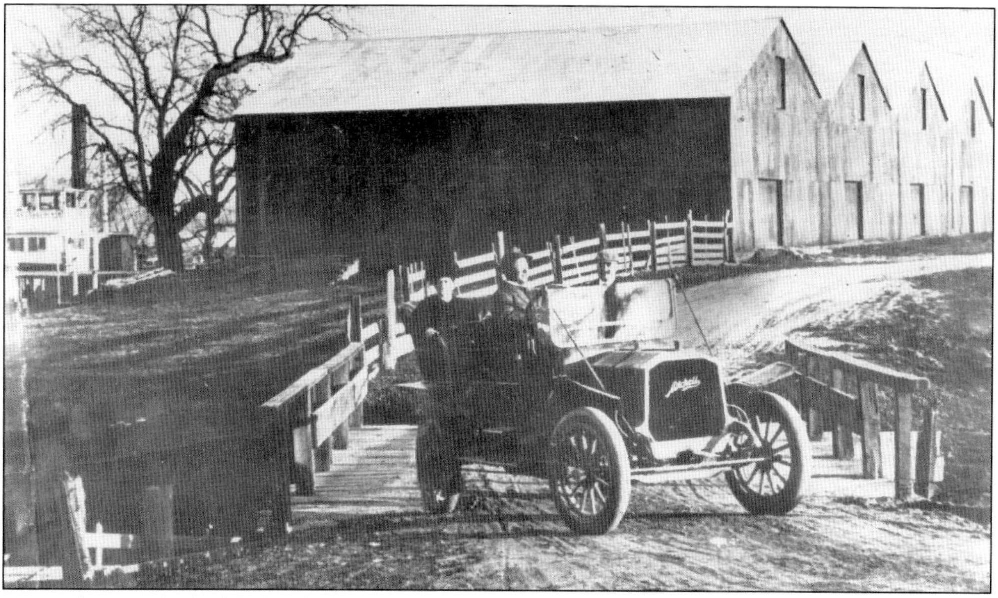

A riverboat is docked behind the large warehouses at Squaw Hill Landing on the Sacramento River, east of Corning, around 1911. These warehouses were built in 1894. In the foreground is Warren Woodson driving a right-handed Mitchell touring car. Woodson drove prospective property buyers around his Maywood Colony in that car. With him are Nina Alice and Livingston Crichton, residents of the community. (Tehama County Library collection.)

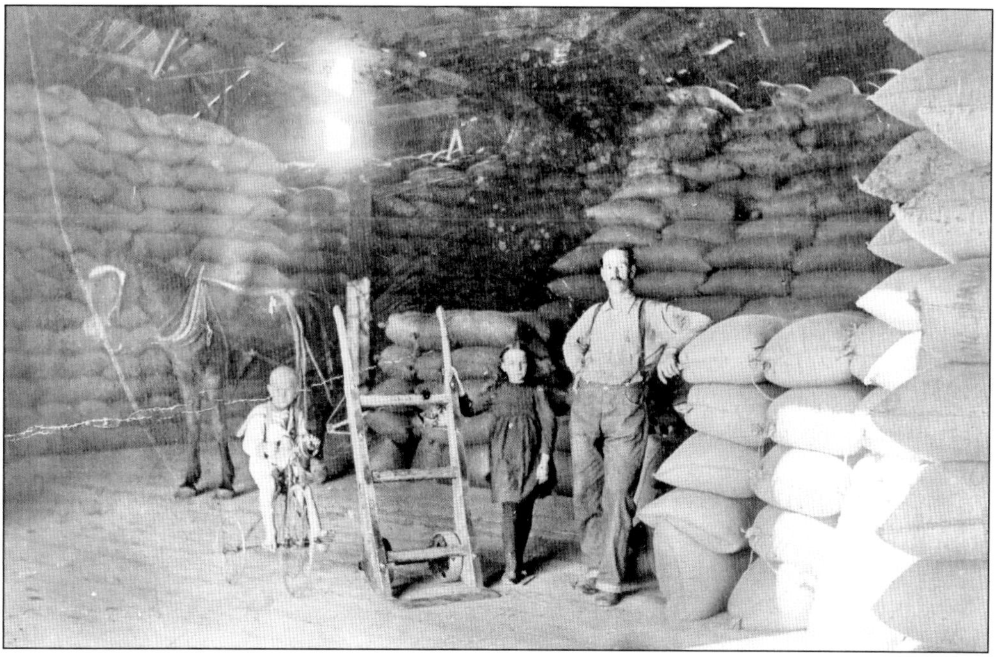

Warehouses along the banks of the river held outgoing cargoes of wool, wheat, and other agricultural products as well as incoming cargoes of hardware, furniture, dry goods, and various items. Ranchers and farmers came from great distances to leave or pick up cargo. By 1916, with riverboat traffic waning, these warehouses were moved south to Princeton in Colusa County. (Tehama County Library collection.)

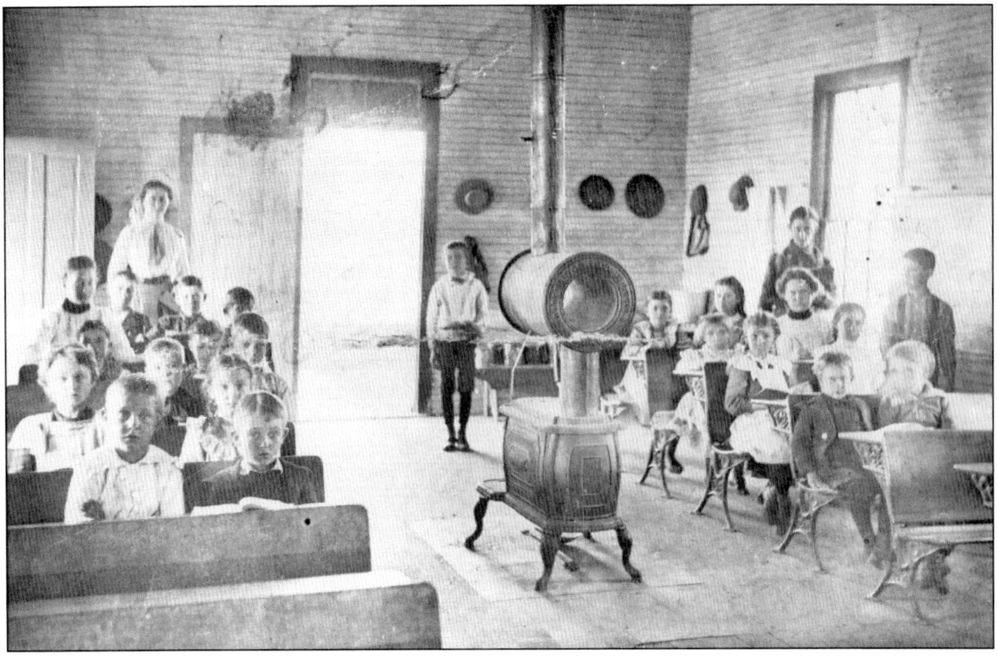

The Squaw Hill community established the Moon School on an acre of property at the corner of Hall Road and Loleta Avenue donated by William McLane. A larger two-room schoolhouse was built in 1905. It was also used as a community hall and a Sunday school for the Corning Methodist Church. Classes were held until 1953–1954, when the school was consolidated with Corning Union Elementary District. (California State University, Chico, Special Collections.)

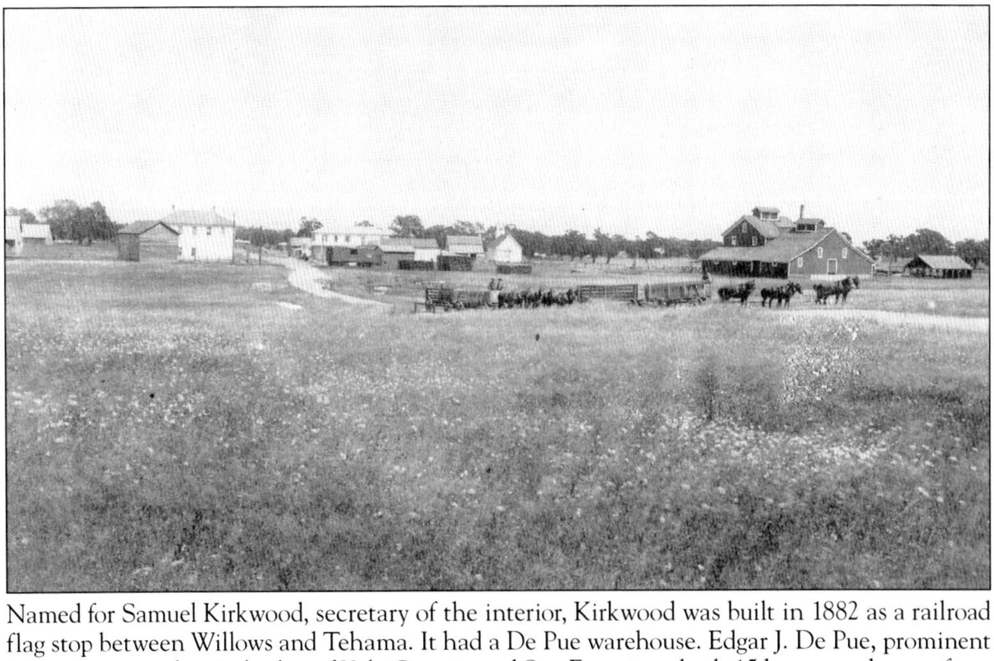

Named for Samuel Kirkwood, secretary of the interior, Kirkwood was built in 1882 as a railroad flag stop between Willows and Tehama. It had a De Pue warehouse. Edgar J. De Pue, prominent businessman and grain broker of Yolo County and San Francisco, built 15 huge warehouses from Port Costa in the Bay Area to Red Bluff. They stood next to railroad tracks where freight could be easily loaded and unloaded. Several still stand today. (Tehama County Library collection.)

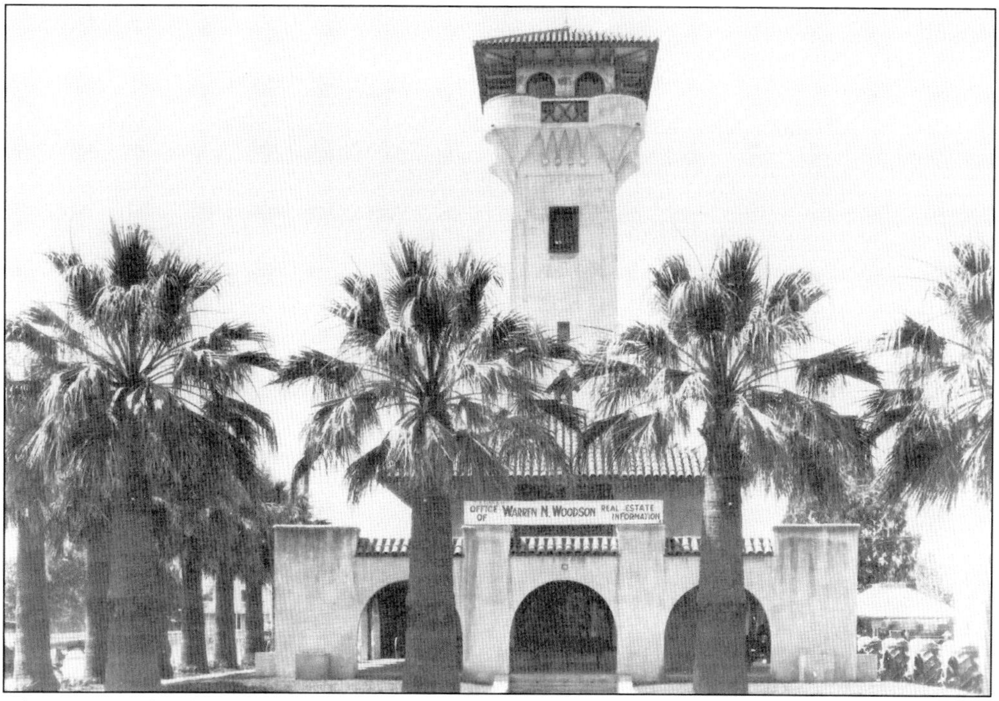


The Maywood Colony Tower was the office of Warren Woodson and a symbol for his Maywood Colony. It was built in the old Spanish Mission style with a red tile roof in 1903. Its observation tower was 75 feet high so prospective buyers could be impressed with the view of the town and surrounding orchards. It was torn down to make way for a used car lot about 1960. (Corning Museum collection.)

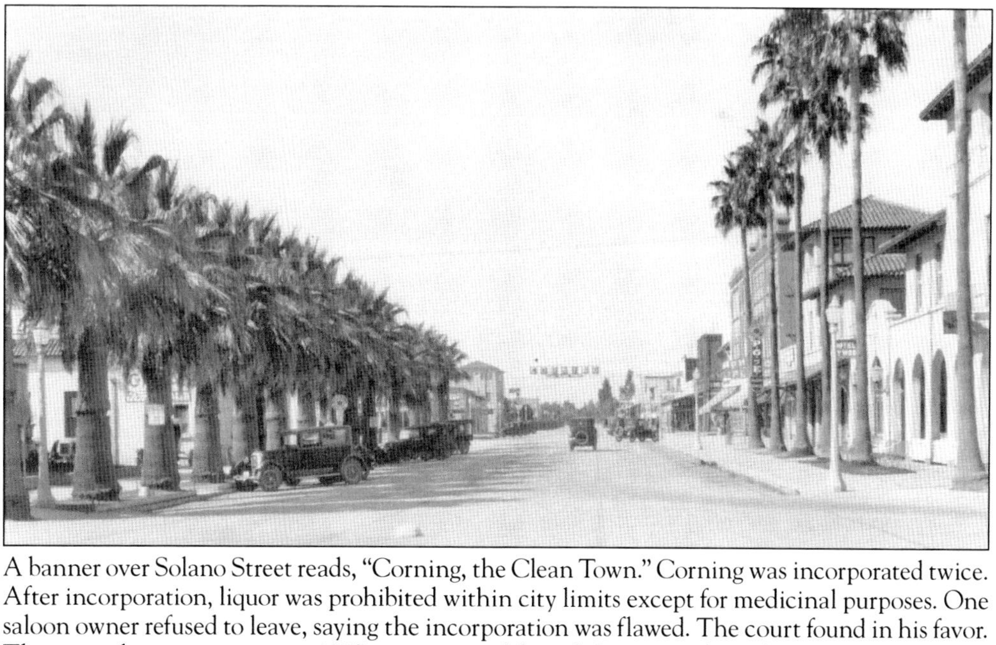

A banner over Solano Street reads, "Corning, the Clean Town." Corning was incorporated twice. After incorporation, liquor was prohibited within city limits except for medicinal purposes. One saloon owner refused to leave, saying the incorporation was flawed. The court found in his favor. The second incorporation in 1907 was successful, and Corning adopted prohibition. Warren Woodson became its first mayor. (Corning Museum collection.)

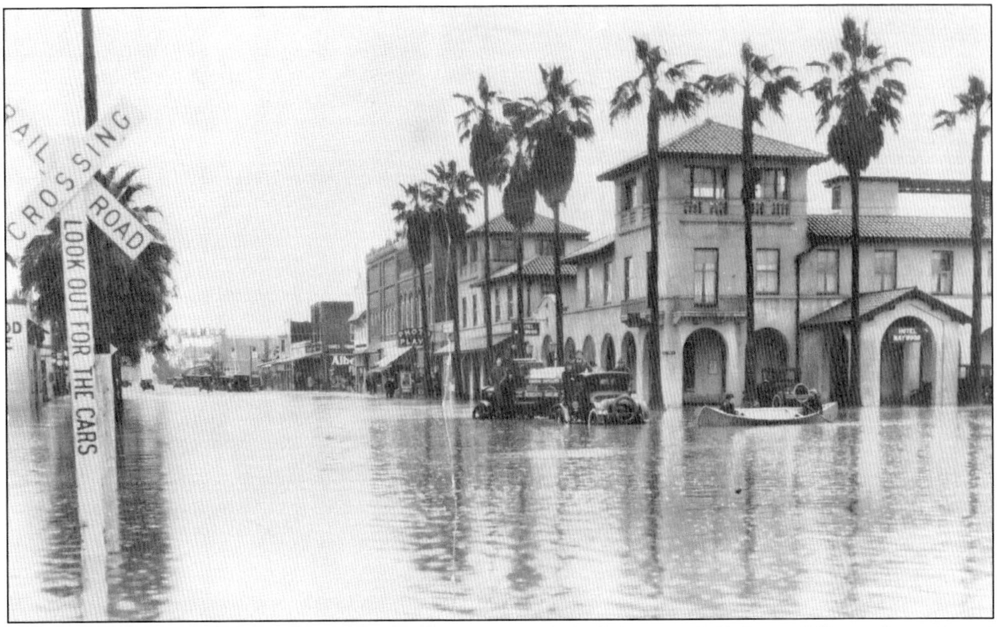


The Hotel Maywood greeted visitors to Corning and the Maywood Colony. When the railroad built Corning, it did not plan for adequate drainage, so the town flooded during wet winters. Tired of the railroad's indifference, locals threatened to dynamite a railroad bridge underpass to improve drainage. The railroad section boss, John Quinn, guarded the bridge with a shotgun and convinced the crowd that the problem would be fixed, which it was. (Corning Museum collection.)

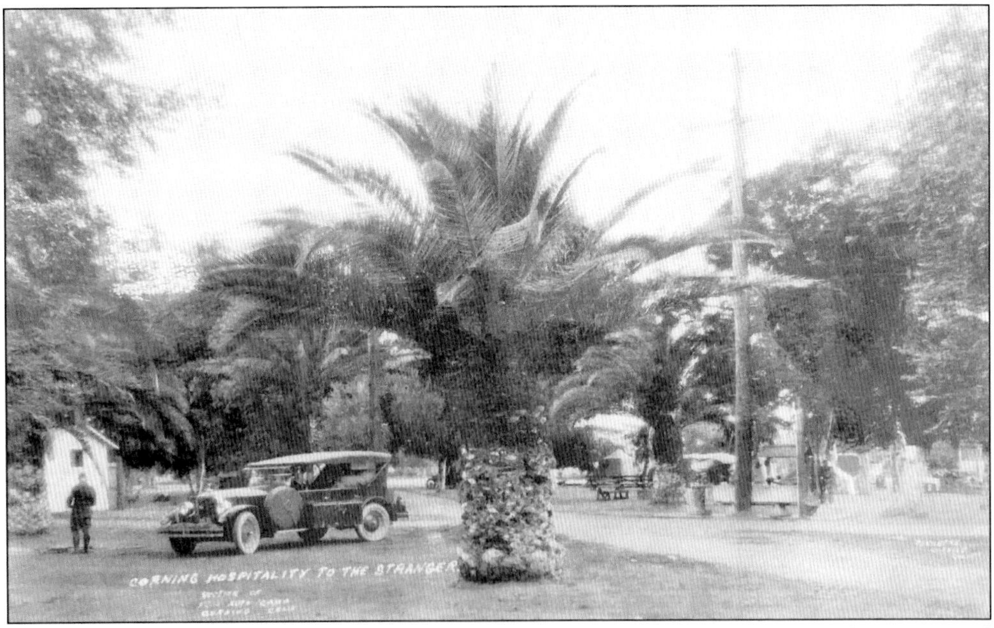


With automobile traffic increasing, a Corning city block was turned into the state's first municipal auto camp in 1900, where travelers could comfortably rest. Showers, laundry facilities, running water, electric lights, tables and benches, large lawns, concrete stoves with wood supplied, and garbage disposal were all provided for 50¢ the first day and 25¢ per day after that. (Corning Museum collection.)

# *Four*

# AGRICULTURE

The wealth of Tehama County has always been its land. Agriculture gives people sustenance and towns permanence. Native Americans gathered native roots, bulbs, fruits, berries, grains, seeds, and acorns every year, but the first agriculture in the county by Europeans occurred when Peter Lassen brought cattle to his ranch on Deer Creek in 1844 and began cultivating the land.

Livestock raised in Tehama County has included horses, mules, cattle, sheep, goats, swine, and turkeys. Early settlers started raising sheep for meat and wool. The Civil War increased the demand for wool, and by the 1880s, about 300,000 head of sheep made Tehama County the largest sheep-producing county in the state. The sheep industry grew until the Great Depression. World War II also adversely affected sheep producers.

The first farming in the county involved wheat, barley, and hay. Large acreages of wheat were grown, and by the late 1860s, wheat surpassed cattle and sheep in annual crop values. When the wheat boom ended in the 1890s, farmers turned to orchard crops such as apples, apricots, cherries, figs, olives, pears, prunes, lemons, oranges, almonds, and walnuts. As early as the 1860s, one of the first fruits planted were peaches. By the 1900s, peaches were the county's principal crop. Grant Merrill of Tehama County was a nationally recognized peach breeder who developed early-ripening peaches. However, local peaches could not compete with those from peach-growing areas to the south, so their importance as a crop declined.

Henry Gerke, from Frankfurt am Main, Germany, crossed the plains in 1847 to California. During the 1850s, he was involved in San Francisco real estate and built one of the first houses in the city. In 1852, he acquired part of the Lassen Ranch and developed the first commercial winery there in the 1860s with his vineyard of 100,000 grapevines. Later, Leland Stanford planted millions of vines on thousands of acres to make his ranch the largest vineyard and brandy distillery in the world at the time.

Currently, the orchard industry of fruits and nuts makes up approximately two-thirds of the agricultural product value of the county, while livestock and poultry are the other third. Walnuts, almonds, olives, and prunes account for nearly all of the fruits and nuts. Cattle account for nearly all livestock.

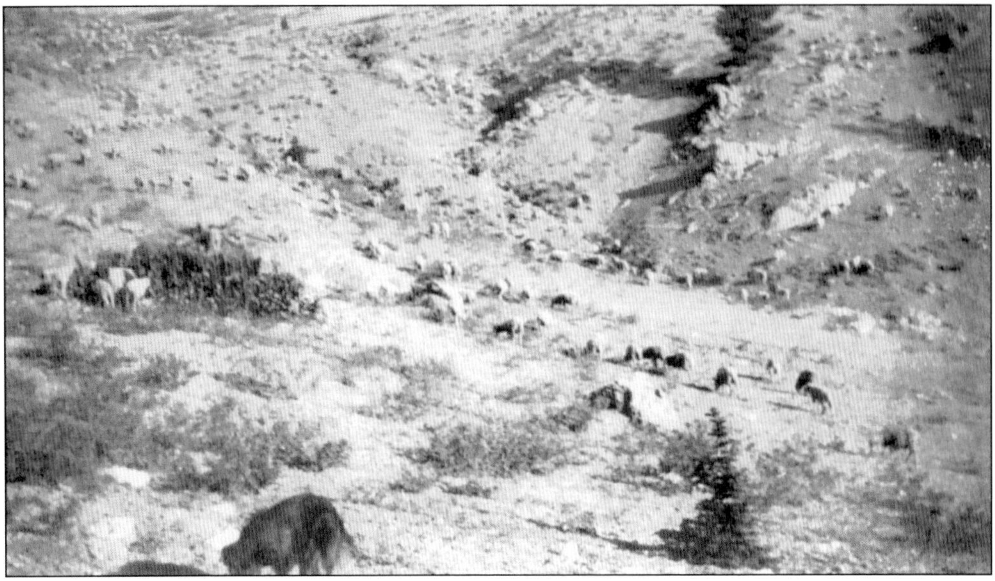

Carroll Irish's sheep are pictured at their summer range in the rugged Yolla Bolly Mountains in Mendocino National Forest near Solomon Peak in western Tehama County around 1921. In Wintun, *yola* means "snow," and *boli* means "spirit." The belief that peaks were the abode of spirits was common among the California Indians. (Wilson family collection.)

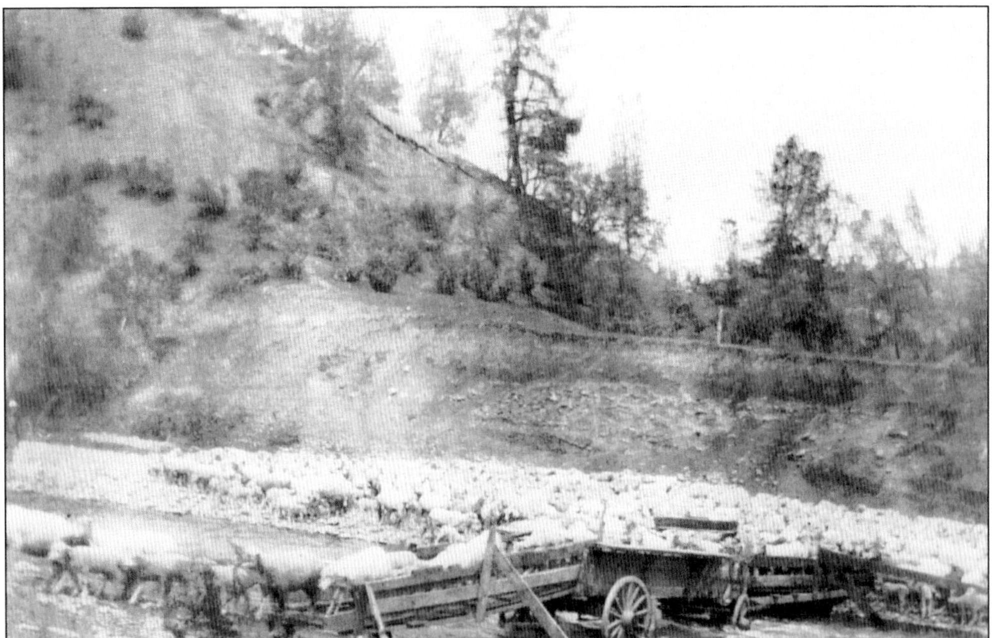

In this image, sheep cross a creek. (Note the wagon used as part of the bridge.) Hobart Moulton recalled that sheep did not like crossing bridges. Sometimes, a sheepherder would have to drag or lead a ewe across before the others would follow. Burros wearing bells were used at times to lead sheep when they were trailed to and from mountain meadows. (Opal Thornton Mendenhall collection.)

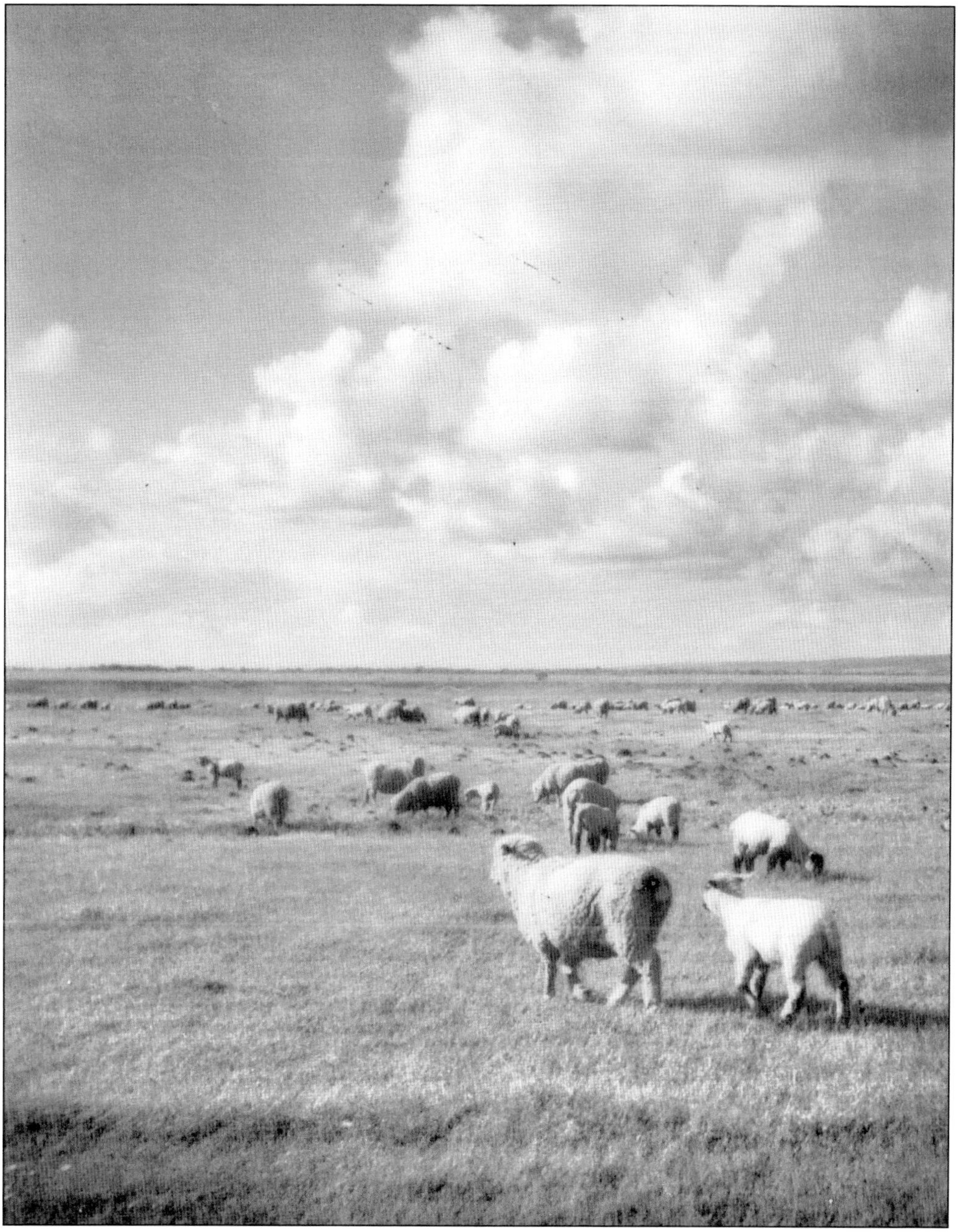

Sheep are pictured on the expansive Vina Plains in southern Tehama County. The Rawson brothers drove 4,000 French Merino sheep into the county in 1857. The county's sheep industry grew steadily until the 1930s, when the Great Depression caused heavy financial losses. Overgrazing, restrictions on the public use of government land based on sharp political differences between advocates of no-use versus wise-use, the federal policy of aggressively fighting forest fires that allowed brush to grow too high for sheep grazing, and the introduction of synthetic fibers after World War II all contributed to the steep decline in sheep numbers. By the 1980s, only 15,000 sheep were left as small farm flocks. Today, the large sheep industry is a thing of the past. (Frances Leininger collection.)

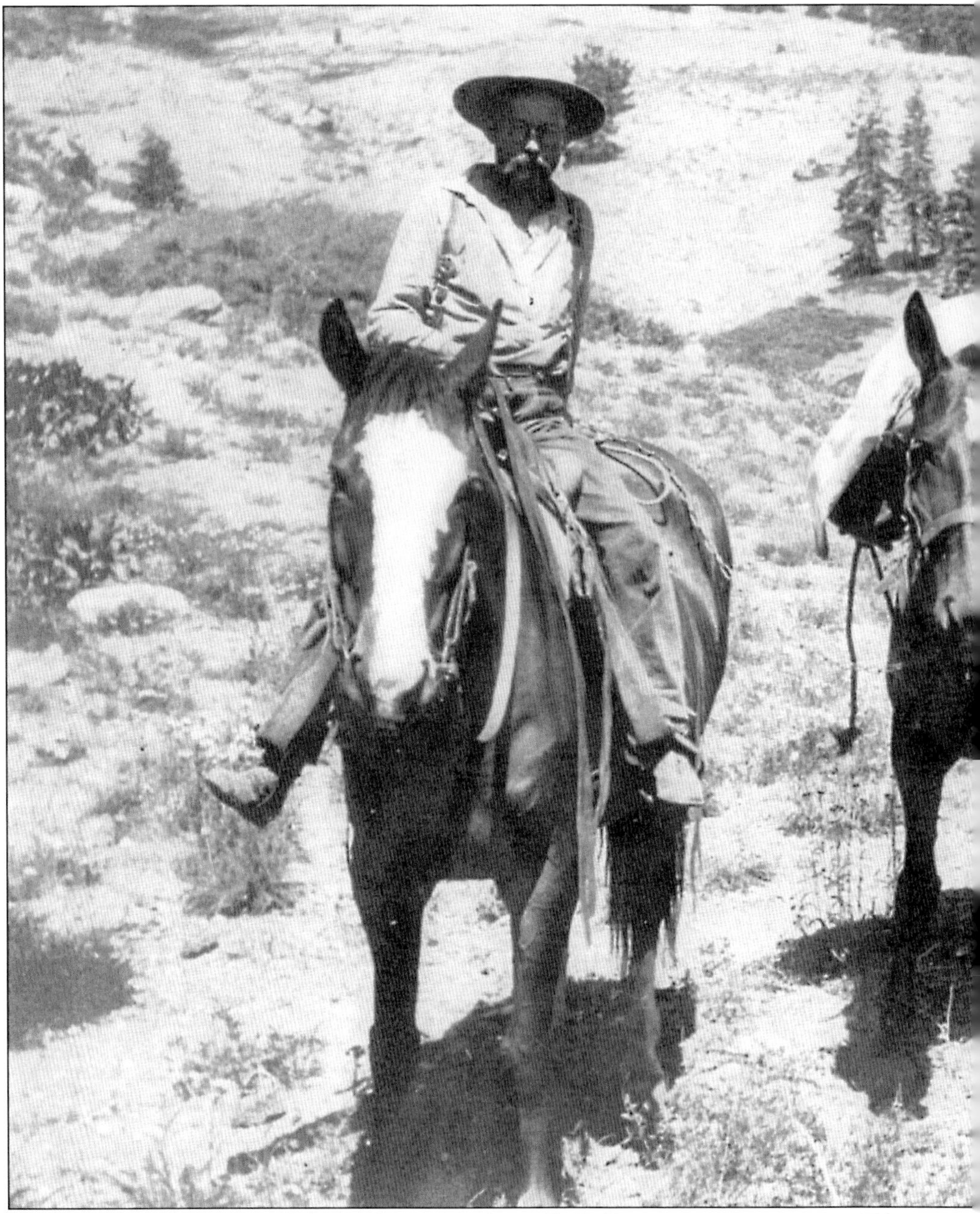

Carroll Irish is seen here with his pack train in the Yolla Bolly Mountains in western Tehama County in the mid-1950s. Valley sheepmen moved their herds to summer pastures in the eastern and western mountains. Strings of mules or horses packed the supplies, which were brought in from the valley every week or two by young men hired as camp tenders. By the 1930s, trucks brought sheep to their mountain grazing areas. The first sheep brought into the northern Sacramento

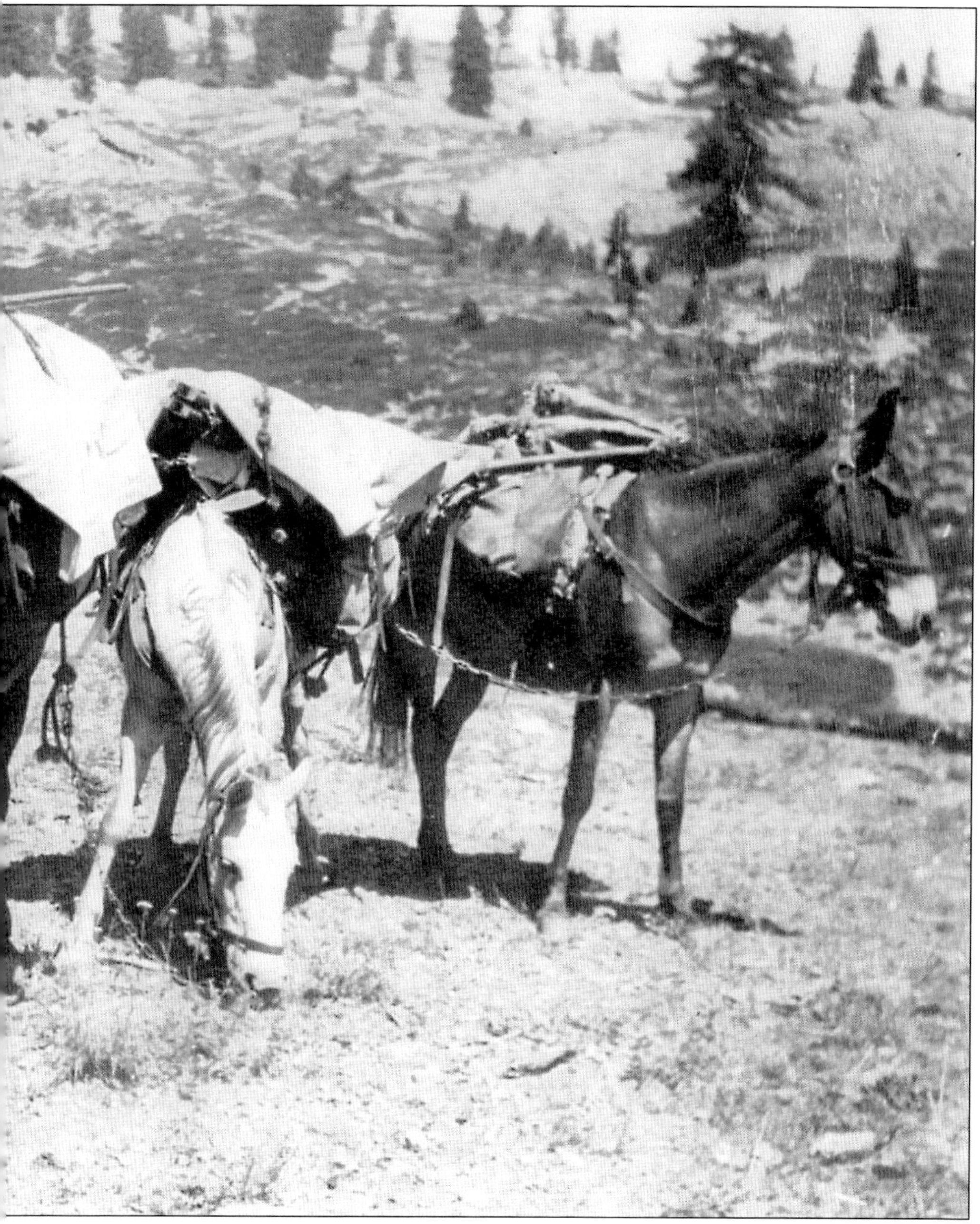

Valley were the coarse-wool Spanish California *churros*. Other breeds soon followed, and between 1851 and 1861, an estimated 75,000 to 100,000 sheep were trailed overland to California. The Gold Rush created a demand for "meat-on-the-hoof." This drove sheep prices from 75¢ per head to $12–14 per head in 1849. After the Gold Rush, the market turned to wool, especially during the Civil War. (Wilson family collection.)

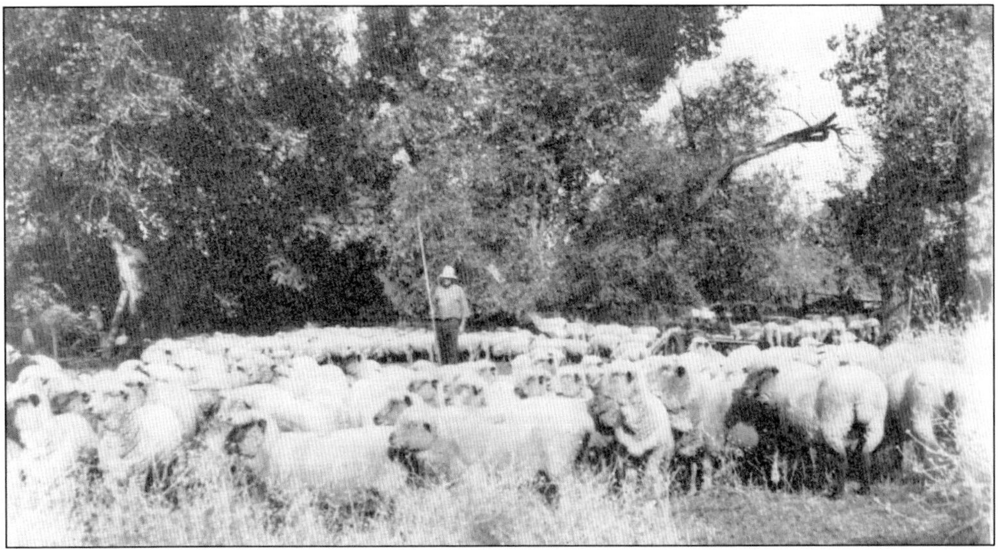

Eph Leininger is pictured with sheep near Vina in this c. October 1937 photograph. The Quong Lee store stood about where Eph is standing. The store started as a Chinese camp. It carried Chinese candy, cookies, groceries, silk robes, slippers, and scarves. One day while he was in town, Lee's store was robbed. After that, whenever he had to leave, he boarded up the windows and padlocked the door. The store burned down about 1926. (Frances Leininger collection.)

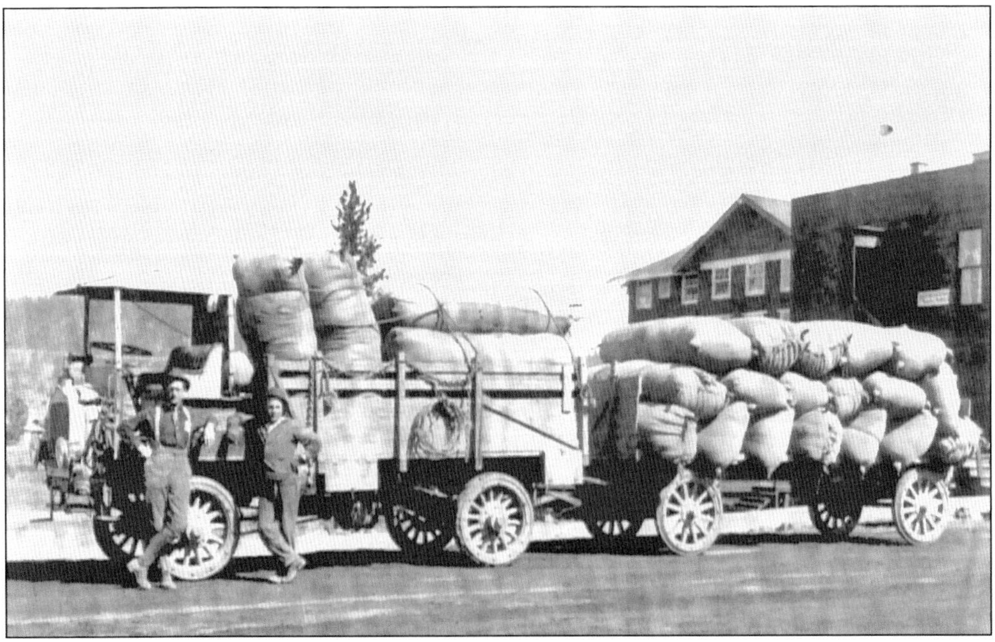

When sheep were taken to their summer grazing range in the mountains, they would often be sheared there too—all by hand. (Shearing 100 sheep in eight hours was considered very good.) The wool would be stuffed into large sacks, branded, and packed out by mules to be loaded onto waiting wagons and brought to town. Later, trucks were used to haul these sacks of wool to town. (Tehama County Library collection.)

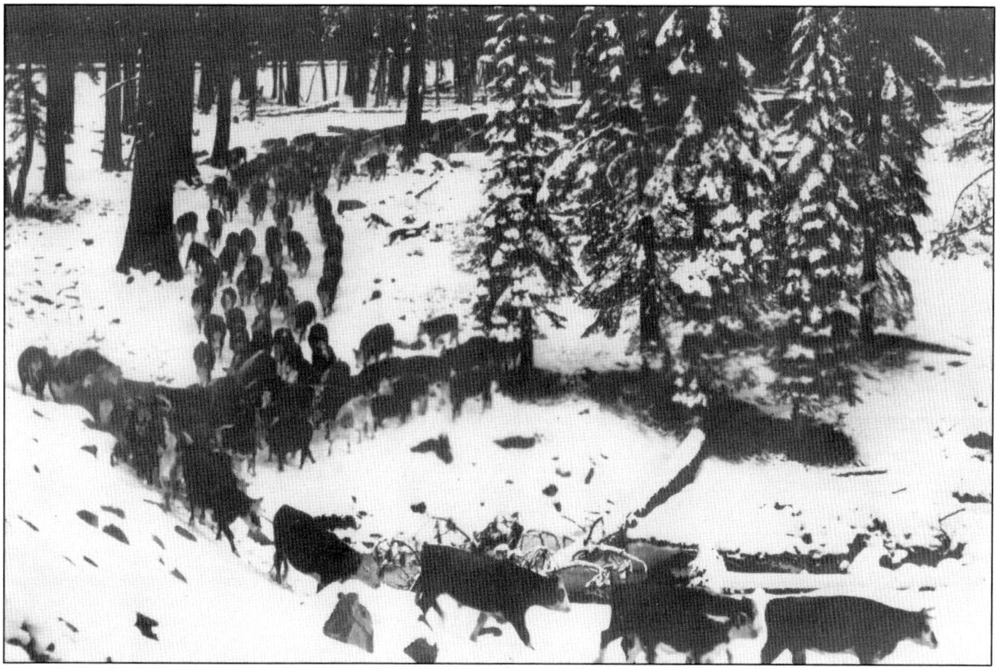

Stover and Conard cattle are pictured on snowy Morgan Summit heading to their winter range around 1938. In 1837, Ewing Young and 16 men drove 700 head of cattle and 40 horses through Tehama County to Oregon. Their trail blazed the way for the California-Oregon Road, the same route used by the railroad, Highway 99, and Interstate 5. From the 1890s until 1950, cattle were trailed to summer ranges. With irrigated pastures, many now never leave the county. (Tehama County Library collection.)

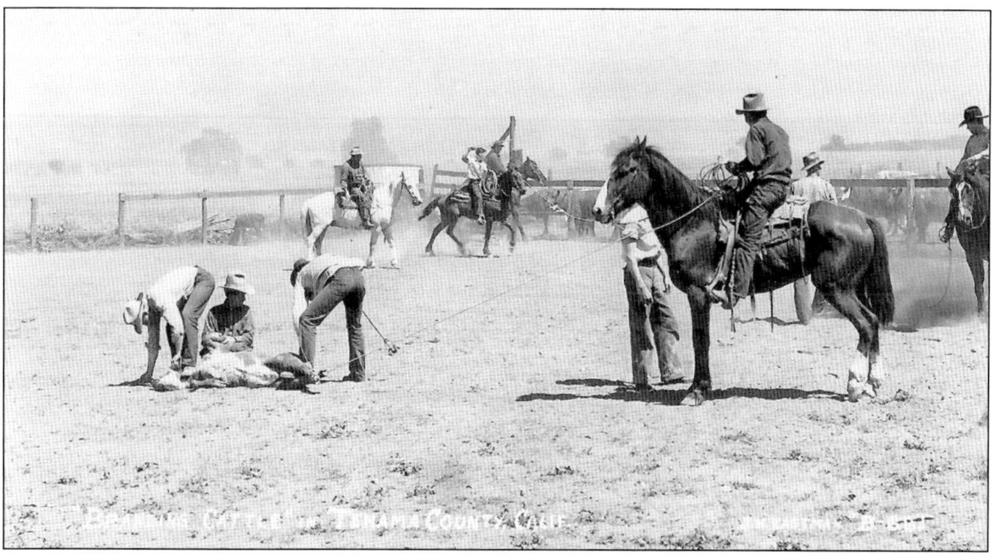


In 1852, California passed legislation providing for the registering of brands. The first brand recorded in Tehama County was by William Allen—a simple "A." Early brands were registered on leather. The shape of a cow's head was cut from leather, and it was branded with the iron being registered. Identifying earmarks were also cut into leather ears attached to the head. This method continued until 1925. (Tehama County Library collection.)

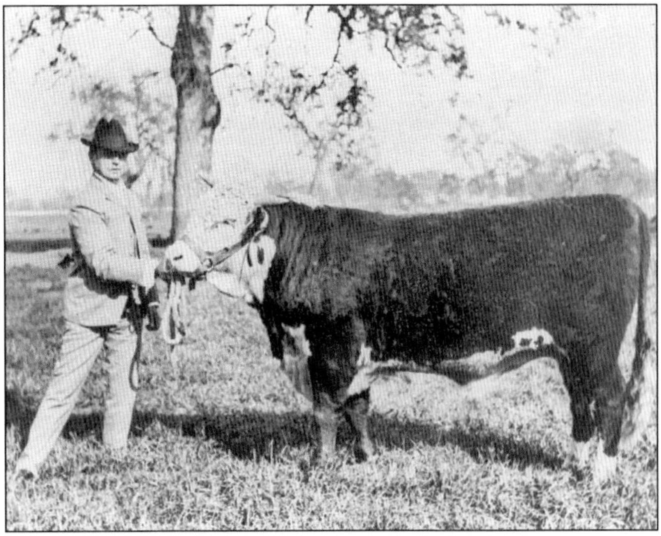

Douglas Cone brought the first purebred Herefords to Tehama County when he purchased 55 head for $8,000 from Gov. John Sparks of Nevada in 1899. Horned Herefords were once the most popular bulls in Tehama County and his Berendos herd was famous. White-faced cattle were such a curiosity that a gentle three-year-old bull named Aaron was kept at the Freeman Stable in Red Bluff for a week in January 1900 to be admired. (California State University, Chico, Special Collections.)

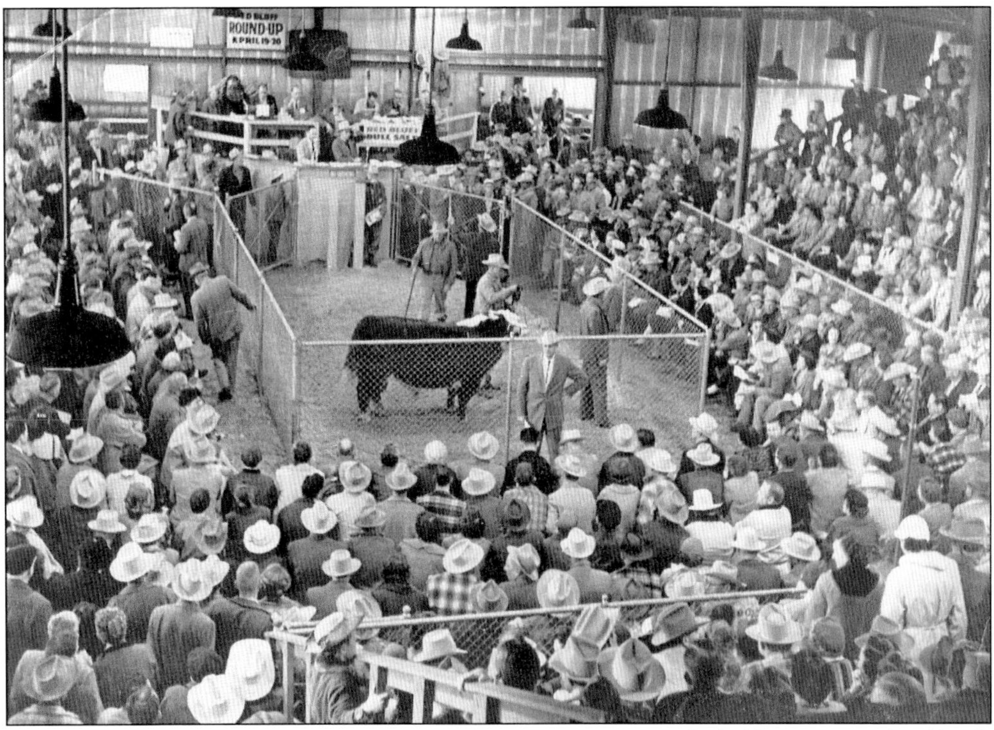


Founded in 1941, the Red Bluff Bull and Gelding Sale was originally held to improve beef herds in the county. The sale has grown into a major event with consignors and buyers coming from nearly every state. It is the largest and one of the oldest stock sales: heifers, bulls, gelding, mules, and herding dogs are sold to the highest bidder. Proceeds benefit charities and community projects. (Tehama County Library collection.)

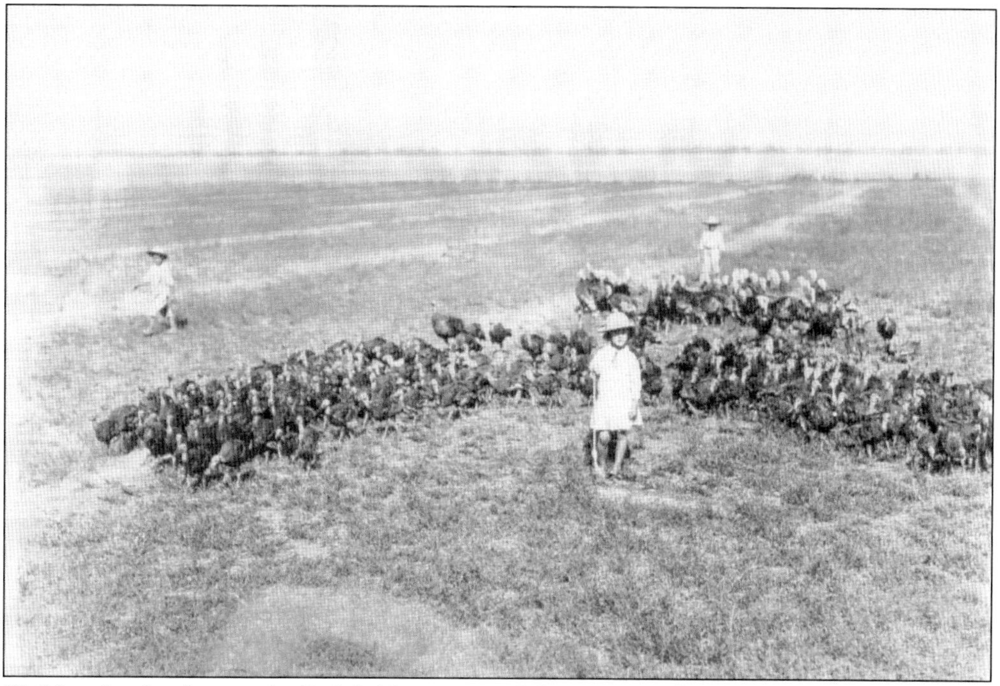

Children herd turkeys in the Richfield area around the 1930s. Turkey flocks were driven into the foothills or alfalfa fields to feed on grasshoppers (to control swarms), seeds, and bugs. Before trucks, turkeys were herded to town when it was time for market. African American pioneer Alvin Coffey raised turkeys. He lived in Tehama County for many years after buying his freedom for $1,000. In an 1892 letter to the Society of California Pioneers, of which he was a member, he wrote, "I sent you a box today by express. It is a stuffed Badger skin to put in your managerie [*sic*]. He destroyed a good many turkeys for me mostly sitting hens in the brush." (Corning Museum collection.)

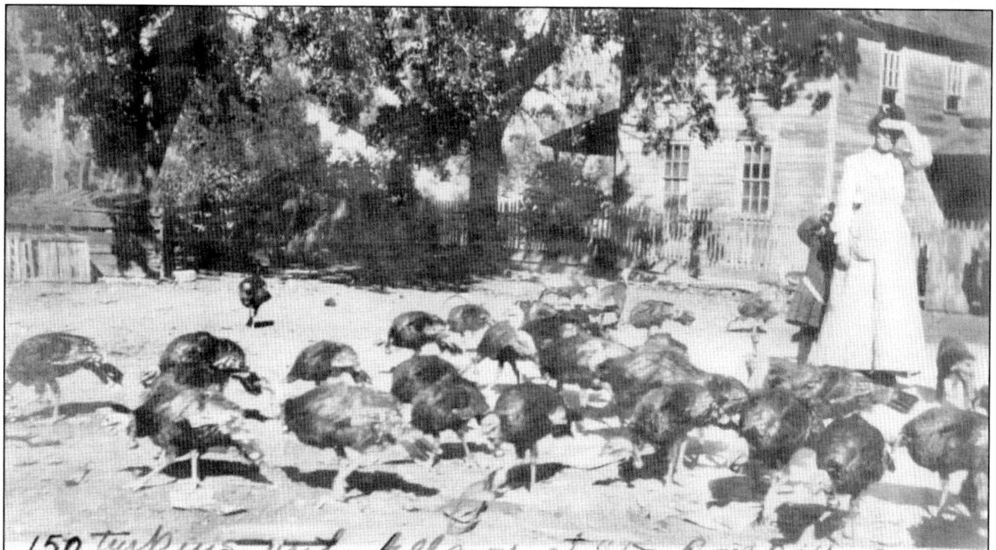

Francis Saunders and her daughter Angie are pictured with their flock of 150 turkeys wearing bells at the Diamond Range House in western Tehama County around 1909. (Saunders family/Opal Thornton Mendenhall collection.)

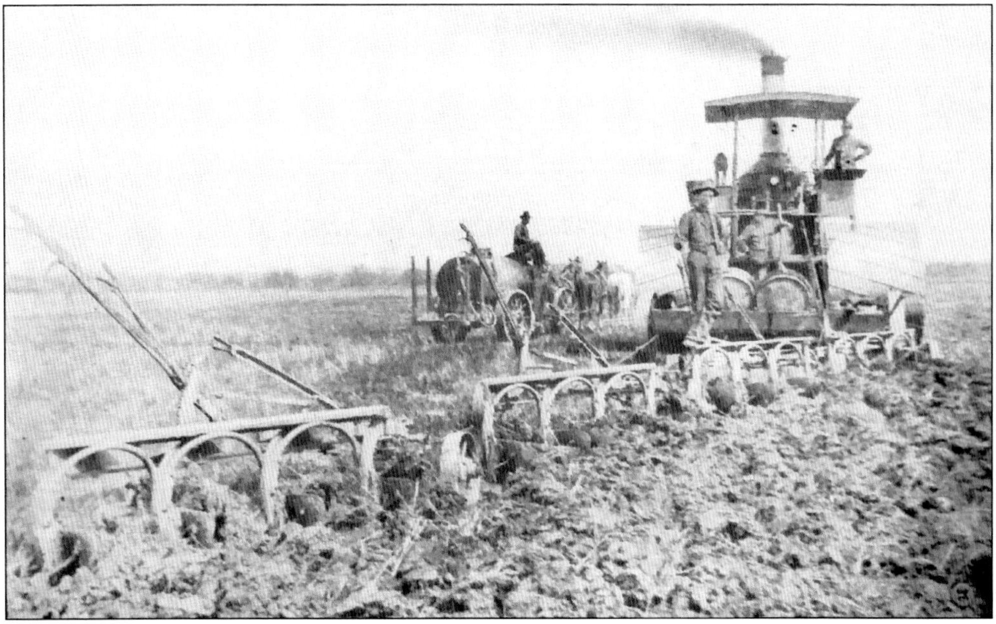

Around 1900, a steam tractor pulls a 16-bottom plow, which is a shovel-shaped implement made of the moldboard (turns the soil), the plow point (cuts the bottom of the furrow), the plow shear (cuts the side of the furrow), and the tag wheel (supports the plow). Daniel Best built the steam tractor for John Moran of Corning. Benicia Iron Works built the plows especially for this tractor. The water wagon filled the steam tractor. (Tehama County Museum collection.)

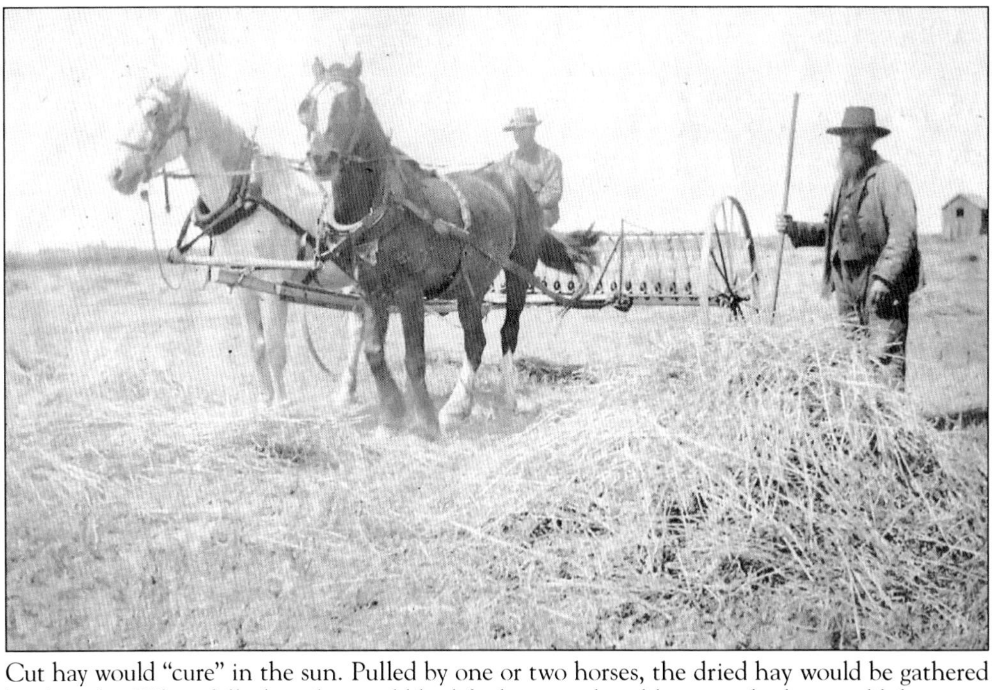

Cut hay would "cure" in the sun. Pulled by one or two horses, the dried hay would be gathered by the rake. When full, the rake would be lifted using a hand lever so the hay could drop into windrows. The rake would be lowered to repeat the process. Eventually, the hay would be raked into long rows and made into haystacks or brought to the barn. (Dan Bayles collection.)

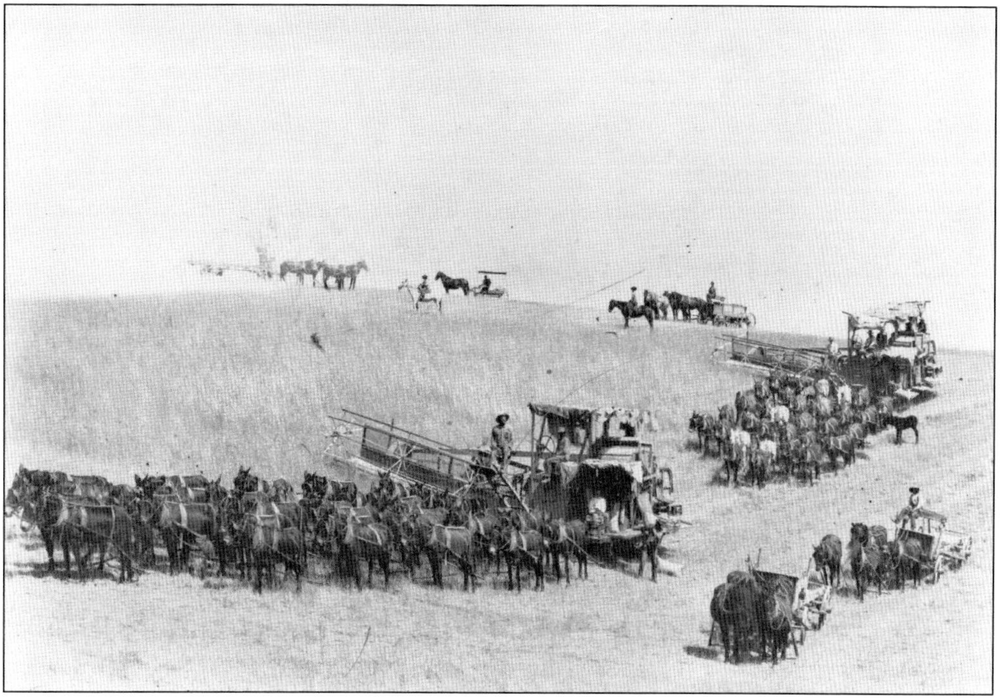

Ralph and Jack Henderson's mule team harvesters are pictured on the Gallatin Ranch around 1910. Albert Gallatin of Sacramento, whose 1877 home became the governor's mansion when acquired by the state in 1903, originally established this 50,000-acre ranch. Albert Gallatin's father (of the same name) was Pres. Thomas Jefferson's secretary of the treasury. The Gallatin River in Montana was named in his honor by Meriwether Lewis. (Tehama County Library collection.)

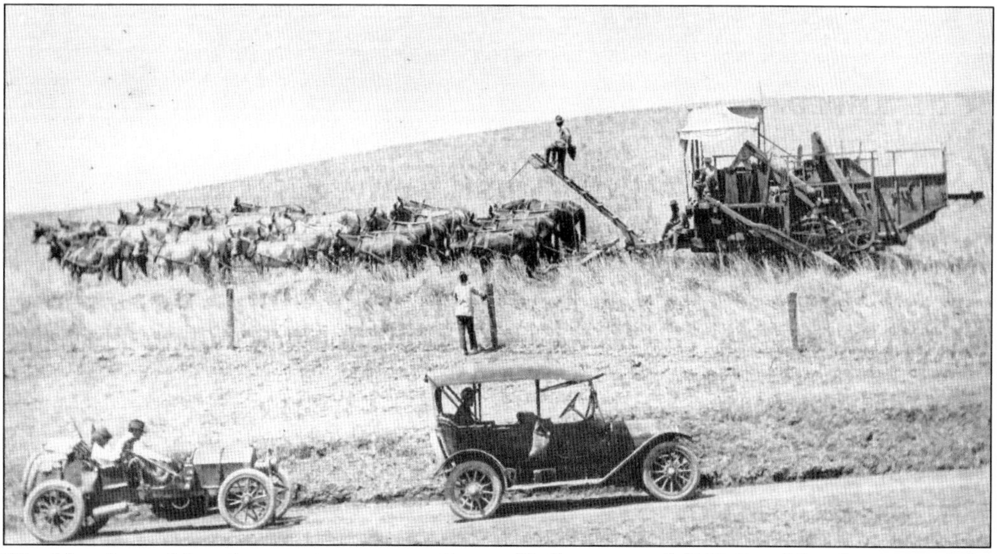

The Houghton 26-mule team is seen near Squaw Hollow around 1920. Ray Houghton stands by the fence with his back to the camera. Tehama County has always been an agricultural county boasting some of the richest land around. A machine with 30 animals and five men could harvest 30 acres per day and between 500 and 1,000 bushels of grain (about 200–300 sacks). (Tehama County Library collection.)

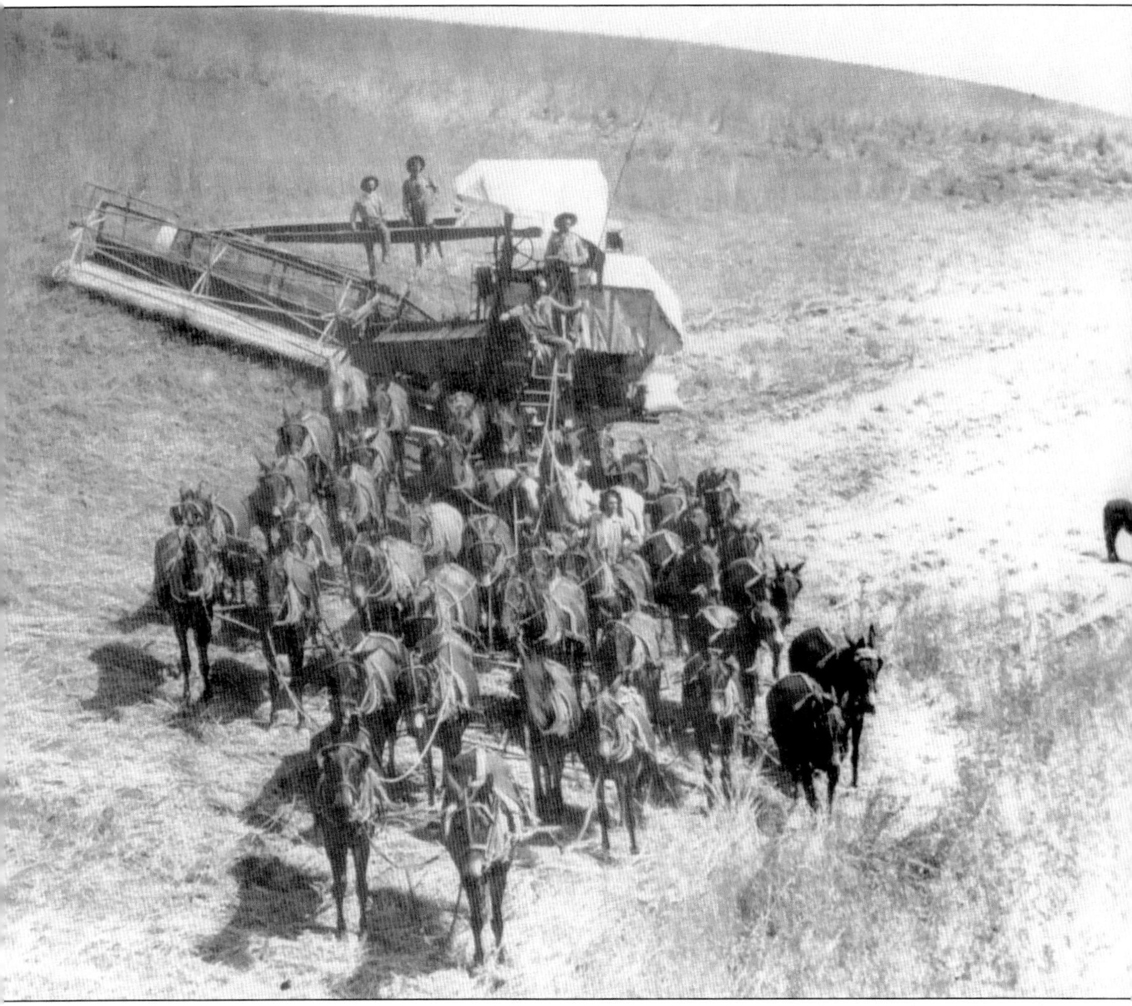

A 40-plus mule team Cushman Harvester works on the Flood Ranch in southwestern Tehama County around 1902. One muleskinner handled the reins of all the mules. A header tender watched the long sickle, beater, and draper that cut the grain and moved it to the separator. A sack sewer assisted by a sack jigger would dump the finished sacks into piles to be loaded into a wagon by the sack buck—a heavy job because each sack could weigh 140 pounds or more. Each man was in charge of eight animals (harnessing and unharnessing, feeding, and getting to the harvester every day). On hot days, the harvester would be stopped every few hours and the mules spread out so the ones in the middle could cool down. Shortly after this photograph was taken, a stampede caused by the cracking of the driver's whip killed one mule and broke the harvester. From top to bottom are Jim Cushman and Tom Flood on the header; Verdie Flood, behind the driver; Lester Flood, driver in seat with long whip; and Bert Hull, riding mule. (Opal Thornton Mendenhall collection.)

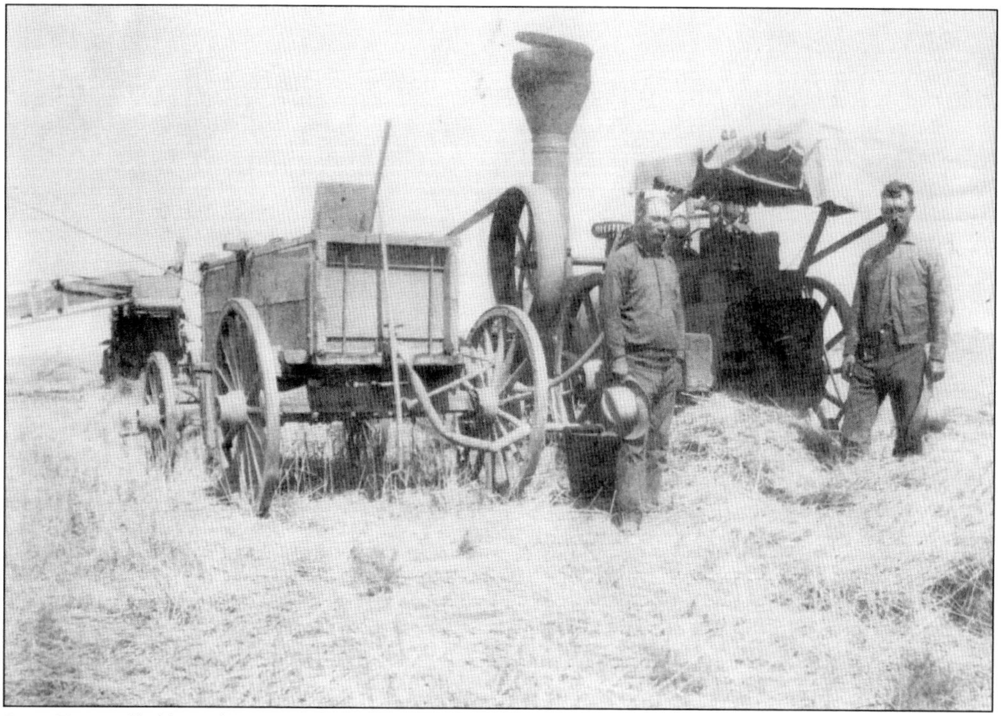

Sam Beaty (left) and James Hughes work a steam-powered threshing machine on the Redfield Ranch near Flournoy. Steam separators could thresh 3,000 bushels of grain a day, the equivalent of 1,200 sacks. The wagon provided water for the boiler, seen behind the men. The thresher is at left in the rear. Cut grain was pitched into these machines from wagons or stacks. Grain was poured into gunnysacks, which were hand-sewn shut. (Opal Thornton Mendenhall collection.)

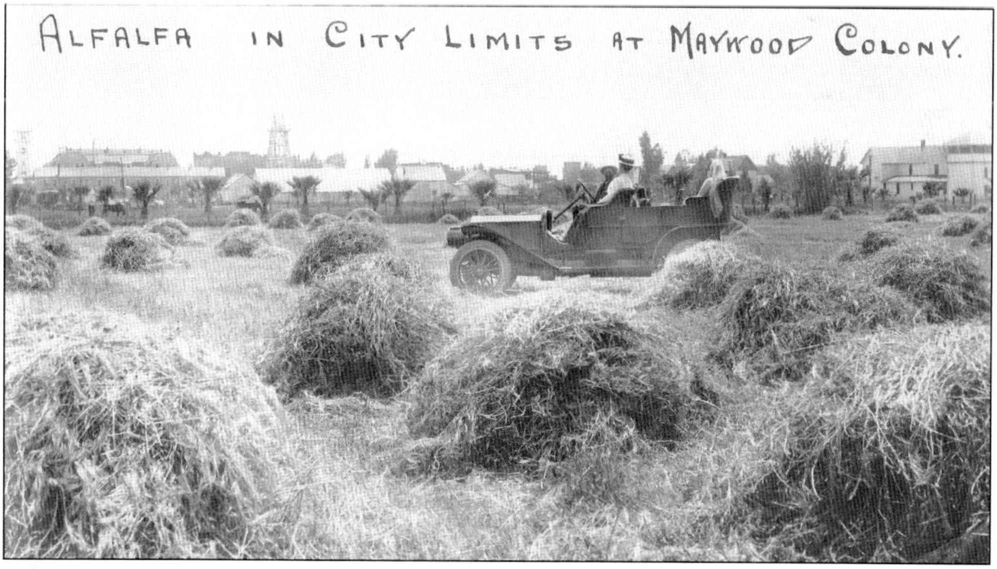


When a wagon was fully loaded with loose alfalfa hay, it could weigh four to five tons. Alfalfa hay was mowed and raked into rows to dry. Then it was either baled for hay or brought to a mill to be made into meal. Depending on growing conditions, an alfalfa field could yield four to five cuttings a year. (Tehama County Library collection.)

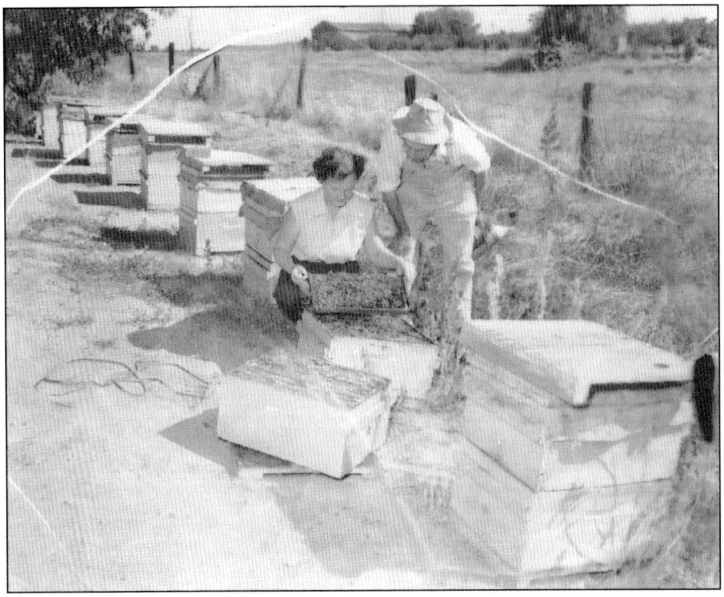

Arthur H. Banta ran the Honey Dale Farm in Los Molinos. He had 3,400 hives that produced 31 tons of honey annually. He developed the Banta queen bee, which produced a gentle but hardworking hive. When his son Jim died, Arthur donated land and funds to construct the Masonic Lodge in Los Molinos in his memory and remarked, "I didn't build this. The bees did!" (Tehama County Library collection.)

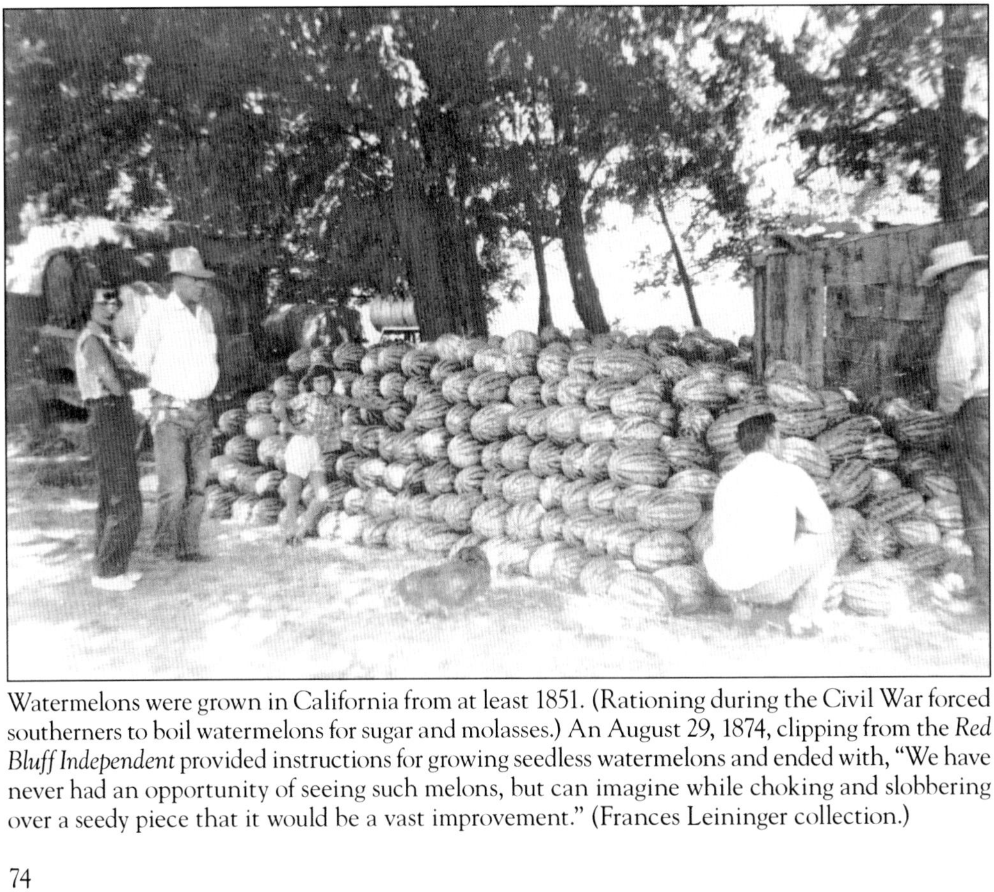

Watermelons were grown in California from at least 1851. (Rationing during the Civil War forced southerners to boil watermelons for sugar and molasses.) An August 29, 1874, clipping from the *Red Bluff Independent* provided instructions for growing seedless watermelons and ended with, "We have never had an opportunity of seeing such melons, but can imagine while choking and slobbering over a seedy piece that it would be a vast improvement." (Frances Leininger collection.)

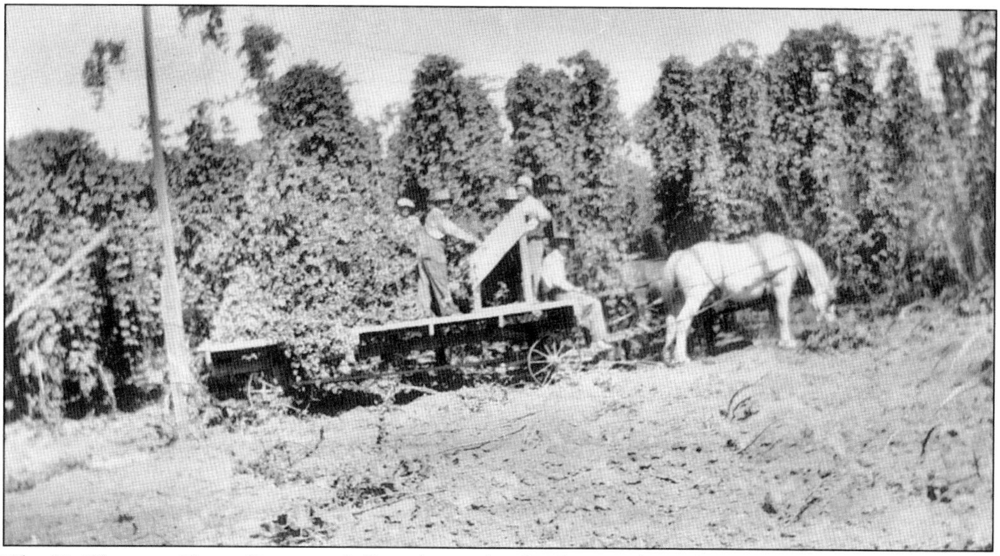

The E. Clemens Horst Company's Ranch south of Tehama planted the first hops in the county in 1904. Men, women, and children pickers were paid \$1 to \$1.15 per hundred pounds of picked hops in 1906. "Picking hops pays bigger wages for less work. Go to Bohemia where money grows on vines for quick pickers," reported the *Red Bluff Daily News* on August 29, 1906. It was called Bohemia because of the seasonal workers. (Opal Thornton Mendenhall collection.)

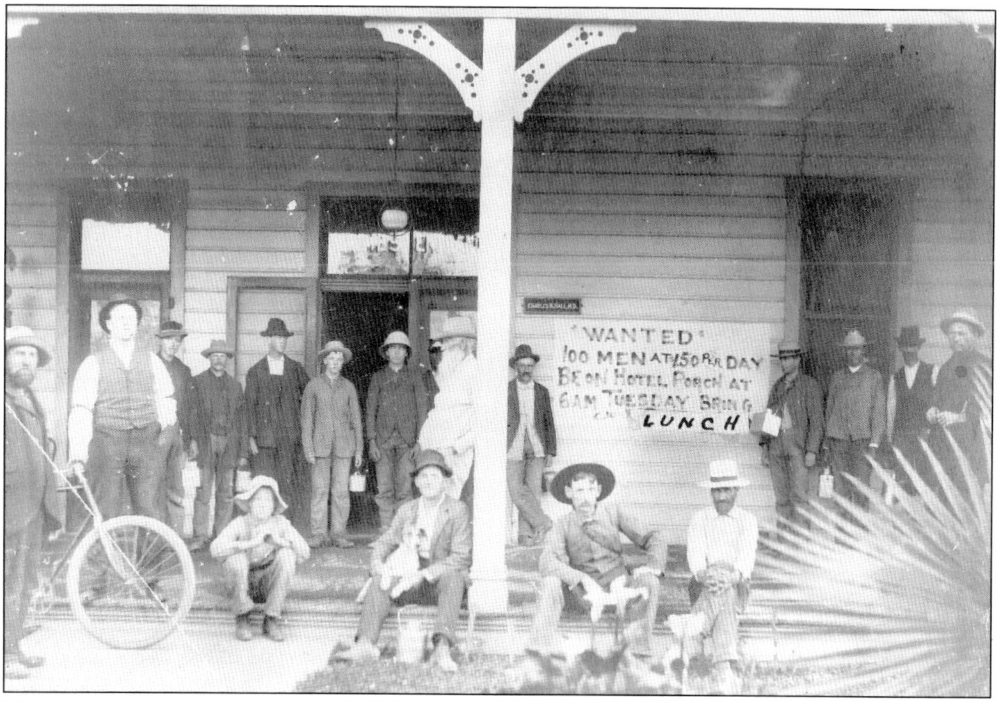


The sign on the front porch reads "Wanted—100 men at \$1.50 per day. Be on hotel porch at 6 a.m. Tuesday. Bring lunch." In 1917, the *Red Bluff Daily News* reported that scarce farm labor was causing a food crisis. To combat this, experts proposed to "close schools earlier; close saloons; compel hobos to work; have young city men spend vacations on farms; adopt a system where 'surplus' city clerks, chauffeurs etc. could be sent to farms." (Corning Museum collection.)

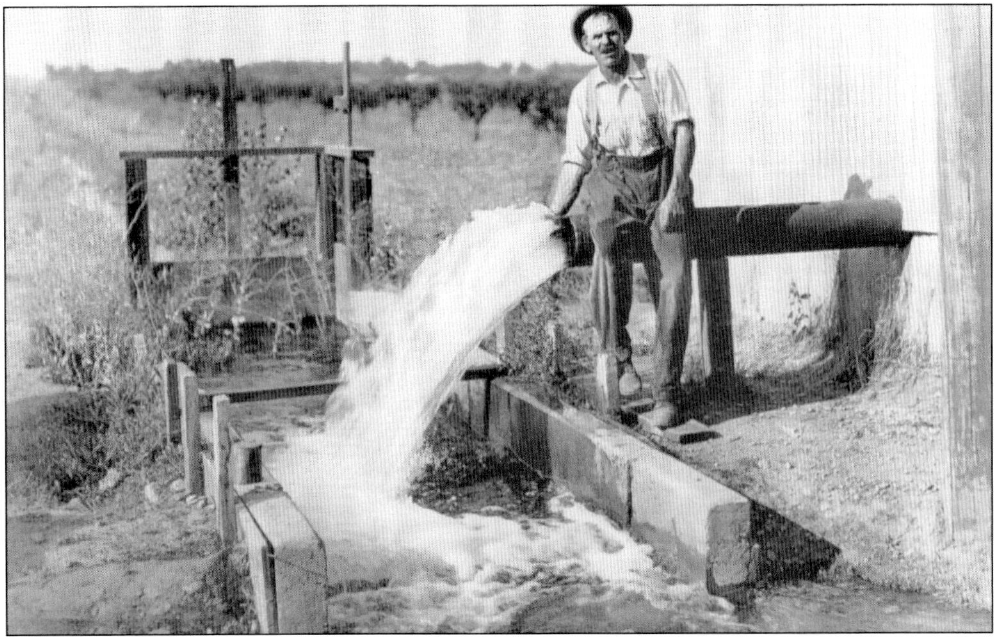

Irrigation and agriculture go hand in hand. The Richfield Land Company developed wells to attract farmers to its colony, which was supposed to be a sugar beet depot, but farmers wanted 10-, 20-, or 40-acre tracts, and these smaller parcels were not suited to sugar beet cultivation. Sugar beets have a high sucrose content and are grown for sugar production. (Corning Museum collection.)

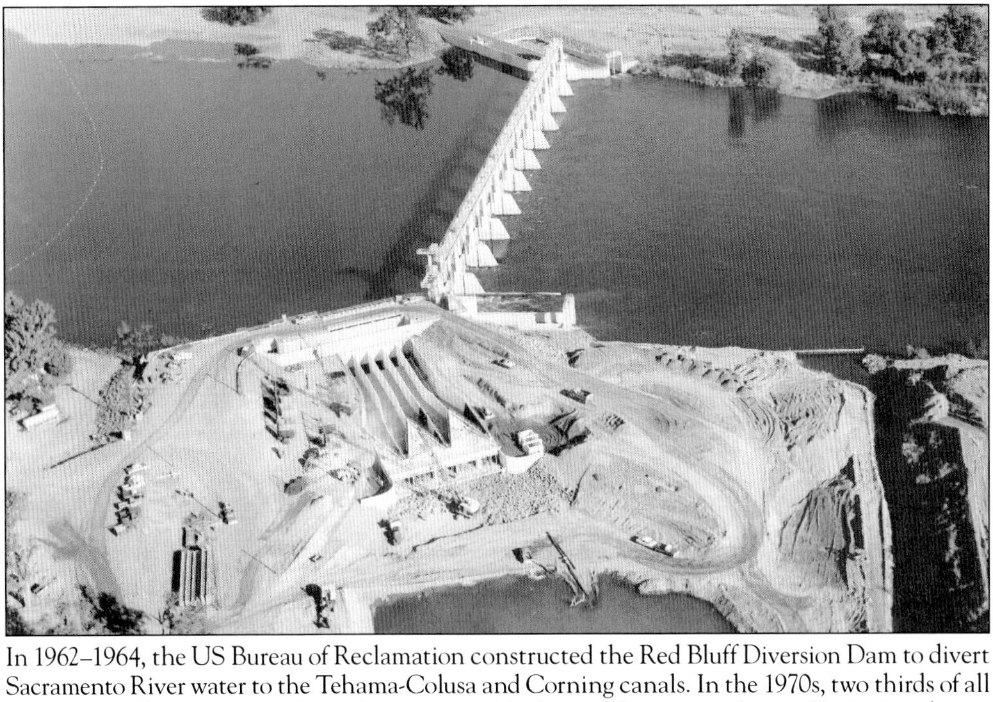

In 1962–1964, the US Bureau of Reclamation constructed the Red Bluff Diversion Dam to divert Sacramento River water to the Tehama-Colusa and Corning canals. In the 1970s, two thirds of all irrigation in the county was by surface water, with the rest from groundwater. Rationing during drought and increased cost for surface water has resulted in more groundwater being used. Now, two-thirds of irrigation is through groundwater pumping. (Tehama County Library collection.)

Horace Greeley said, "Fruit growing is destined to be the ultimate glory of California," and Warren Woodson took that to heart. The 40,000-acre Maywood Colony grew one million fruit and nut trees (oranges, almonds, walnuts, peaches, figs, olives, apples, lemons, plums, pecans, black walnuts, pears, cherries, and apricots, to name a few). Other crops, fruits, and vegetables were also planted. Photographs of produce were used to promote the rich agricultural opportunities the colony offered. (Corning Museum collection.)

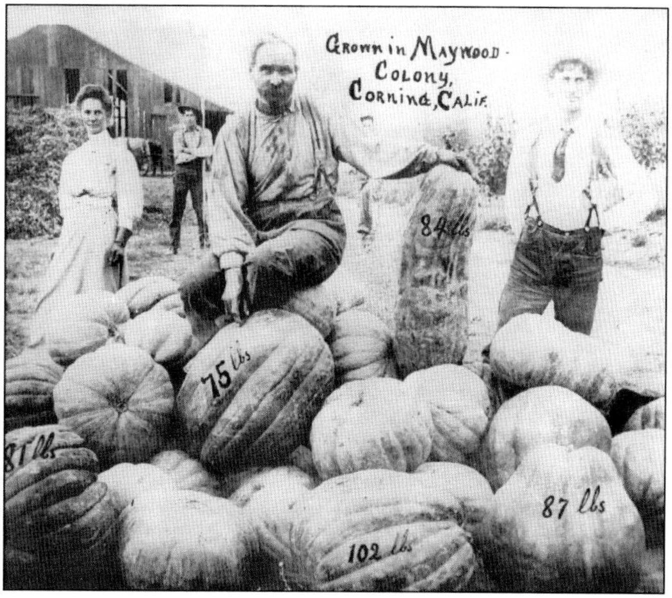


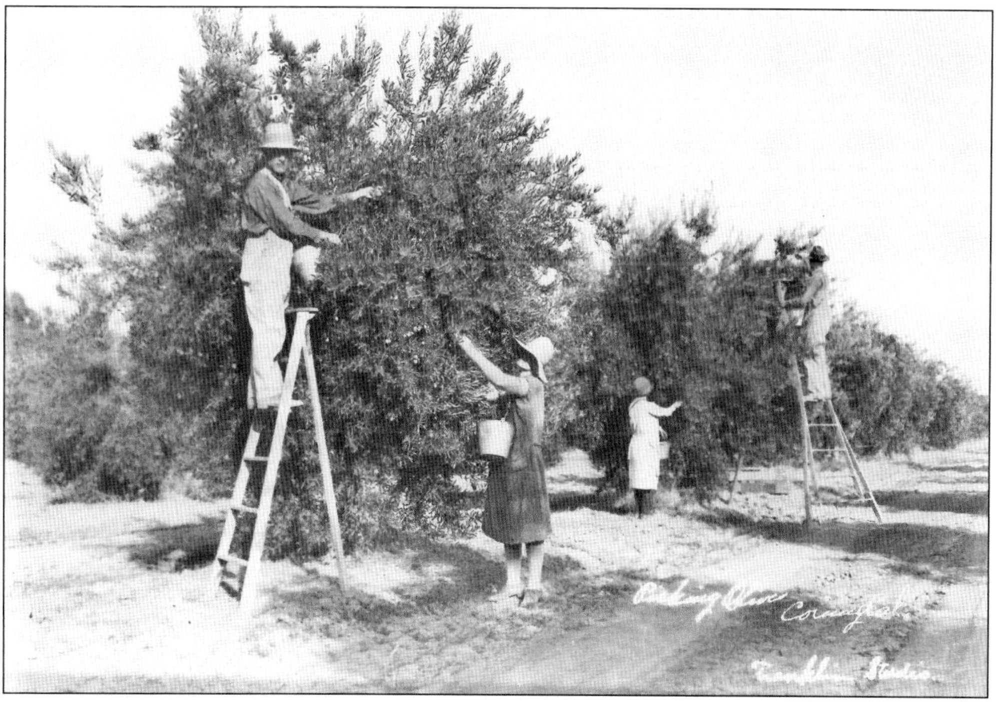

Drought, disease, and pest resistant, olive trees grow well in the soil and climate of the area and require little care. Olives were planted after the disastrous year of 1897 when hordes of grasshoppers and rabbits damaged other fruit trees. An unknown variety produced olives the size of plums: the Sevillano Olive. It soon became the queen of all olives, and Corning was dubbed "Olive Town." (Corning Museum collection.)

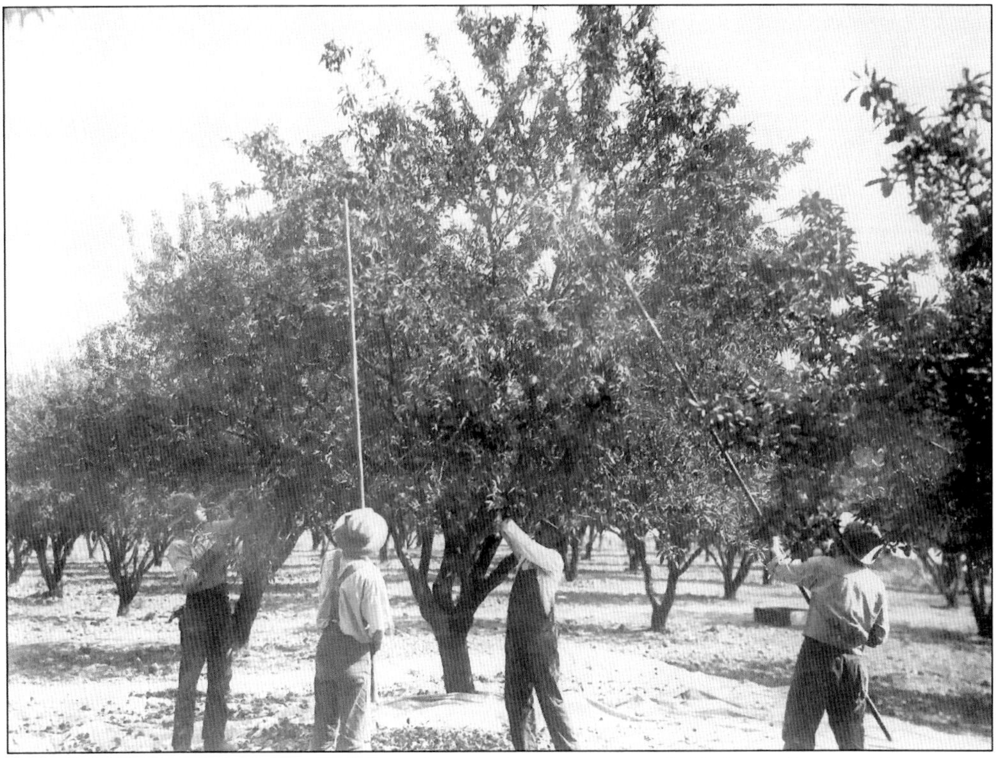

Before modern machinery, almonds were knocked out of trees with 18-foot poles or rubber mallets onto canvas. (Today, a mechanical shaker vigorously shakes the nut-laden trees.) The nuts were then collected and brought to a shed or shade tree where they were hulled by hand, laid out to dry under the sun, and then bagged for shipment. (Sacramento Valley Museum collection.)

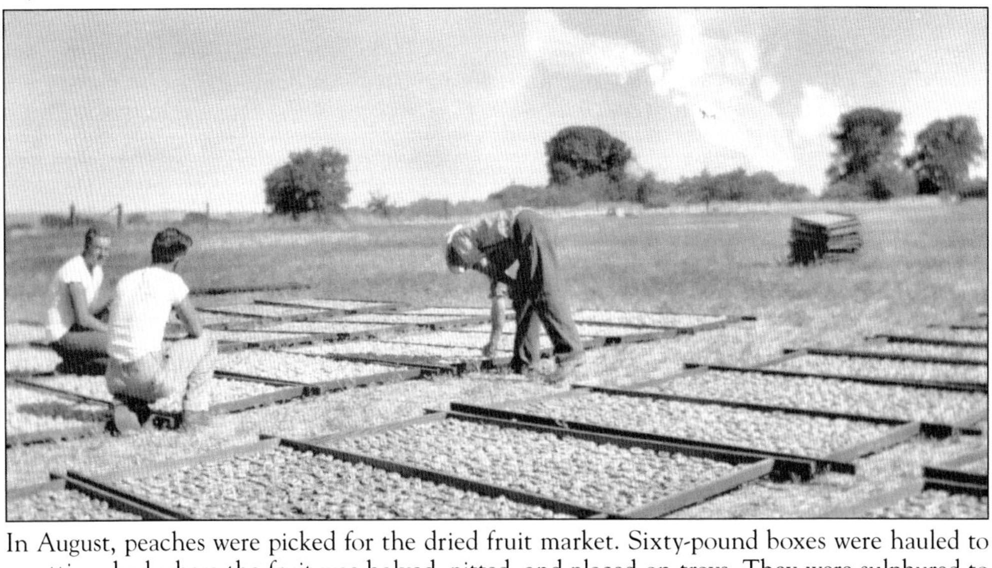

In August, peaches were picked for the dried fruit market. Sixty-pound boxes were hauled to a cutting shed where the fruit was halved, pitted, and placed on trays. They were sulphured to preserve color and keep insects away, and the trays set out under the hot sun in drying yards many acres in size. Once dried, the peaches were put into sacks and hauled to market. (Dan Bayles collection.)

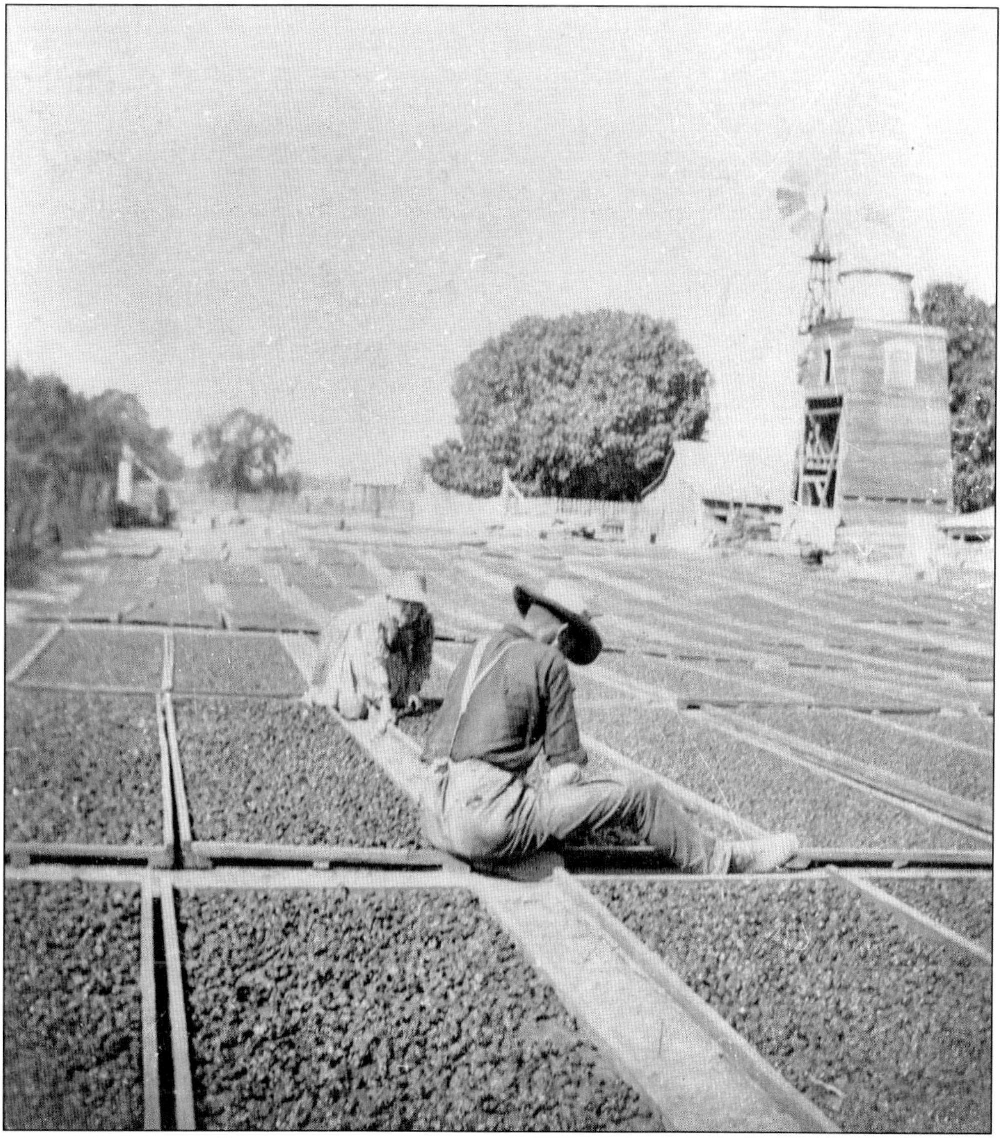

Max and Mattie Muller are pictured in their prune-drying yard at C Street in Tehama around 1900. The Mullers grew 400 trees that produced six tons of fruit yearly. Plums were knocked to the ground, usually by men, in September and collected to fill 60-pound boxes. The boxes of sweet, ripe plums were loaded onto wagons, hauled to vats to be dipped for a few seconds in scalding lye water, then laid on trays to dry in the sun to become prunes. There were not many dryers (or evaporators, as they were called) in those days, but there was plenty of clear, bright sunshine. Dryers were used for late harvests of fruit. Depending on the weather, it could take a week to dry prunes. In case of rain, the trays would be stacked and covered until the rain passed. (California State University, Chico, Special Collections.)

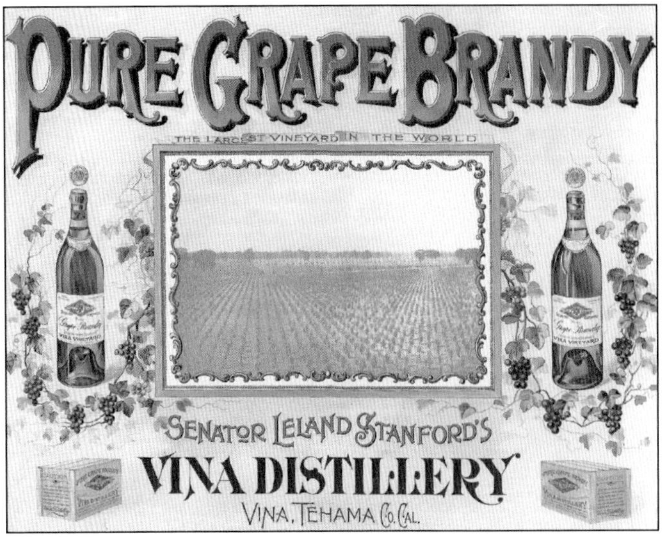


Henry Gerke planted European grapevines and produced brandy, sherry, claret, angelica, and a very popular Riesling. Railroad magnate, governor of California, and US senator Leland Stanford bought Gerke's ranch in 1881 (Gerke lost interest after his wife died, sold out, and died a year later.) Stanford hoped to produce wine to rival the great vintages of Europe. He failed, but the soil and climate produced excellent sweet wines and brandy. (Author's collection.)

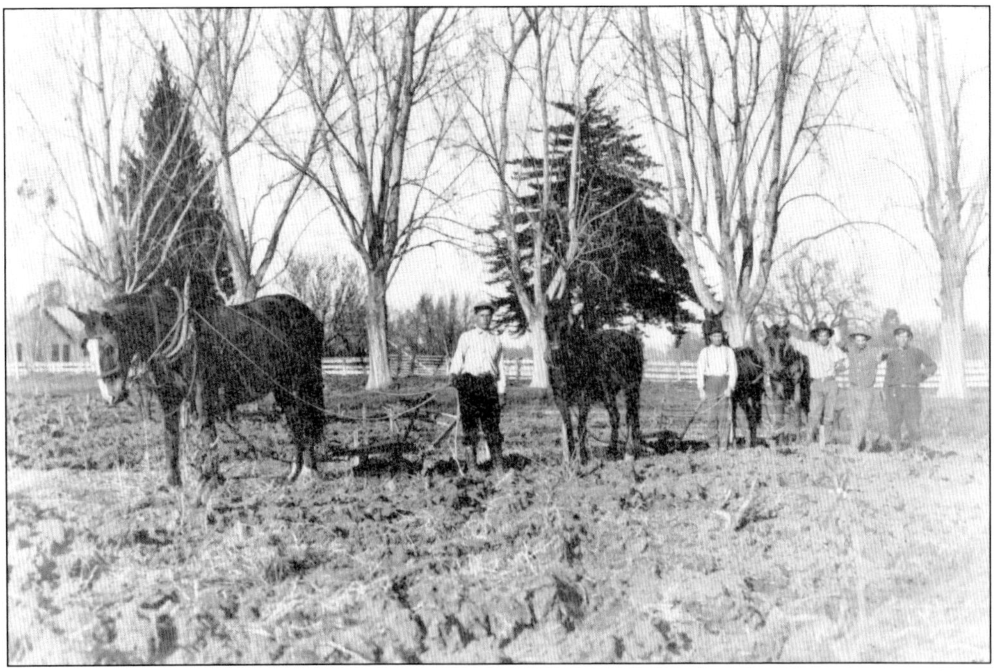

At one time in the late 1800s, Leland Stanford's Vina Ranch (approximately 59,000 acres) was the world's largest brandy distillery, winery, and vineyard, with almost three million vines on 3,600 acres. After his death in 1893, the vineyard and ranch declined. The grapes were pulled out in 1915 and replaced with alfalfa. From left to right are Sid "Pinky" O'Brien, John Gilbert, Matt O'Brien, Cecil Newman, and John O'Brien. (Frances Leininger collection.)

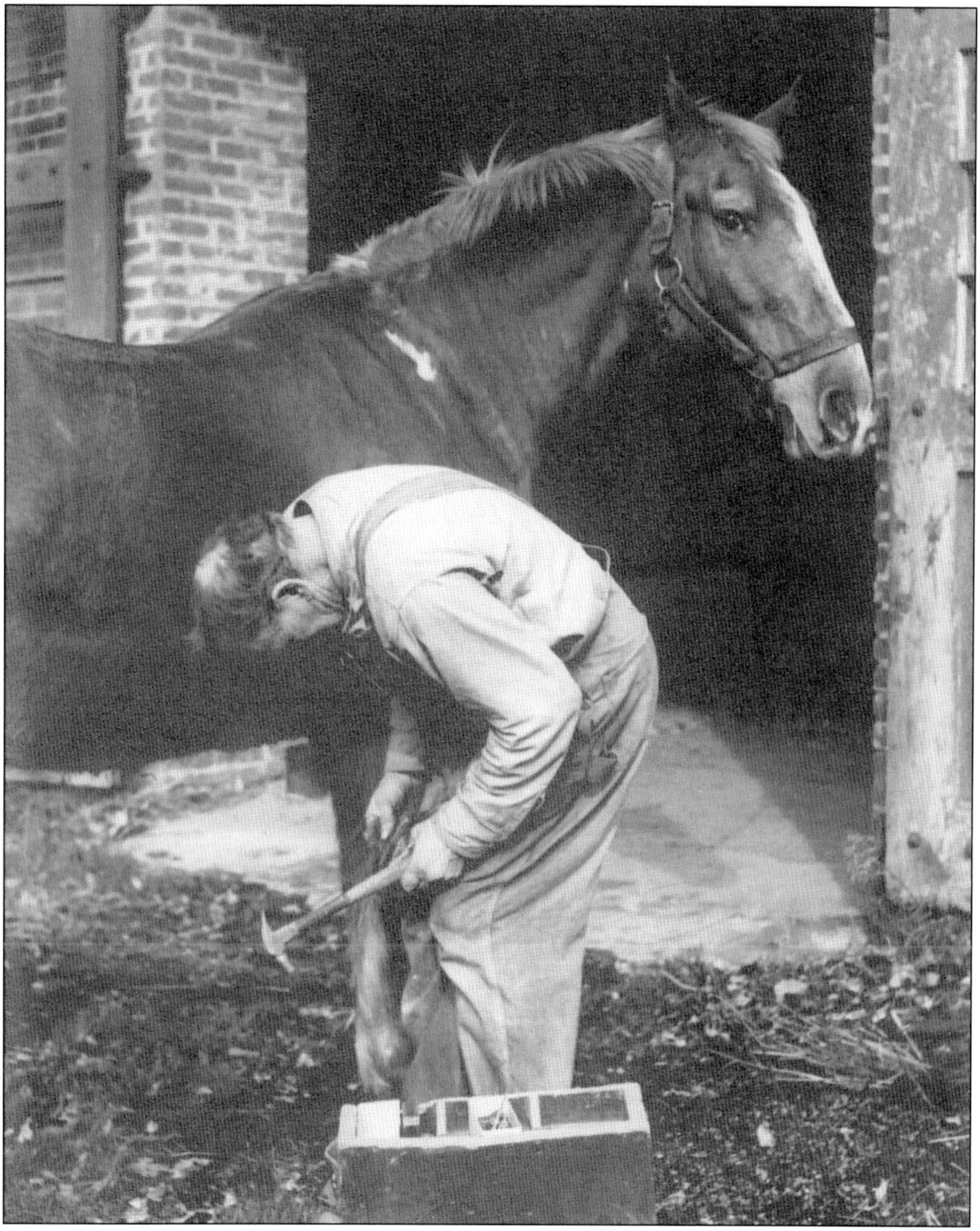

Gus Ackerson shoes a horse by the winery doors. Leland Stanford housed thoroughbred harness horses at this ranch and built a quarter-mile training track for them on the north side of Deer Creek. His love for horses was not just for thoroughbreds. The story goes that while staying in the town of Sisson (now the town of Mount Shasta), the locals considered him a "railroad monopolist" and ignored him by not engaging in hat lifting or bowing when they passed him on the street. One day, he noticed an old, blind, lame horse wandering the streets. He asked if anyone knew who owned the neglected horse—no one did. Going into a local tavern, he put five gold twenties on the bar and told the tavern owner that the money was to be used to care for the horse. Word soon spread of his kindness and generosity toward the horse, which gained the respect of the locals, who became more friendly to him during his stay. (Frances Leininger collection.)

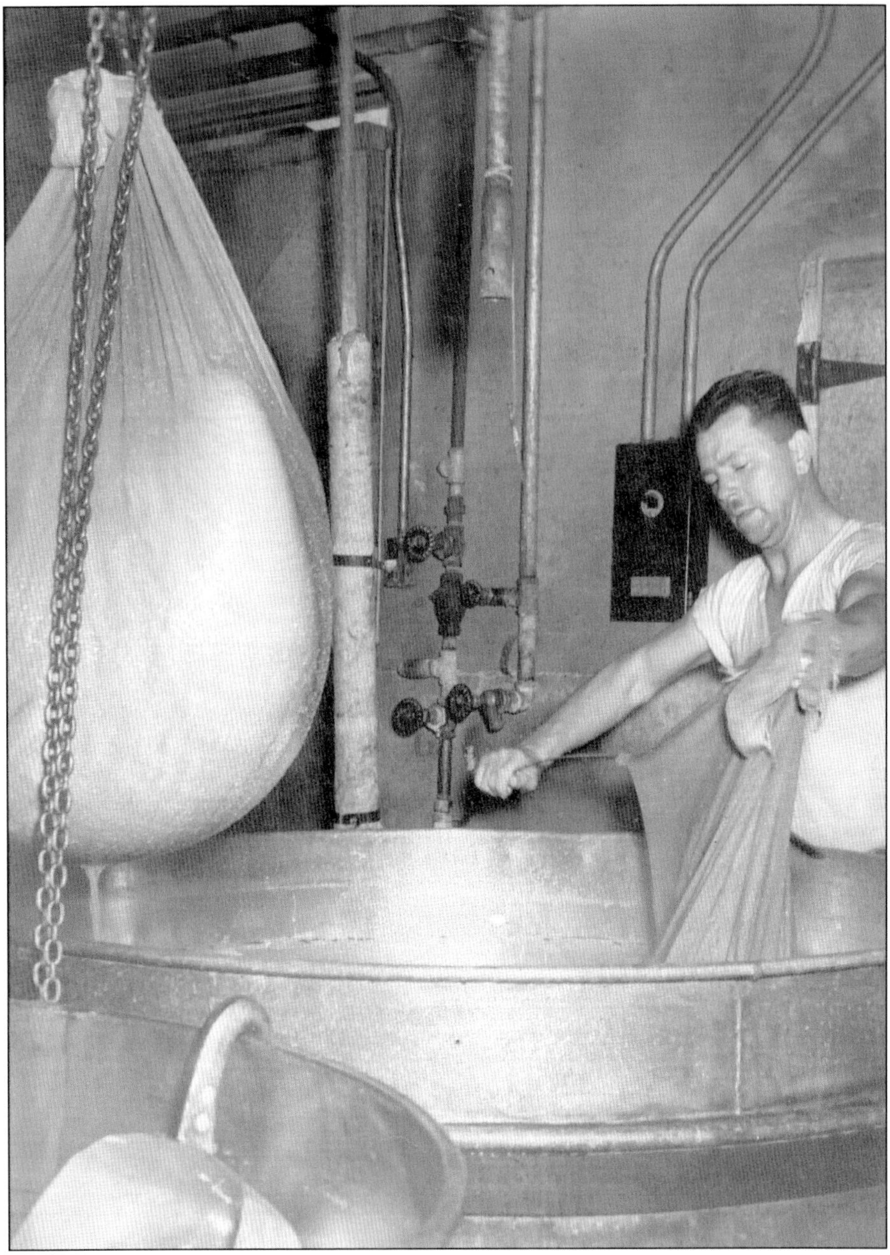

The "cheese room" was at the northeast corner of the winery. In the early 1880s, Leland Stanford developed his herd of 500 registered, purebred Holstein-Freisian dairy cows imported from the Netherlands. Some of the milk produced was made into the celebrated Vina butter. The dairy was one of the ranch's few profitable operations. When the herd was sold in 1917, buyers came from as far away as Chile. The average price per cow during the sale was $175, but one three-year-old—Lady Spotlight Ormsby—sold for $675. In an official test, she gave 25 pounds of butterfat in one week. (The average for a three-year old cow of the same breed in 1899 was 12.1 pounds per week.) Butterfat is what butter is made from, and its size and content in milk also determines the type of cheese made from it—a large amount of big globules of butterfat in milk is good for soft and semi-soft cheeses, while small globules are good for hard cheeses. (Frances Leininger collection.)

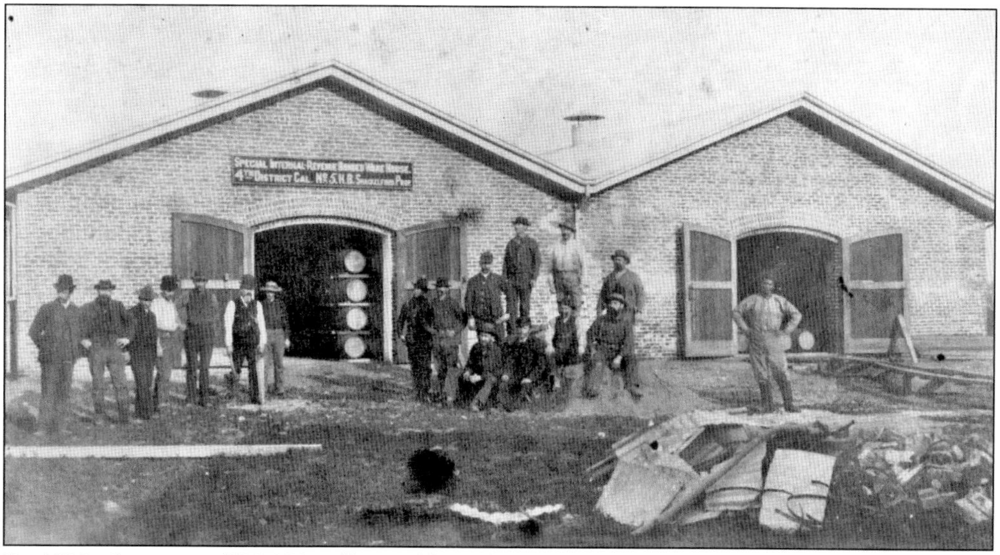

By 1890, there were 700,000 gallons of brandy stored in the Internal Revenue brick bonded warehouse at Stanford's Vina Ranch. Federal law required brandy to be aged under lock and key and then taxed when removed. Two dams on Deer Creek, a reservoir, and 150 miles of ditches/canals (some cut through solid rock) supplied the hydropower used to run the winery and distillery and provided irrigation for 12,000 acres of grapevines, orchards, and other crops. (Frances Leininger collection.)

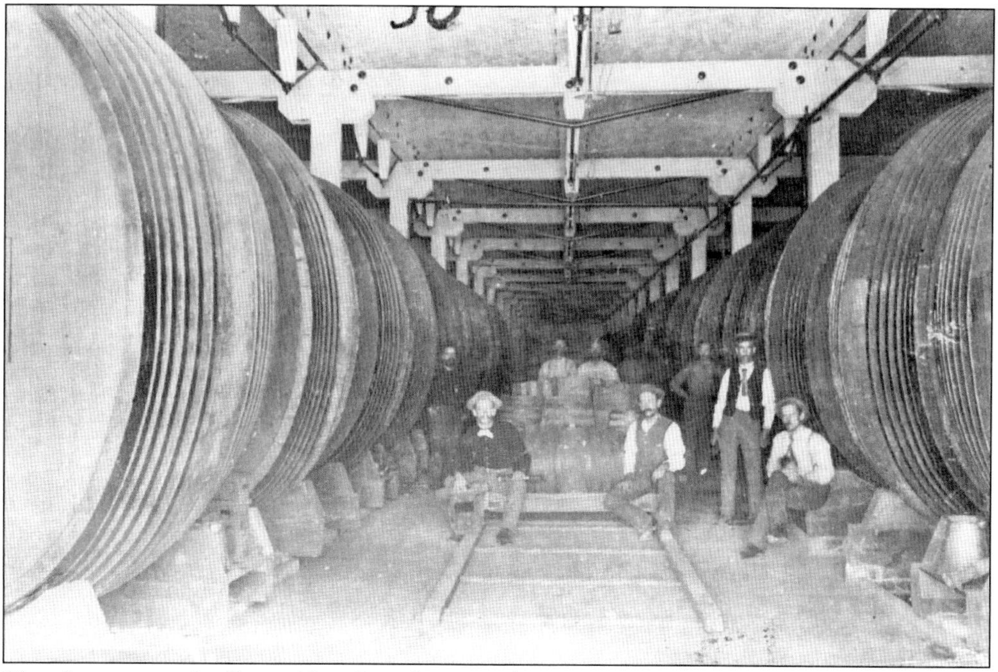

The above-ground cellar at Vina Ranch covered two acres, had double walls 30 inches thick, and could hold two million gallons. The fermenting tanks were redwood, while the storage tanks were oak. The vineyard was laid out in blocks separated by avenues lined with trees of walnuts, apricots, peaches, and plums. Down the center of each avenue was a 15-foot-wide ditch with 12-foot-wide roadways on each side. (Frances Leininger collection.)

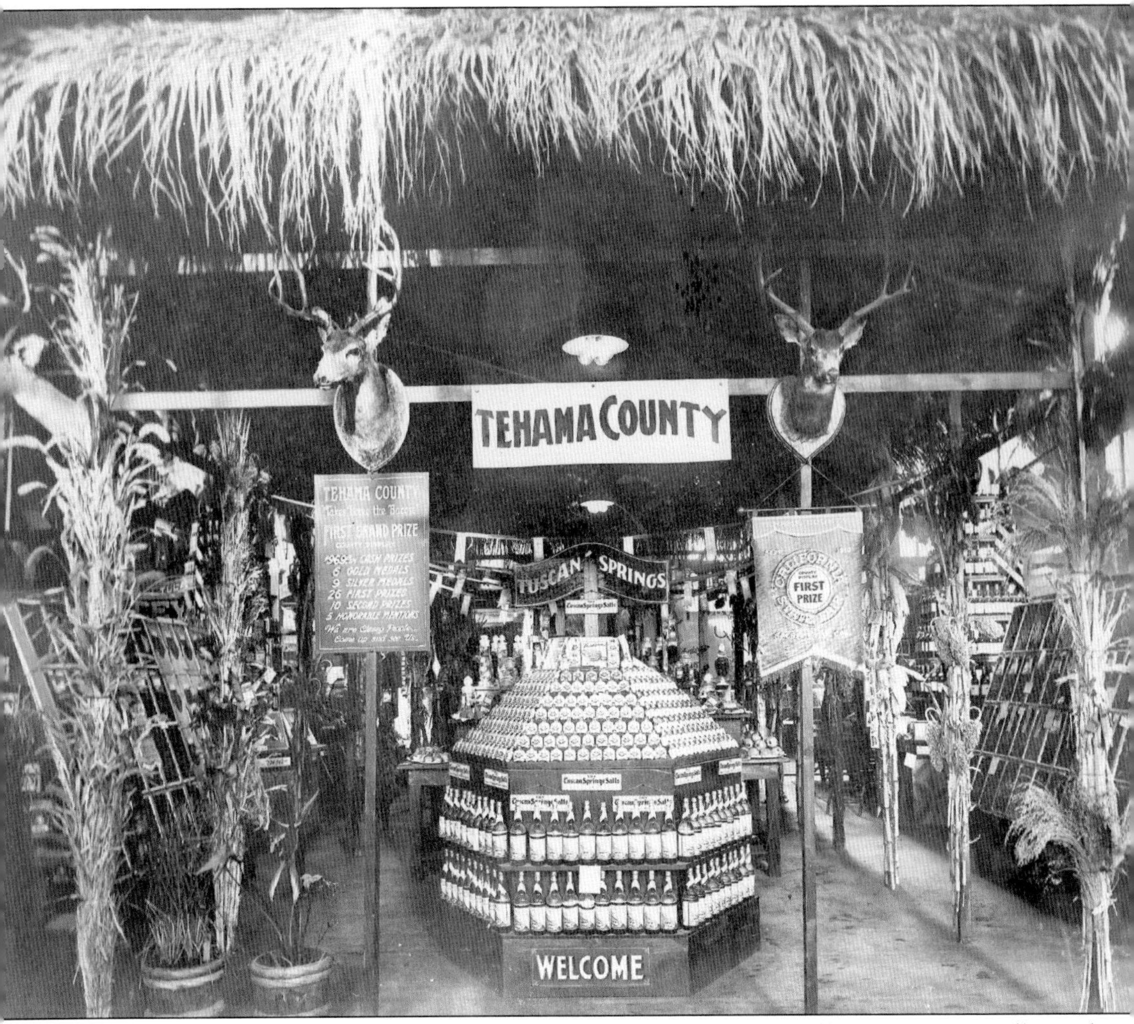


The first state fair was held in 1854 at San Francisco and then in different cities annually until given a permanent home in Sacramento in 1860. Tehama County's horticultural display at the 1910 state fair won the grand prize. Lumber, palm leaves, and deer heads from the county were used in its construction. Fish, flowers, and fruit were displayed in a 400-pound block of ice. The sign at left reads, "We are a classy people. Come up and see us." (Corning Museum collection.)

# *Five*

# Southwest

This corner of the county is rural and very agricultural. The communities of Elmore, Burton, Red Bank, Flournoy, Henleyville, and Lowrey were homesteaded by settlers in the 1860s and 1870s looking for land to farm and ranch because much of the valley belonged to a few men who had been given Mexican land grants. The rolling plains were used to raise grain, while the oak covered hills were suited for grazing livestock.

Families developed close relationships. This neighborliness meant people came together to help each other. Since there wasn't any refrigeration in those days, it was difficult to keep meat. Members of the community took turns butchering livestock and sharing portions with neighbors. It was not uncommon for families to bring back supplies for each other from town.

Toward the western mountains, John Colyear homesteaded on property that contained cold-water springs, some clear and some containing sulphur, which was considered medicinal. Dr. J.A. Owen of Red Bluff attempted to make the area into a mountain health sanitarium, but steep roads and difficult access disappointed his dreams.

The name for the little town of Paskenta is derived from a Wintun word meaning "down under little hills." Sitting in the foothills near the Coast Range Mountains, it began in the 1850s as a trading post. Ranching and lumbering were major enterprises for the area. Electricity did not reach the town until 1939. Just to the north was the 25,000-acre Nome Lackee Indian Reservation.

Groves of Australian Eucalyptus trees can be seen along Interstate 5. They were planted during a period of timber speculation in the late 1800s and early 1900s. It was expected that these trees would produce the same fine lumber as their Australian counterparts, and since they grow quickly, money could be made fast—but it did not turn out that way. The wood from the trees grown here is inferior, only good for fence posts, railroad ties, or firewood. A large 10,000-acre grove of these trees was planted as an experiment in the 1980s to produce paper. Known as the Tehama Fiber Farm, the grove can be seen near Corning west of Interstate 5.

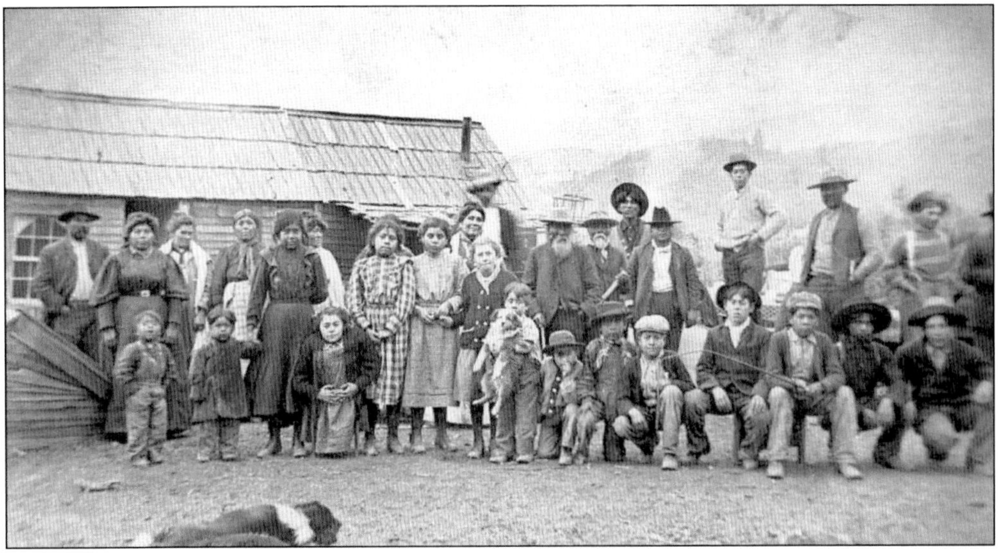

Wintun Indians at the Freeman home in Paskenta are seen in this 1912 photograph. Identified in the first row are Lizzie Frank (third from left), Edith Hayward of Hayfork (fourth from left), and Rena Hayward (seventh from left). When the Nome Lackee Indian Reservation closed, the *Red Bluff Independent* considered it a failure, declaring in its December 29, 1863, issue, "The large tract of land comprising the Nome Lackee Reservation will present great inducements for settlers." (California State University, Chico, Special Collections.)

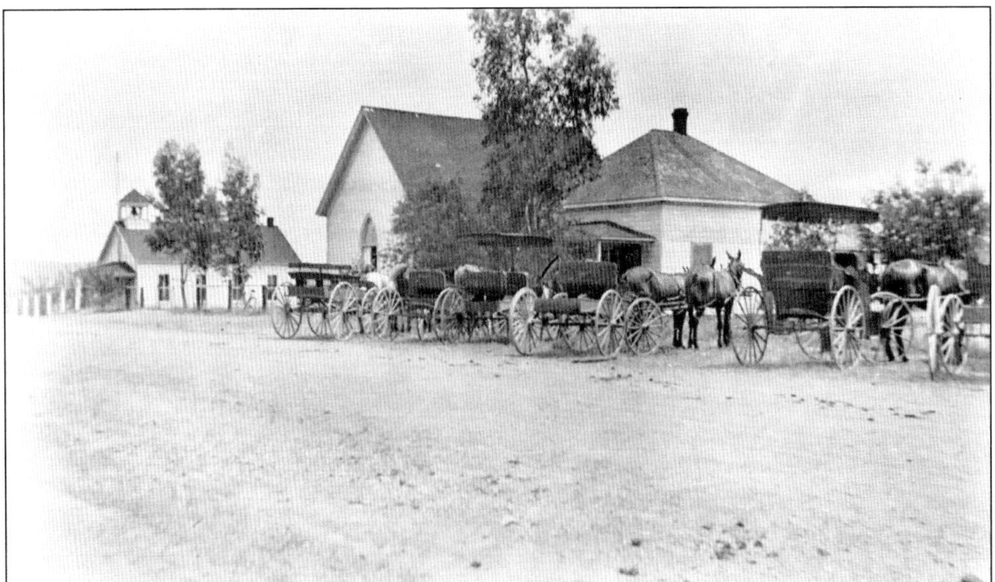

Horses and buggies are pictured by the Henleyville church around 1915. In 1887, a site for a state Normal School, where future teachers were taught the "norms," was being scouted. Henleyville offered five to ten acres for the school and forty acres for professors to raise poultry in their spare time. Chico was selected for the new site, and the Normal School became California State University, Chico. (Tehama County Library collection.)

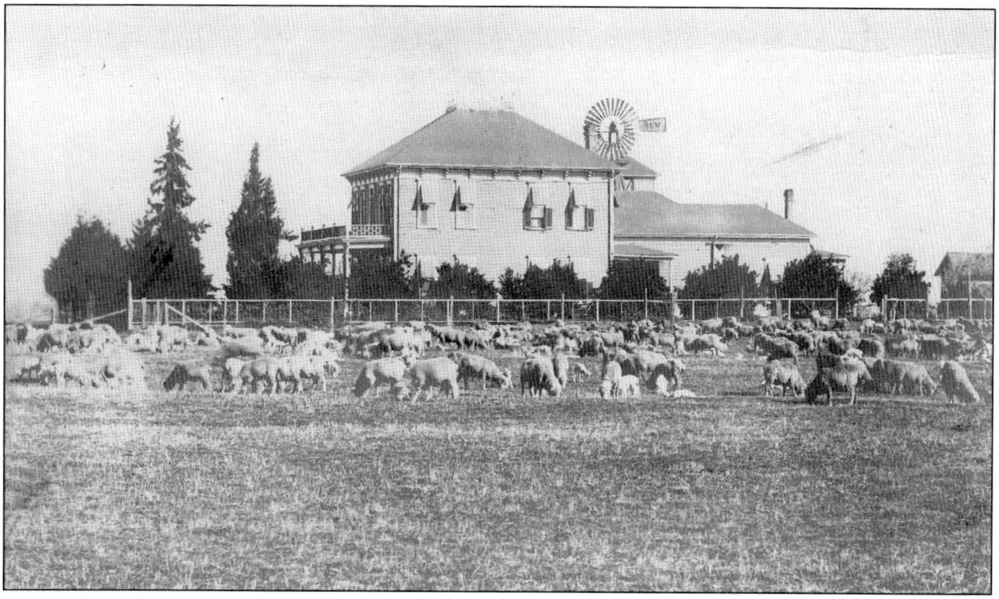

James Howell arrived in California in 1859 with one dollar in his pocket and built this ranch home in 1893 at Henleyville for $10,000. He worked odd jobs until he could buy a half interest in a band of 1,100 sheep. Howell owned 5,000 head of thoroughbred Spanish and Rambouillet sheep that he trailed to Lassen County and Howell Camp, located west of Paskenta in the Coast Range Mountains. (Tehama County Library collection.)

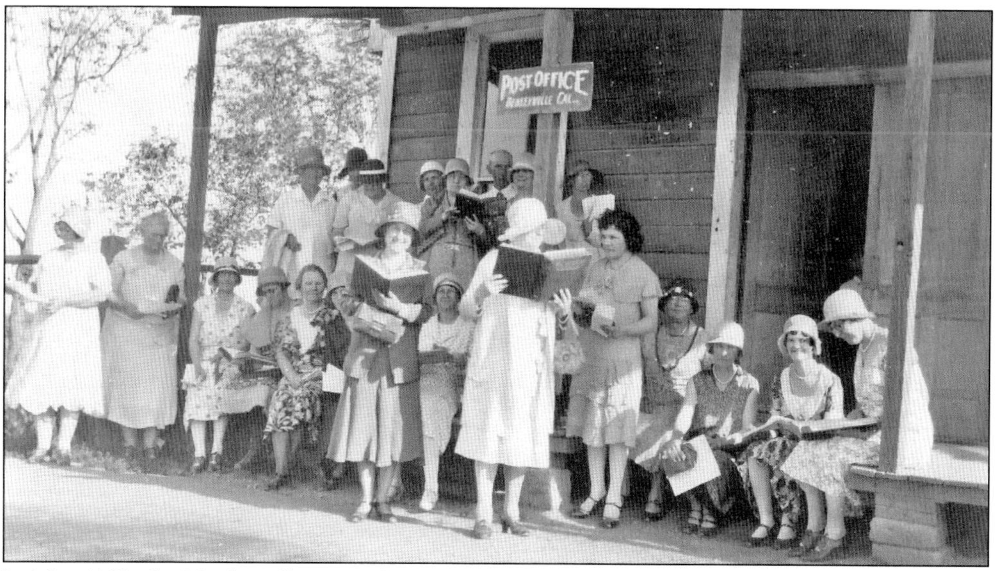


In May 1873, the Henleyville post office was established and occupied the same building as the general store. In December 1878, it was moved three miles west to Gleasonville but returned in 1880. It was closed in November 1936, and mail service was received by rural route from Corning. By the 1940s, the general store, blacksmith shop, church, and school were gone. (Tehama County Library collection.)

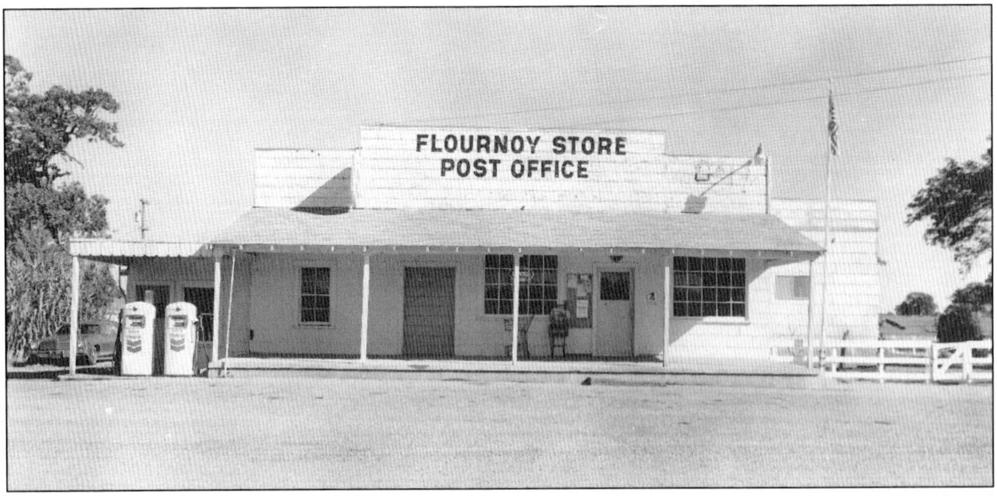


Flournoy was named for the Flournoy family who settled the area in the 1870s. In 1922, local ranchers captured a "wild man" suspected of stealing chickens and vegetables. When asked how he made a living, he answered, "Oh, I just go out and get it. The world owes me a living anyway." The man, Martin Aldrich from Washington state, was committed to the state hospital for the insane in Napa. (Tehama County Library collection.)

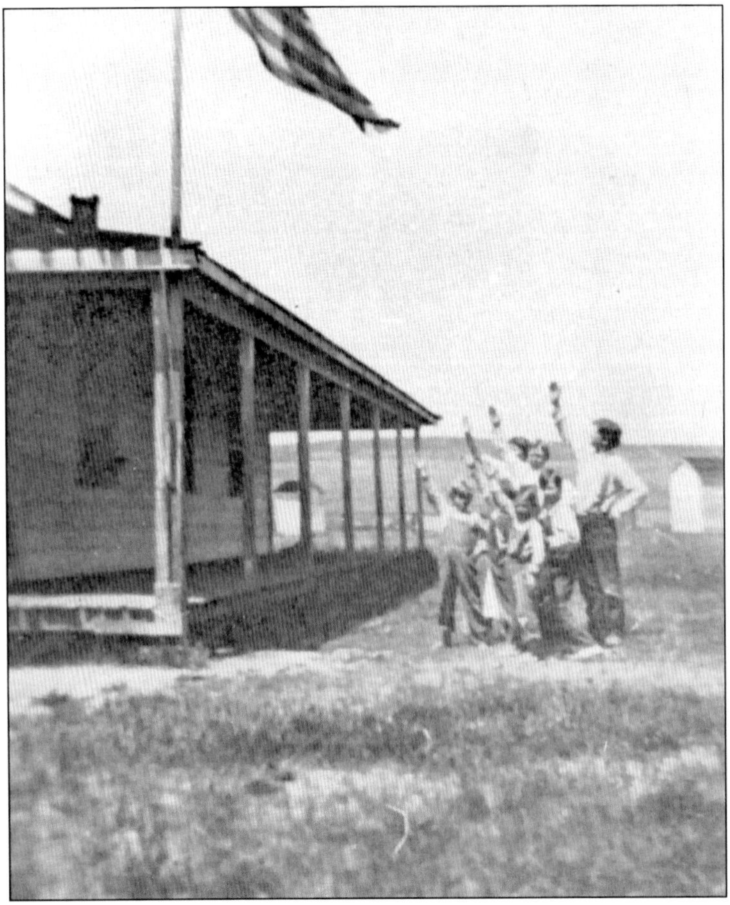

Elkhorn School students Charles, Eldon, Robert, and Ray Azevedo; Floyd and Virgil Rannells; and Henry Flournoy salute the flag using the Bellamy salute, in which the arm is stiffly extended. Because it resembled the Nazi salute, Congress instituted the hand-over-the-heart gesture in 1942. In the background are the boys' and girls' outhouses. Opal Thornton Mendenhall recalled boys would throw rocks at the outhouse when girls used it. (California State University, Chico, Special Collections.)

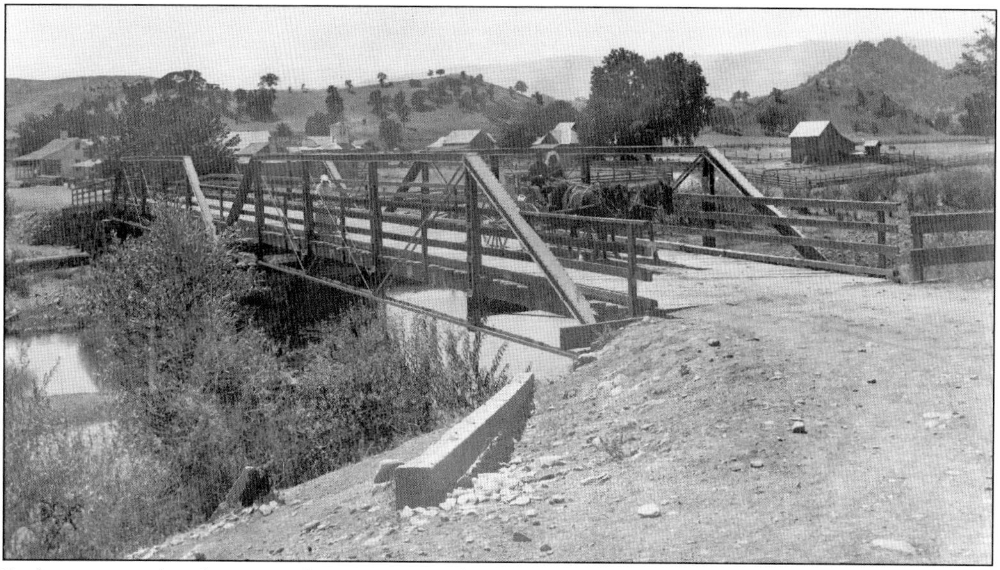

Paskenta was a bustling town boasting several general stores, two blacksmith shops, two saloons, a butcher shop, hotel, Chinese laundry, a cheesemaker, a large hall used for dances and roller skating, a school, and men's and women's baseball teams. The town supplied many ranches in the area along with pack trains. Sometimes, 80 to 100 pack trains passed through Paskenta for the cattle and sheep mountain camps. This c. 1900 view looks southwest. (Tehama County Library collection.)

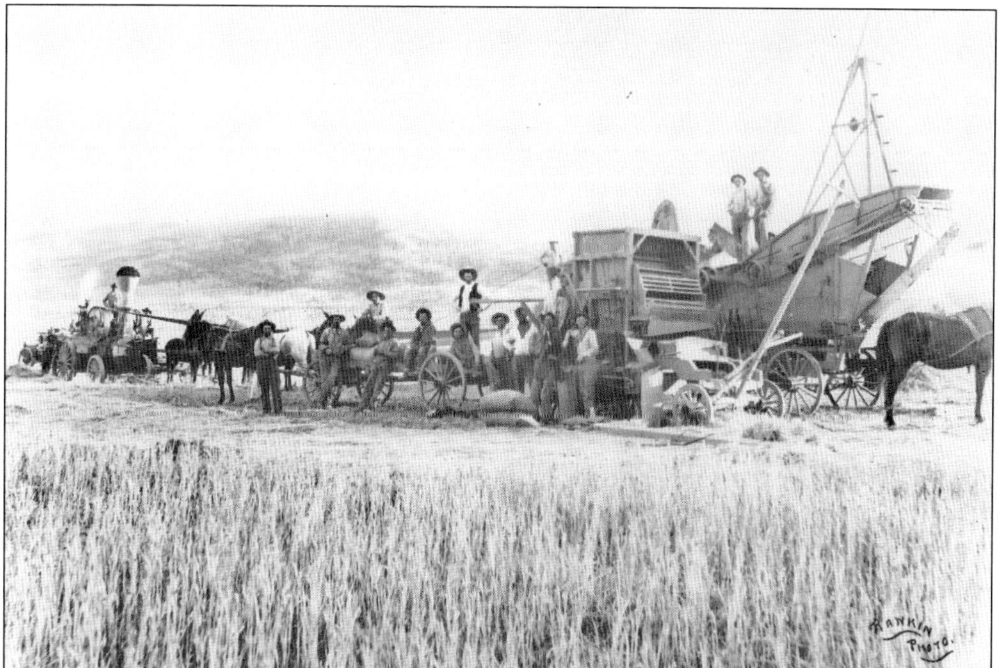

In this photograph, grain is being threshed in the Paskenta area. The most important grain crops were barley and wheat. With long, hot summers, a hardy dry wheat was grown that could withstand the rigors of export. In 1883, Paskenta resident Martin Wilcox received a patent for an improved grain separator "to separate wheat from barley, oats, and small grains or seeds after the grain has been cleaned from the straw and chaff." (Tehama County Library collection.)

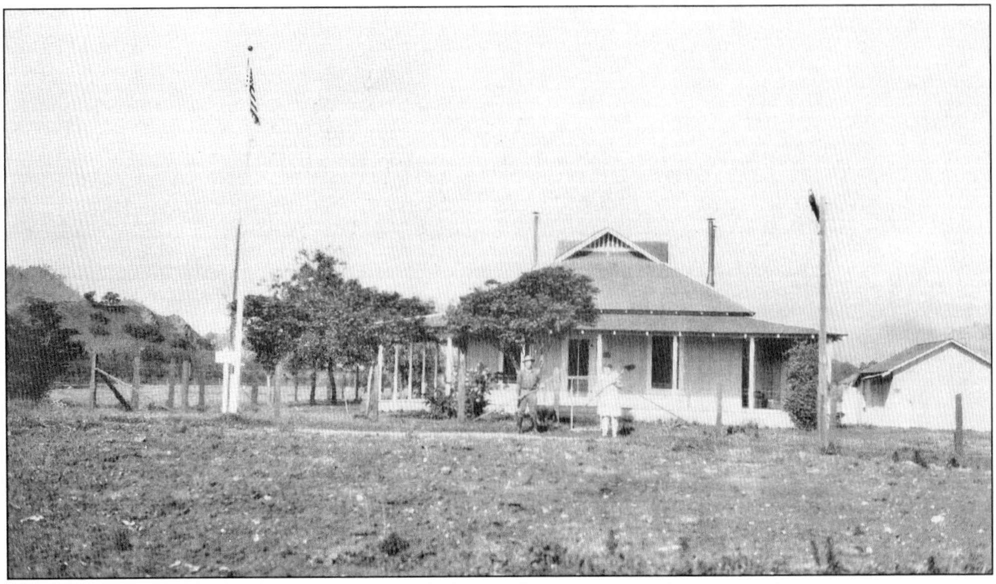

The Wilder Ranger Station was originally built about seven miles west of Paskenta on Covelo Road in the early 1900s. In the 1920s, it was moved to the south side of the creek and moved again in the 1930s. It is claimed the house was later moved south to Stonyford in Colusa County and is still there. (Opal Thornton Mendenhall collection.)

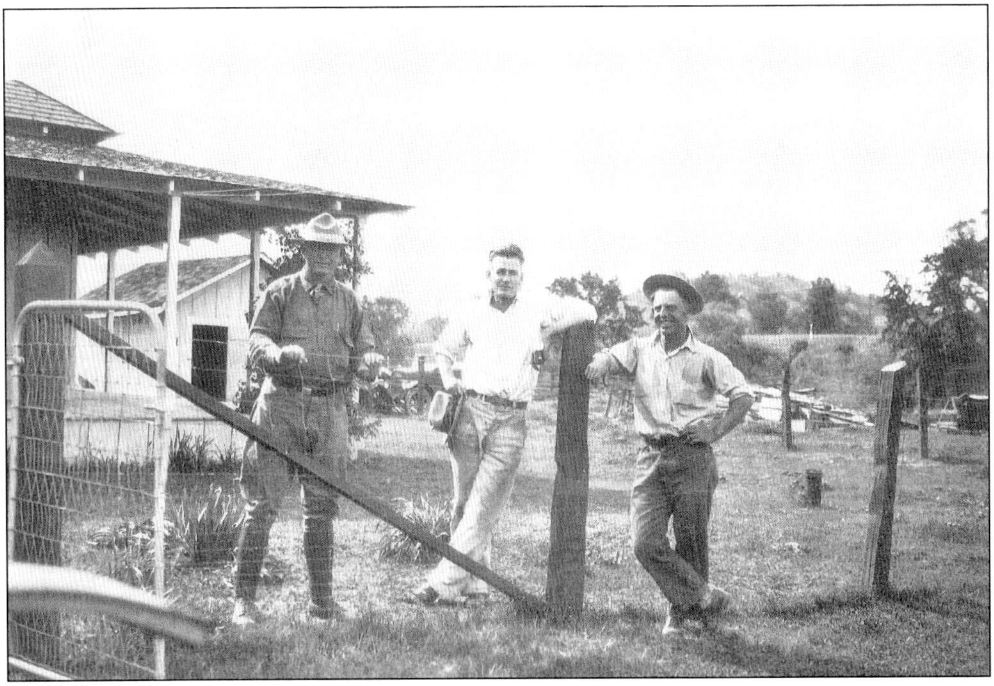

The Wilder Ranger Station at Paskenta was the first US Forestry Service station in the area. From left to right are Bill Clifford, Clarence Oaks, and Cap Whitlock in about 1930. The first district US Forestry Service ranger was Charles "Bud" Adams, who served from 1926 to 1927. (Opal Thornton Mendenhall collection.)

Buried at the Elmore cemetery is Cordia Jobe. On October 4, 1901, the *Red Bluff Daily News* reported, "The first death from lightning that has ever been known in Tehama County occurred four miles west of Henleyville. Cordia Jobe, 18 years of age, was struck dead by a bolt of lightning while shoeing a horse at the [blacksmith] shop. [It] also killed the horse he was shoeing." (Patti Oakley McFarlin collection.)

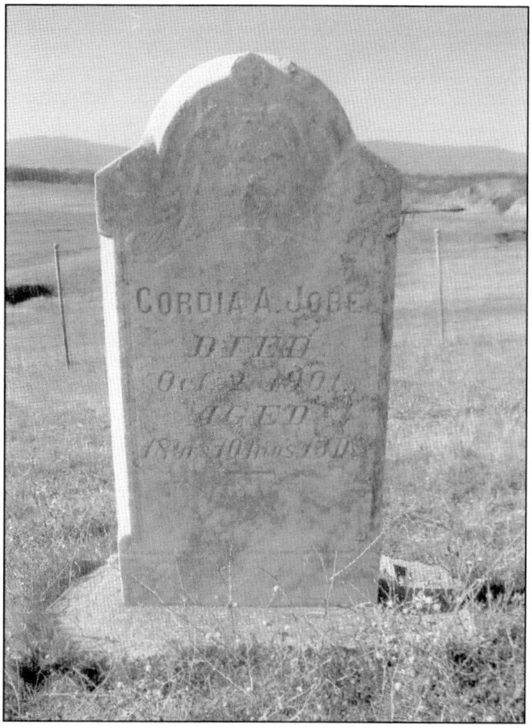


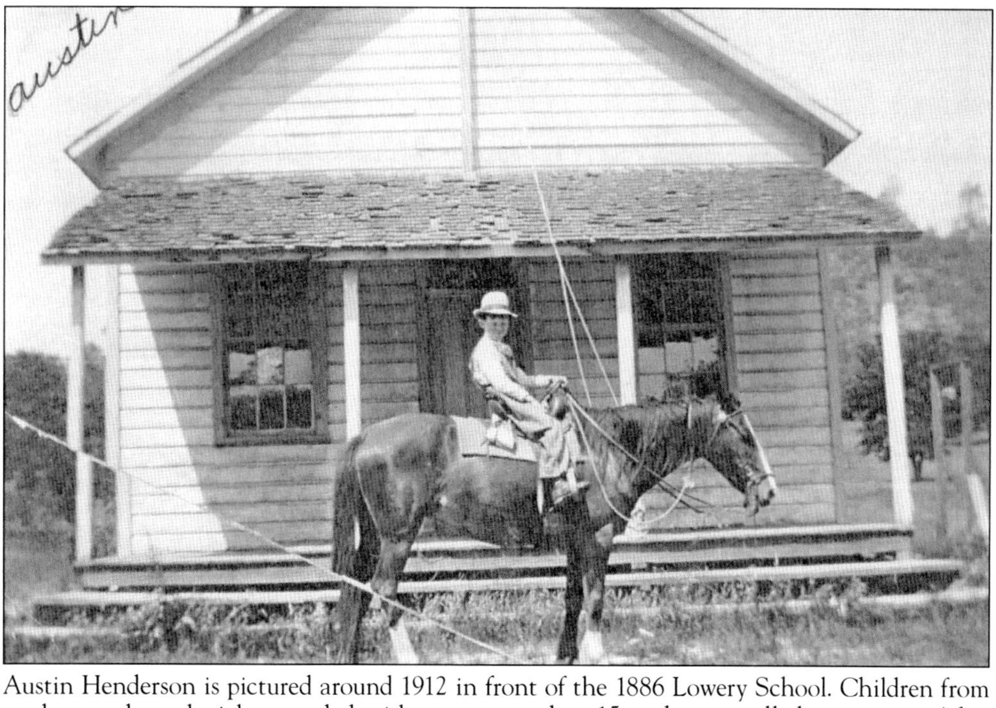

Austin Henderson is pictured around 1912 in front of the 1886 Lowery School. Children from grades one through eight attended, with never more than 15 students enrolled at one time. After eighth grade, students were transferred to other high schools. Transportation to the school ranged from walking, mule-drawn carts, or horseback riding. Over time, attendance declined, and the school was closed in 1944. (John A. Bedford collection.)

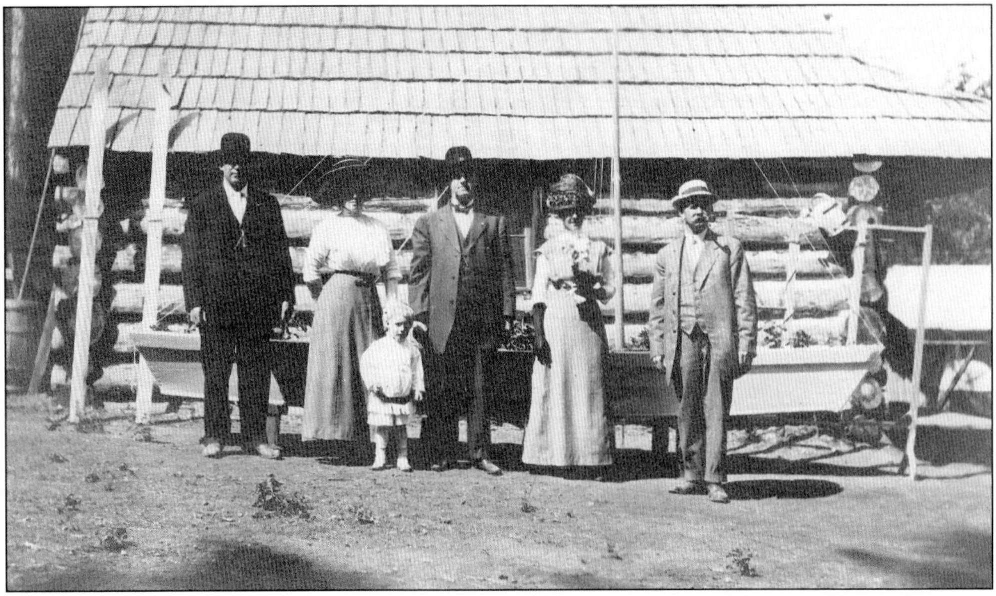

Colyear Springs, located 35 miles west of Red Bluff, was named for John G. Colyear, who came to Tehama County in 1851 from Kentucky. By 1904, several cabins were built as retreats from the summer heat of the valley. The area was used for several years as a mountain resort because of the cold water and sulfurous springs in the area. (Tehama County Library collection.)

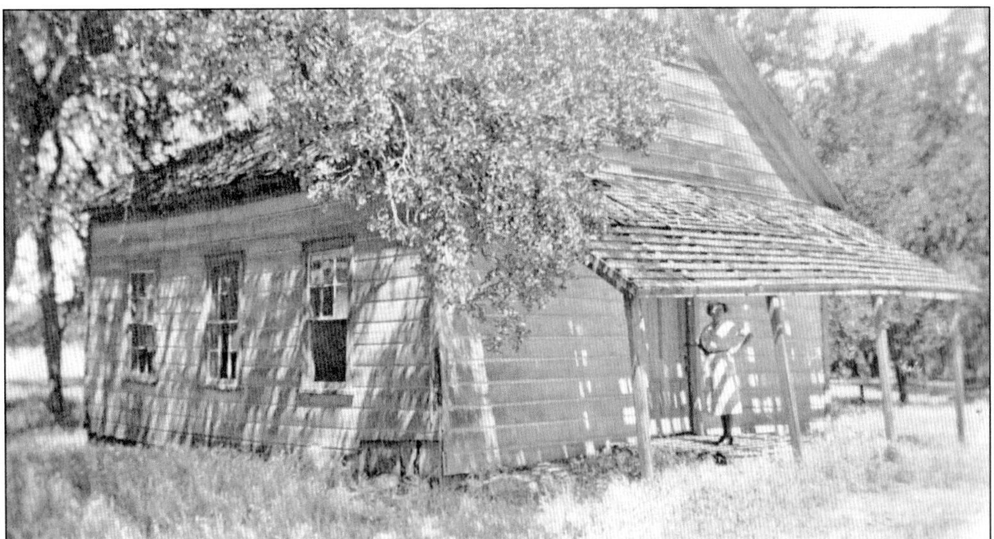

In 1882–1883, the Colyear School was established and served students until 1914. The school house doubled as a community center for many years, even after the school no longer existed. The building was used for dances, special community events, group meetings, and even a polling place. Eulalia (Eaton) Rogers stands by the door. (Opal Thornton Mendenhall collection.)

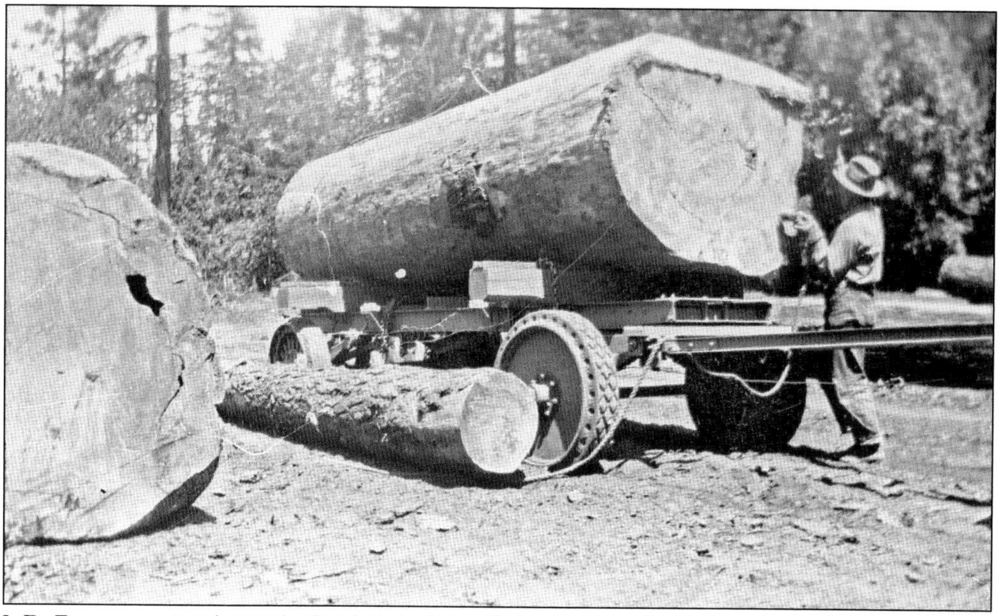

L.D. Fox prepares a log to be hauled to the mill. Lumbering thrived in the Paskenta area. The Patton mill was built in 1858 and ran without steam or electricity—it was completely water-driven. The mill was powered by a waterwheel 40 feet in diameter and 12 feet wide using water from Mill Creek, a tributary of Thomes Creek. The mill operated until 1897. (California State University, Chico, Special Collections.)

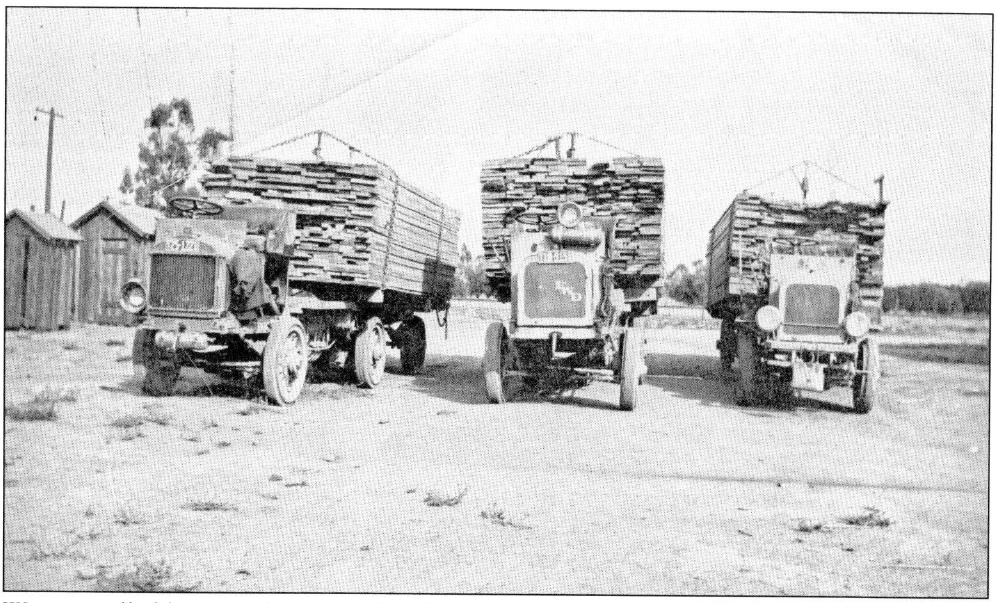

Wagons pulled by oxen, horses, and mule teams were used to haul lumber out of the western mountains. In the 1920s, lumbermen started using trucks with solid rubber tires. To help brake the trucks as they came down the narrow and steep mountain roads, a tree would be dragged behind the truck. (California State University, Chico, Special Collections.)

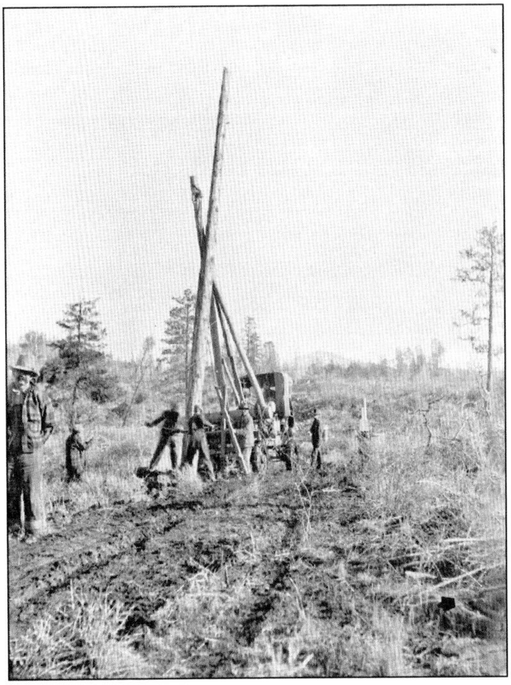

L.D. Fox and crew are raising poles for the electric company using a McVey loader. Built in 1936 by the McVey Machine Shop of Klamath Falls, Oregon, it was a 1921 Mack Bulldog truck with a 46-foot fir boom. To power the loader, the truck's chain drive to the rear wheels was removed and reattached to hydraulic drum winches on the bed. Electricity came to Tehama County (first to Red Bluff) in 1888 and to Paskenta in 1939. (Tehama County Library collection.)

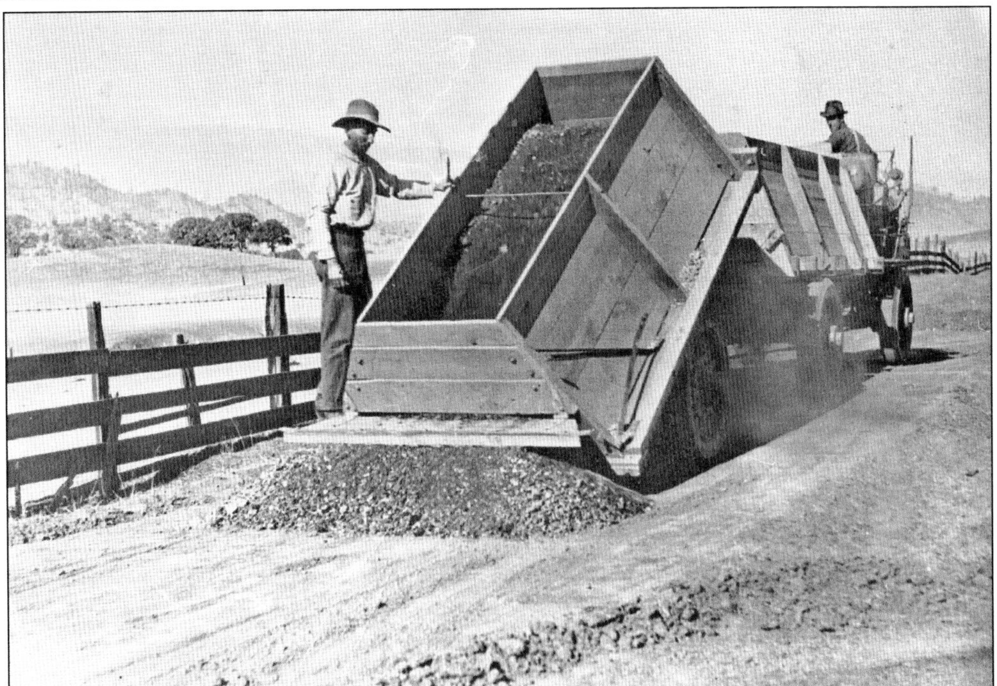

County supervisors contracted with local men to build and maintain county roads. Driver L.D. Fox and Bose Miller are dumping gravel on a road by Paskenta around the 1920s. The Nome Lackee Reservation Road, built in the 1860s, was one of the first roads in the state built and paid for by the US government. It ran from the reservation to the old Colusi Road. (California State University, Chico, Special Collections.)

# *Six*

# Recreation

There has always been a wide variety of entertainment for the hardworking residents of Tehama County to enjoy: dances, touring theatrical groups, parades, sports, and picnics, to mention a few. At home, families spent evenings playing various musical instruments, engaging in parlor games, reading, or visiting nearby friends and neighbors.

The beautiful Sacramento River has always been an integral part of life in Tehama County, whether for agriculture, commerce, or recreation. Flowing through its center, it is the living heart of Tehama County. Waterskiing, fishing, kayaking, or boating on its smooth surface are just some of the countless recreational opportunities it offers. Not to be outdone, the rugged mountains mantled with the Lassen National Forest to the east and both the Mendocino and Shasta-Trinity National Forests to the west offer year-round recreation with skiing, snowshoeing, sledding, and snowmobiling in the winter and cool respites during the hot summer for hiking, camping, fishing, and hunting.

State hunters backed a bill requiring hunting licenses starting in July 1907, with the money applied toward game preservation; fishermen were exempt. Licenses cost $1 for residents, $10 for out-of-state residents, and $25 for foreigners. Hunters had to display elliptical metal tags stamped "Hunting License No.—, State of California, Expires June 30, 19—." These tags were aluminum for residents, copper for out-of-state residents, and brass for foreigners.

If the river is the heart of the county, rodeo is its soul. The Red Bluff Round-Up is a popular yearly event that has thrilled hundreds of thousands of rodeo fans since 1921. The rodeo is a natural expression of a cowboy or cowgirl's skills honed on the ranch and displayed in the arena. The Red Bluff Round-Up grew out of informal rodeo gatherings at local ranches. The earliest was held at the Clough Ranch east of Los Molinos in 1918. Then Jess Bennett and Ivy Bell held an informal roping and bronc-riding contest in 1919 at their ranch near Vina. These gatherings were so successful that the Northern California Round-Up Association was formed in 1920 and continued until 1925. From these traditions, the Red Bluff Round-Up Association was formed in 1921.

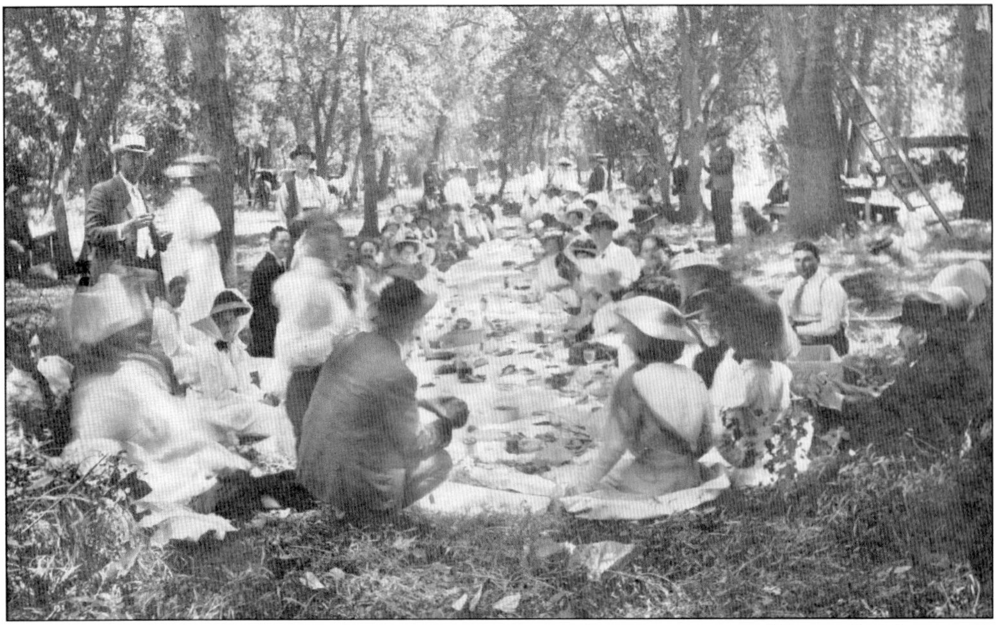

May Day picnics were very popular community events that everyone could attend. Along with picnics, there were foot races, wheelbarrow races, horseshoe pitching, tug-of-wars, and gunnysack races for kids. Parades and baseball games between towns were also enjoyed. No particular day was May Day, which allowed communities to pick days that did not interfere with each other so people could attend more than one. (Frances Leininger collection.)

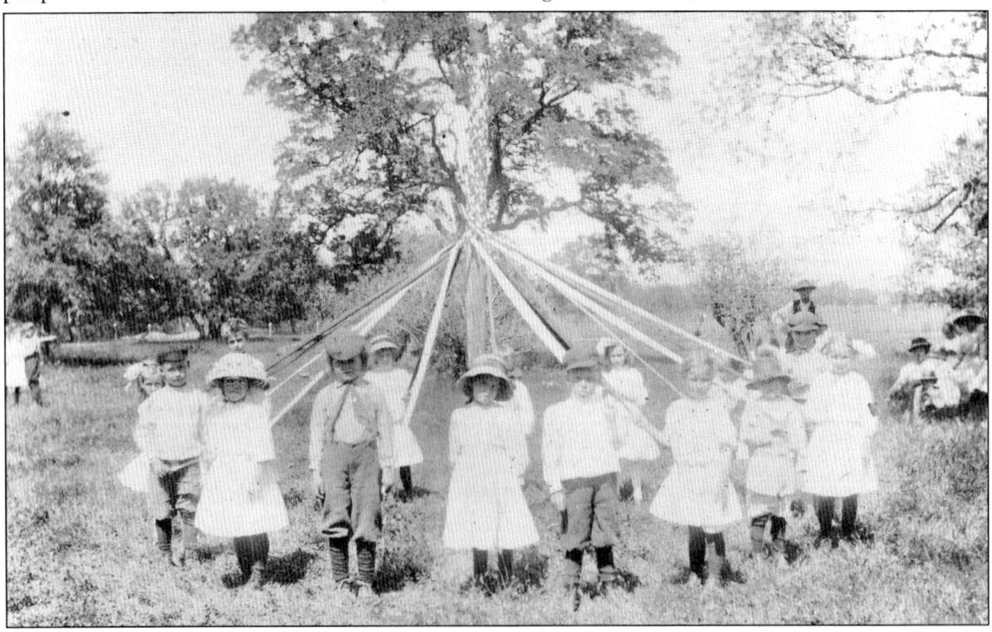

The May Pole dance was a springtime celebration for local schools and communities. Here is a May Pole dance at Los Molinos on May 1, 1912. From left to right are Viola Carrington, James Carrington, Pearl Moore, Robert Stryker, Alfred Davis, Nita Porter, Althea Kennedy, two unidentified boys, Alice Moore, Jewel Summers, Lester Williams, Guy Pittone, and Irene Stryker. The man in the background is Mr. Summers. (Tehama County Library collection.)

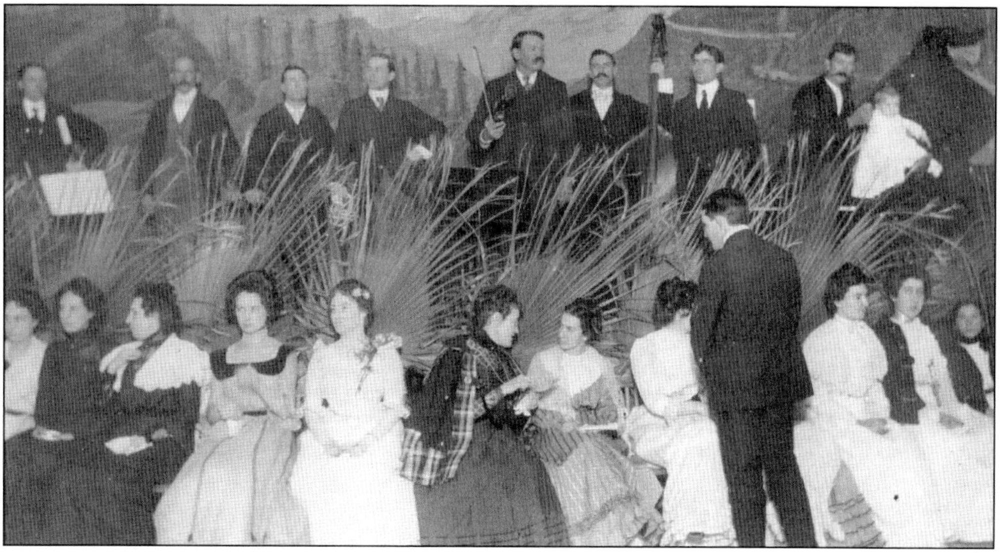

A Christmas Night Ball was held at Liersch House Hotel in Corning on December 25, 1901. Balls were very popular social events that lasted all night, with supper usually served at midnight. Dances included the waltz, quadrilles, and polkas. Apperson's Orchestra from Willows provided the music for this ball, with leader John A. Apperson on violin, Charles Eilerman on coronet, Henry Summers on bass fiddle, and Lenus J. Klemmer on piano. (Corning Museum collection.)

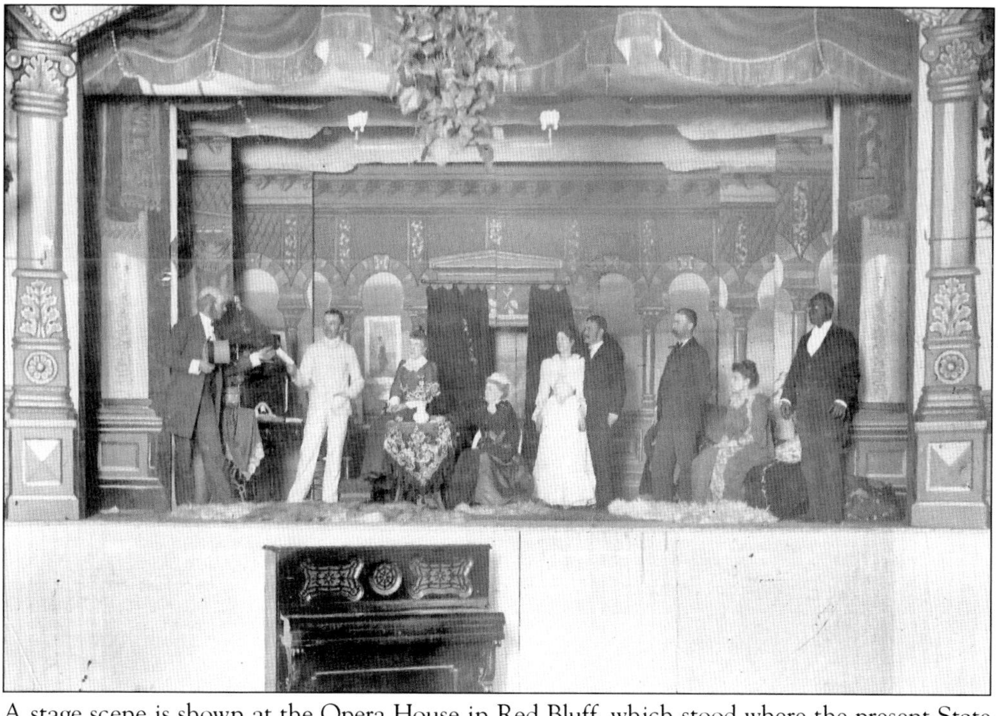

A stage scene is shown at the Opera House in Red Bluff, which stood where the present State Theater now stands. The Jessie Shirley Company, which toured the United States and Canada, produced weekly plays while appearing in Red Bluff. Gas jets (seen above the actors) provided the stage lighting in this c. 1900 photograph. Price for admission ranged from 10¢ to 75¢. (Tehama County Library collection.)

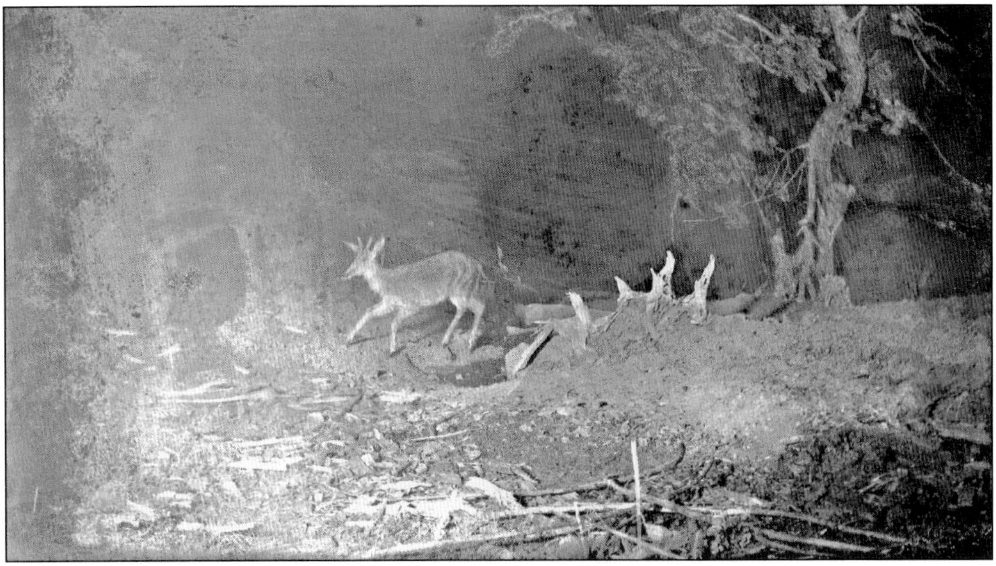

This deer took a picture of itself at night when it triggered a remote-control camera on July 23, 1896. This may be one of the earliest examples of "flash-light photography," as described by newspapers at the time. When the animal tripped a wire, it ignited the flash and triggered the shutter. This "rapidly developing art" was written about in several publications in the 1890s. (California State University, Chico, Special Collections.)

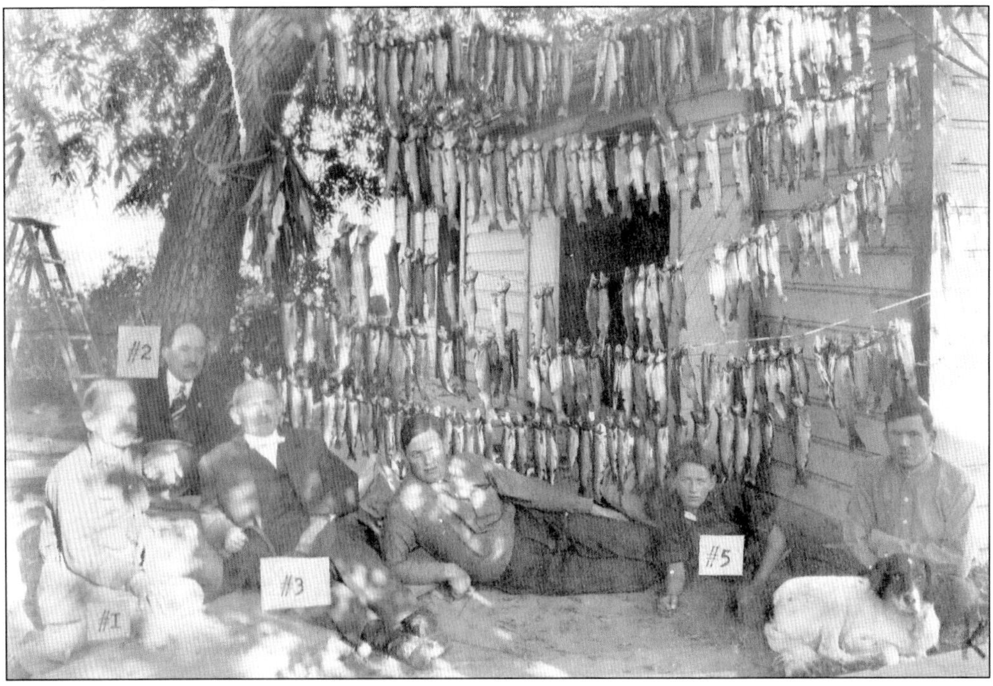


Over 200 trout are pictured here. From left to right in this c. 1908 photograph are Tehama County assessor Louis Winter, Dr. F.L. Doane, Dr. N.I. Paxton, Dr. Paxton, Mr. Winter, and Dr. Bagley. One of the finest fly-fishing rods in the world, the Powell split-bamboo fly rod, got its start in Tehama County in 1918 when E.C. Powell developed strong, lightweight rods based on the hexagonal shape of beehive cells. (Tehama County Library collection.)

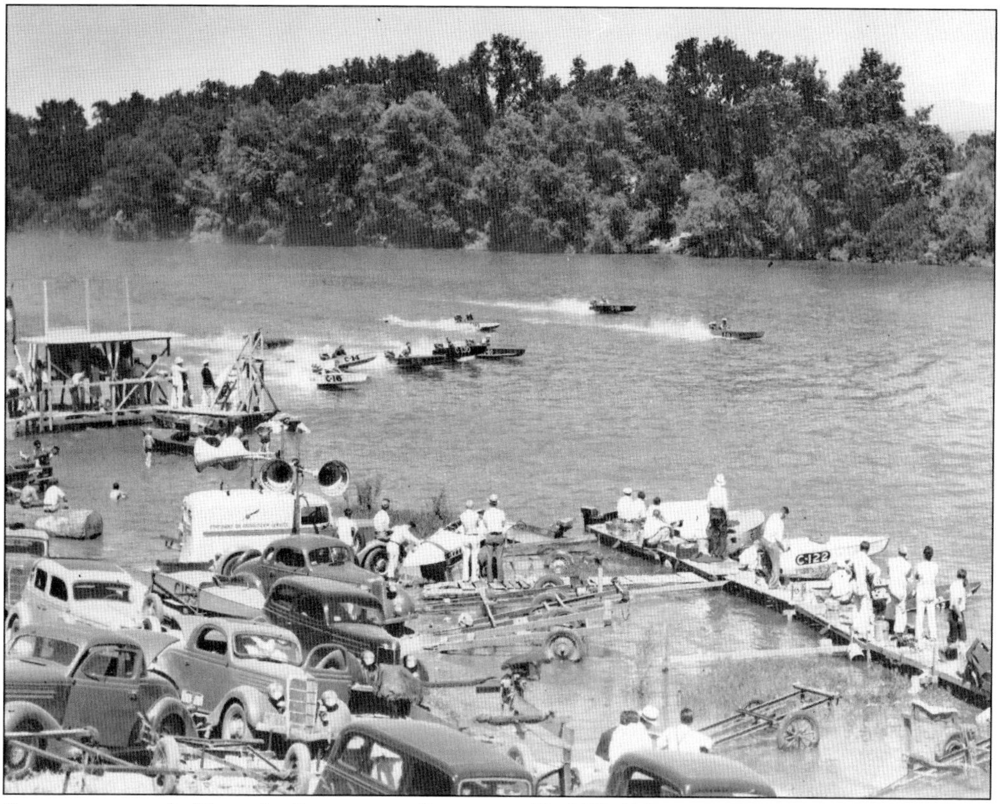

Boat races were held on the Sacramento River near Red Bluff during 1932 to 1941. These 12-foot runabouts reached speeds of 50–60 mph. Later, the popular Red Bluff Nitro National Drag Boat Festival began. Boats raced up to 200 mph on a temporary lake formed when the Bureau of Reclamation lowered the gates of the Diversion Dam. A federal court order protecting endangered salmon ended the races in 2009. (Tehama County Library collection.)

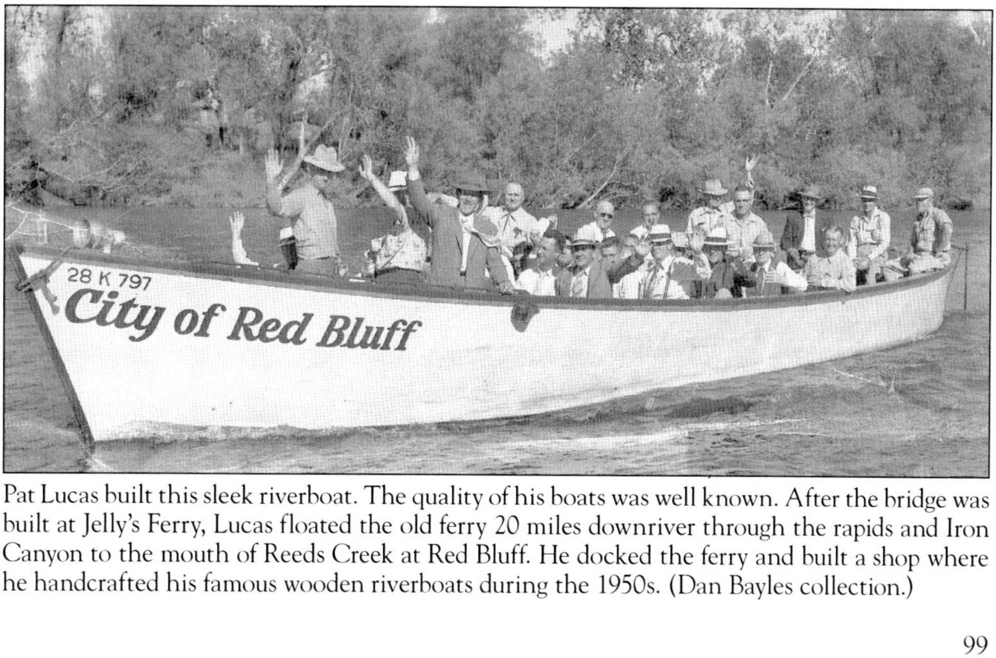


Pat Lucas built this sleek riverboat. The quality of his boats was well known. After the bridge was built at Jelly's Ferry, Lucas floated the old ferry 20 miles downriver through the rapids and Iron Canyon to the mouth of Reeds Creek at Red Bluff. He docked the ferry and built a shop where he handcrafted his famous wooden riverboats during the 1950s. (Dan Bayles collection.)

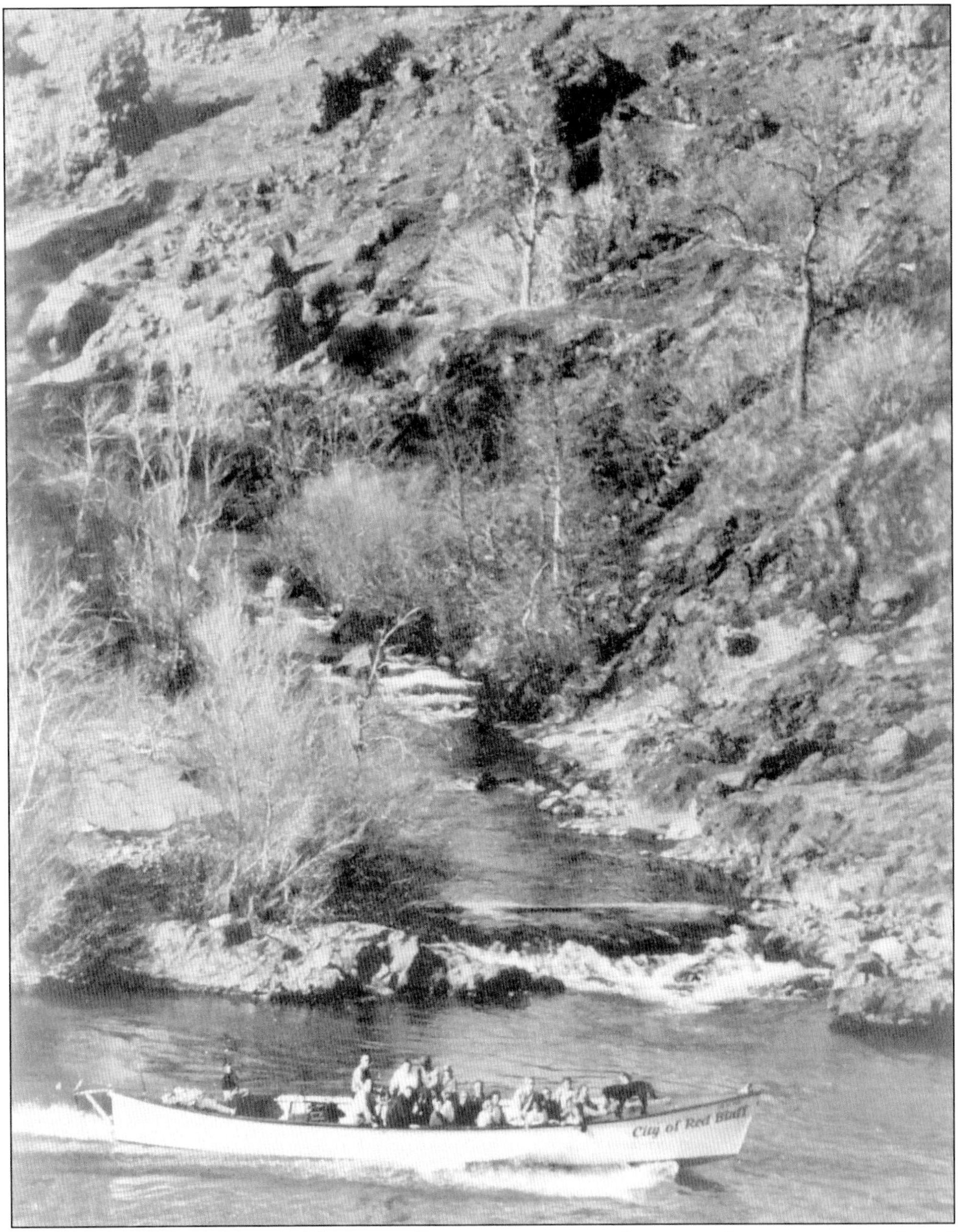


In the 1940s and 1950s, one of the most pleasant ways to spend a summer's evening was to board the *City of Red Bluff* (or "the Big Boat") and cruise up the Sacramento River. The owner, builder, and pilot of the 45-foot tour boat was Pat Lucas, who owned the marina at the Red Bluff River Park. It was a Rogue River–style boat made to run shallow water. (Lucas came from family that pioneered the Rogue River area in Oregon.) His boats had frameworks made of Port Orford cedar and plywood hulls. The engine was a Buick Fireball In-Line Eight, and the propeller could be lifted by stepping on a foot lever. The vessel carried 20 or more people and made daily trips for a dollar a person up the river through Iron Canyon as far as China Rapids. These river tours were so popular that *Sunset* magazine wrote two articles about them. (Dan Bayles collection.)

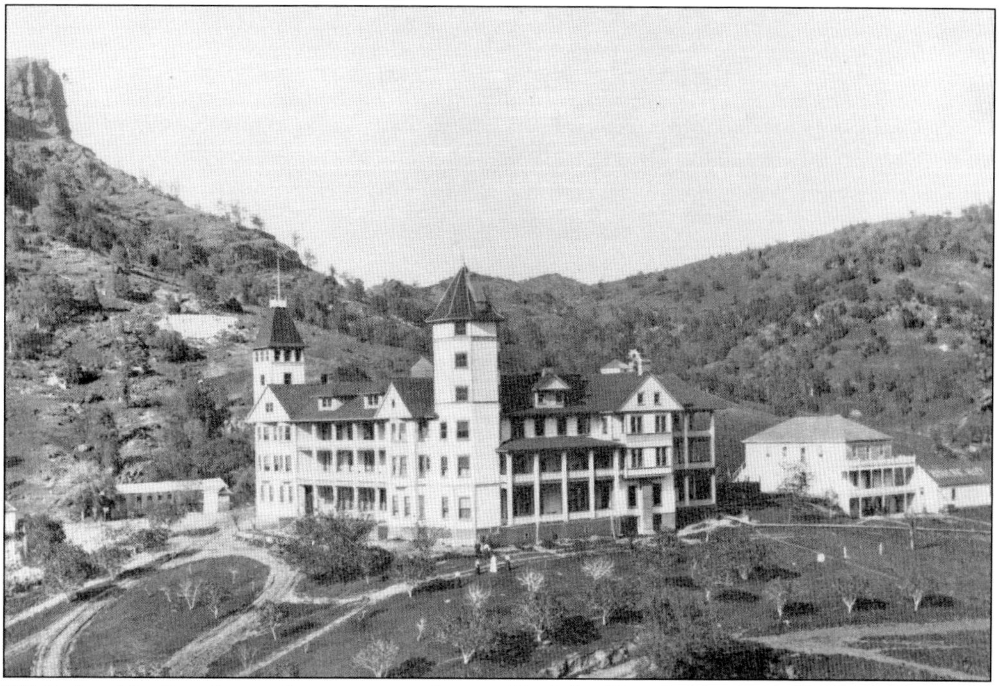

While local Indians knew these springs, chemist Dr. John Veatch "discovered" them on January 8, 1856. The Tuscan Springs Resort was built and flourished for 50 years. At its height, the resort boasted a four-story hotel, post office, telegraph/telephone offices, a saloon, two dining rooms, billiard and club room, bridle paths, hunting and fishing, a water bottling plant, and bathhouses that took advantage of the medicinal qualities of 50 springs. (Charles Hughes/California State University, Chico, Special Collections.)

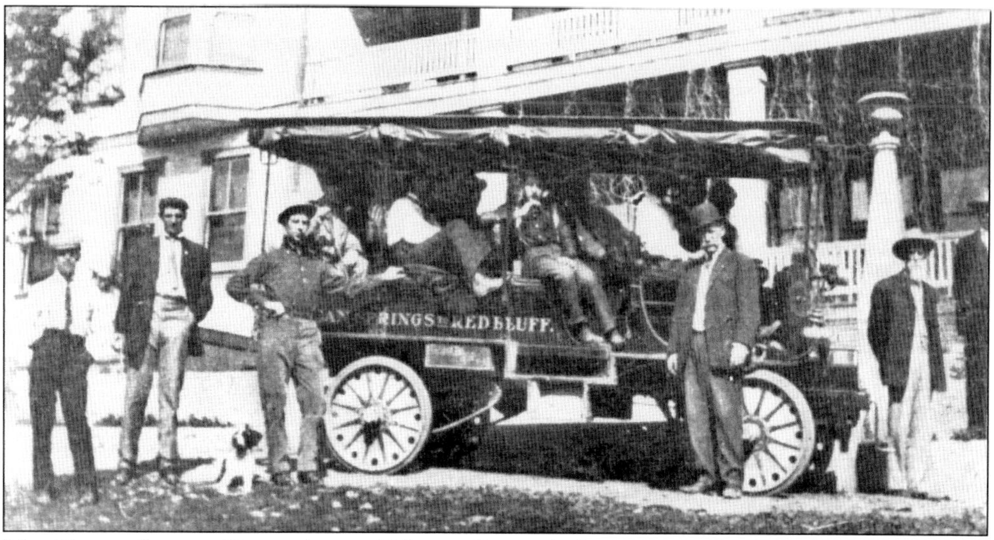

The Tuscan Springs Resort began Tehama County's first commercial car service that could carry eight people between Red Bluff and the very popular resort/spa seven miles to the east. However, in 1916, a fire destroyed the hotel. It was underinsured, never rebuilt, and gradually fell into ruin. Today, scant traces remain of this once magnificent destination. (Tehama County Library collection.)

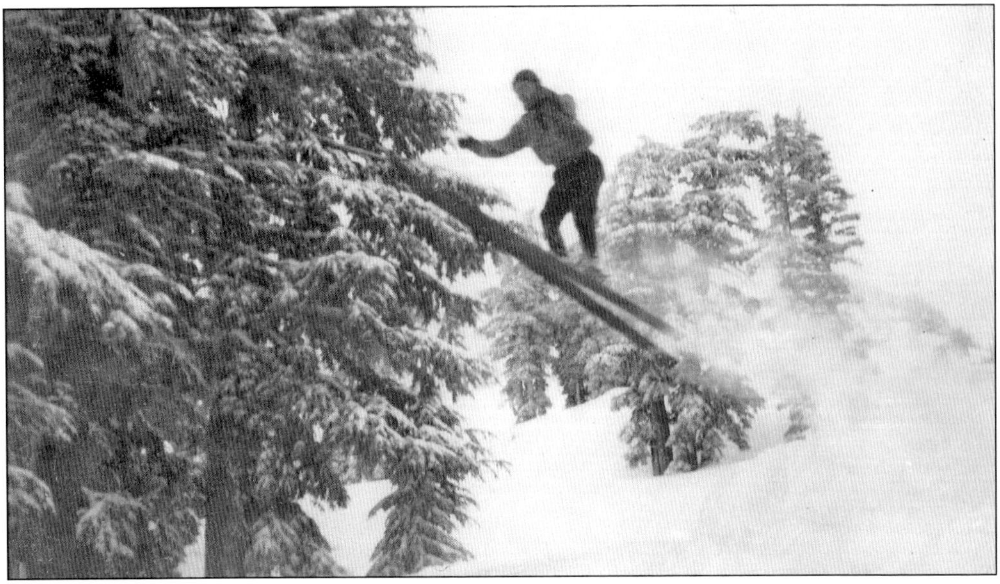

In 1935, the California State Ski Jumping Championships were held at Mineral. Norwegian lumbermen and skiers working for the Red River Lumber Company in Westwood helped construct the ski jump. Modern Olympic jumping form had not been perfected yet. Early jumpers would wave their arms in the air, known as the Kongsberger technique, to extend their jumping lengths from 148 feet to 330 feet. The jumper in this photograph is unidentified. (Dan Foster collection.)

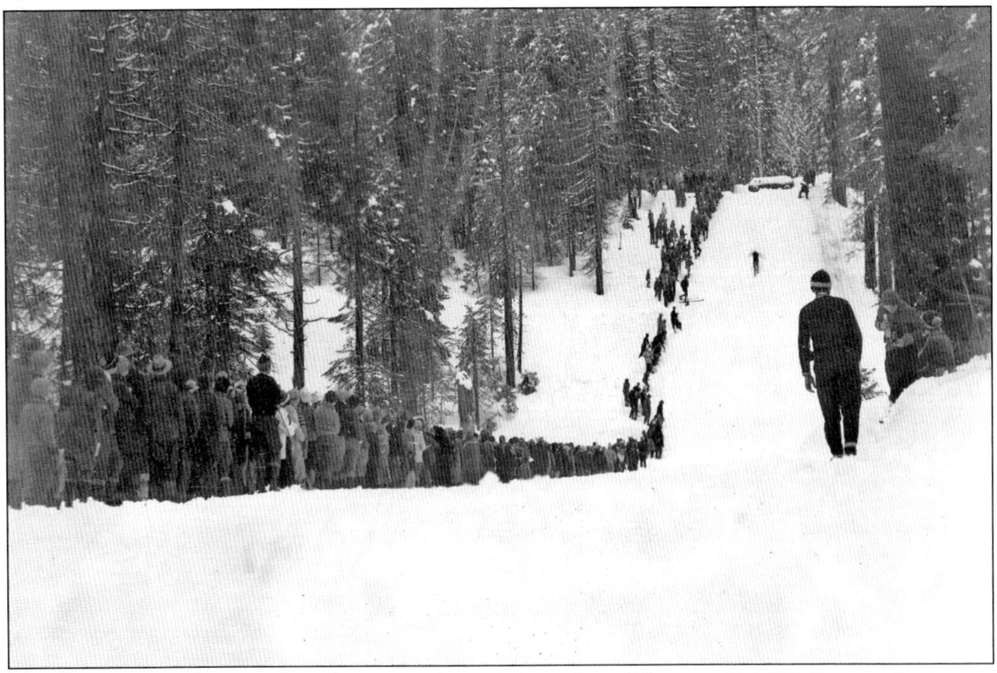

A crowd watches a ski jumping championship at Mineral on February 17, 1935. On nearby Lassen Peak, five US Olympic Ski Team members skied the spectacular July 4th Inferno Ski Race—snow was still abundant even then. The ungroomed course, with four gates and two turns, started near the summit at 10,500 feet and ended near the park road at 8,500 feet. One competitor remembers skiing it with eight-foot long Army surplus skis. (Dan Foster collection.)

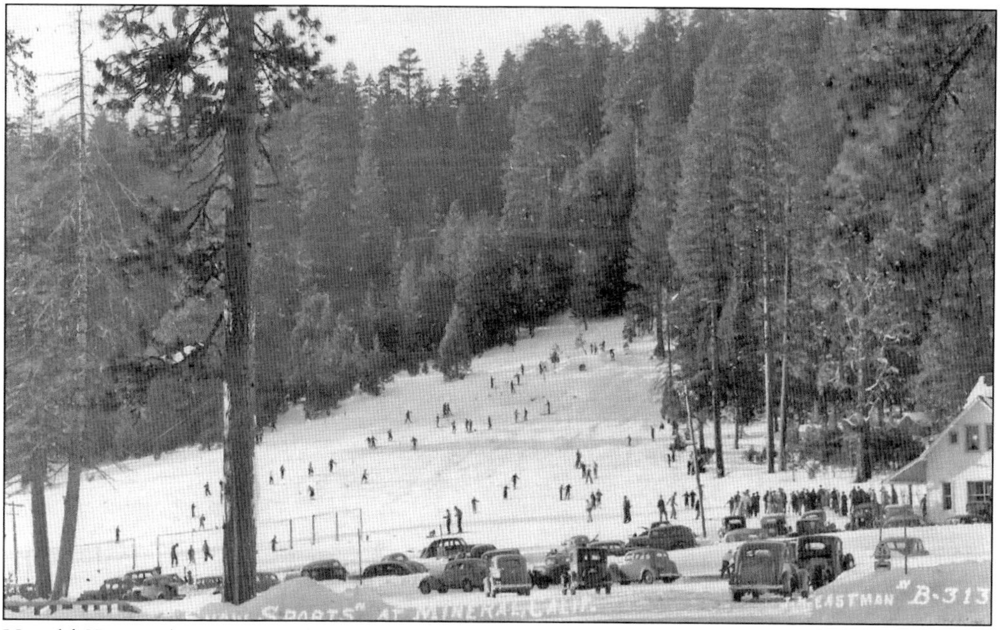


Harold K. "Husky" Beresford owned and managed the Mineral Lodge. He introduced skiing to the area about 1932 and promoted many regional skiing events in the Mineral area in the 1930s–1940s. He installed lights to enable nighttime skiing. Here are skiers on the hill just west of the lodge around 1934. (Tehama County Library collection.)

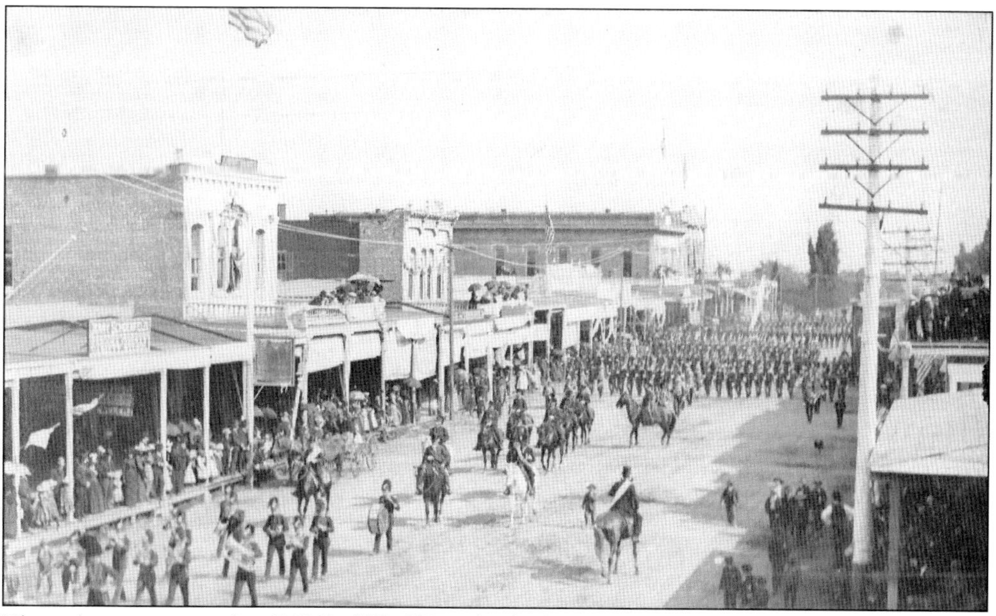

The military group in this 1898 Red Bluff Fourth of July parade is described as "Shafter's Advanced Guard" in the original caption. Maj. Gen. William Shafter was the commander of the Fifth Army Corps, which included the Rough Riders. Fourth of July events were all-day affairs with parades and races, including hose-cart contests between fire departments. The day would close with fireworks and a fancy dress ball. (Tehama County Library collection.)

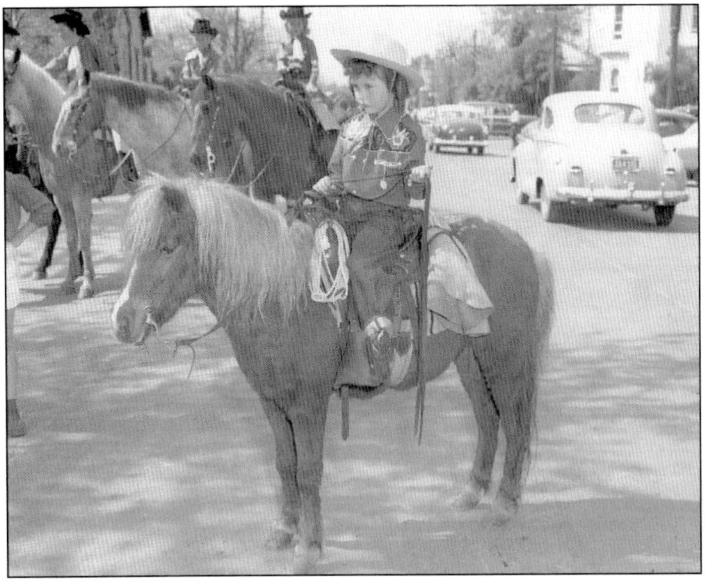

During the 1930s–1940s, a Kiddies Parade was held during the Red Bluff Round-Up. Children would participate, either costumed or otherwise, sometimes with a family pet. Each entrant received a pass to the State Theatre and a ticket to the Round-Up. The route went east on Walnut Street, south on Main Street, and ended at the courthouse where the judging for prizes took place. (Tehama County Library collection.)

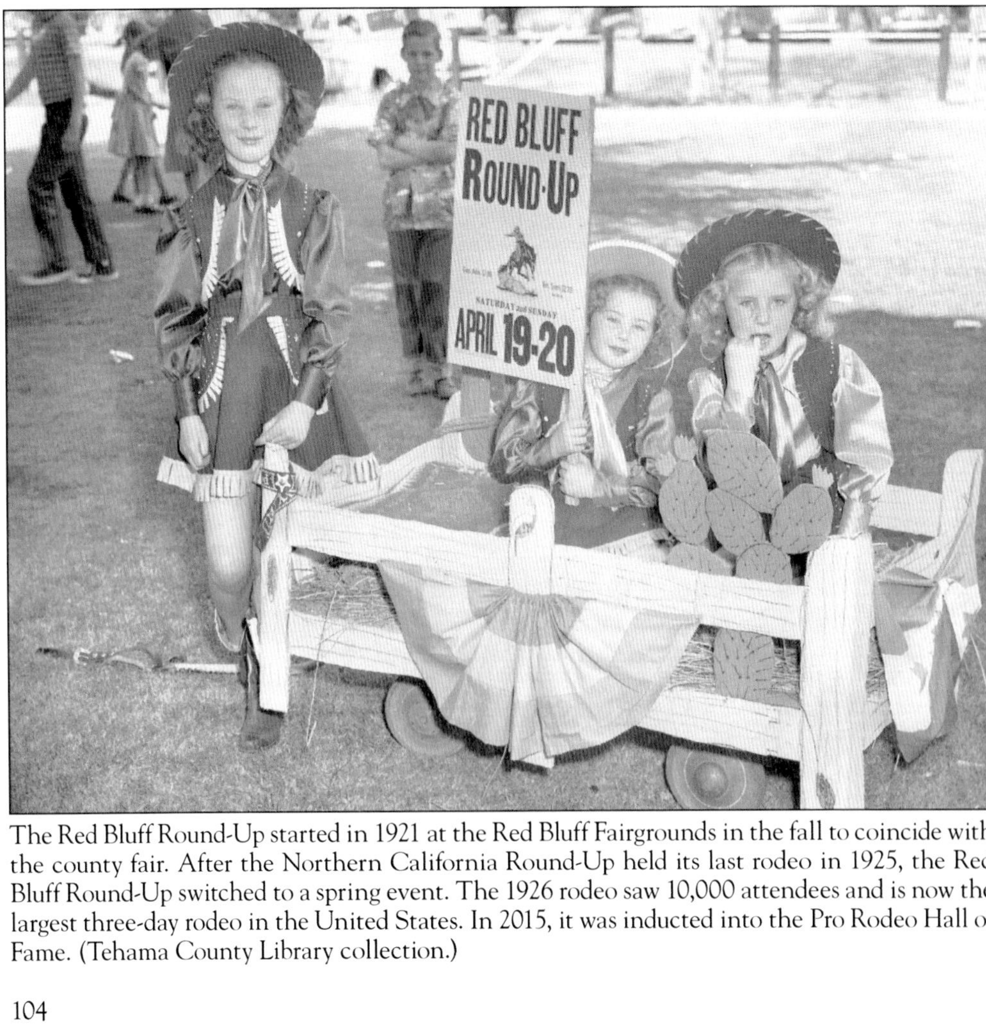


The Red Bluff Round-Up started in 1921 at the Red Bluff Fairgrounds in the fall to coincide with the county fair. After the Northern California Round-Up held its last rodeo in 1925, the Red Bluff Round-Up switched to a spring event. The 1926 rodeo saw 10,000 attendees and is now the largest three-day rodeo in the United States. In 2015, it was inducted into the Pro Rodeo Hall of Fame. (Tehama County Library collection.)

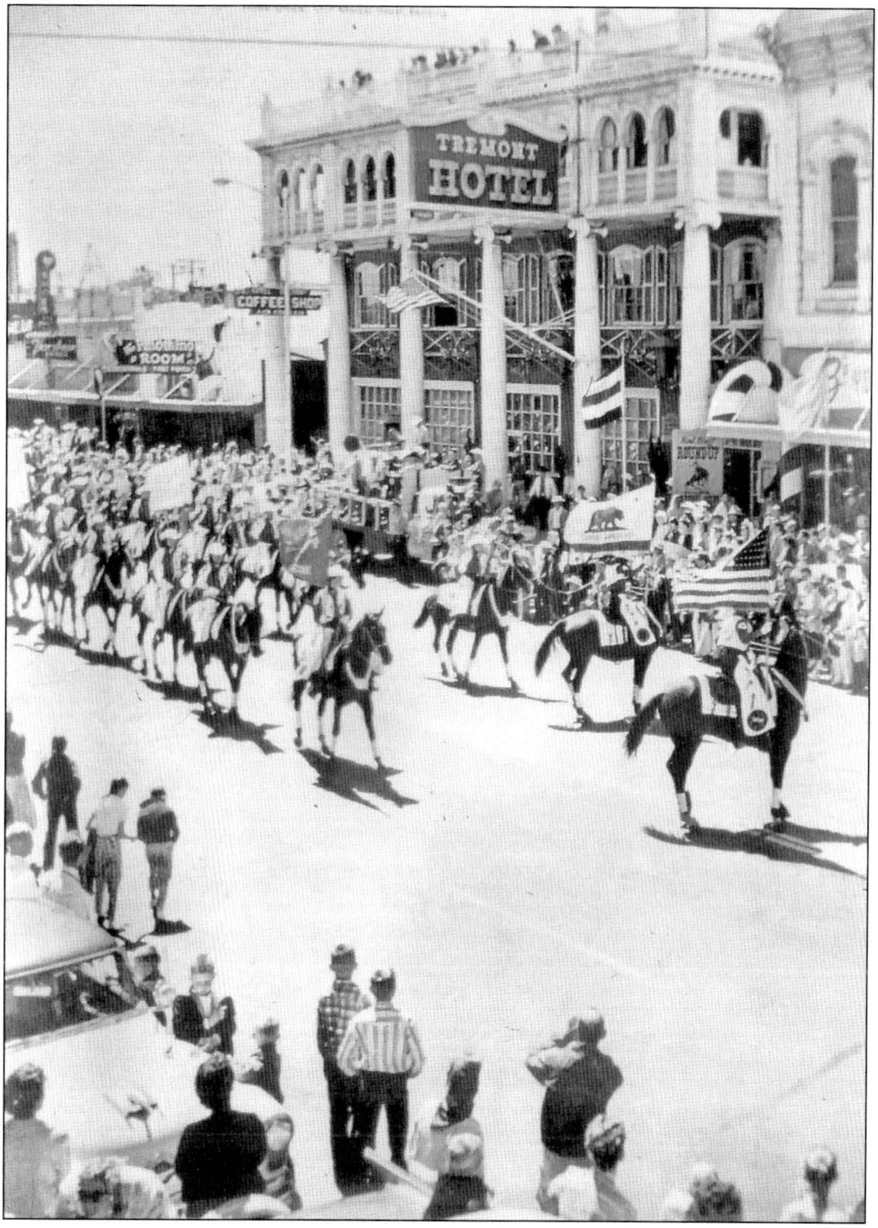


A big part of the Round-Up was (and still is) the parade in Red Bluff. In 1922, the Flying Squadron, a publicity parade of rodeo boosters dressed in cowboy outfits, drove highly decorated cars to valley towns to promote the Round-Up. On September 8, 1922, the *Red Bluff Daily News* published this cheeky itinerary: "Chico, for dinner and where they will shoot up the city horribly. Then, pursued by the wrathful citizens of Chico, they'll take refuge in Willows, only to obliterate the capital of Glenn County entirely. Then north to Orland where every man, woman, and child will be made to take an oath to attend the Round-Up or face banishment to Igo. Then to Corning where they can rest before heading north to attack Cottonwood, Anderson, and Redding." Later publicity parades involved 50 cars. With a saddle on its hood, the lead car's siren led the way. Announcements made through the first car's megaphone were echoed by another megaphone 49 cars back. This caravan effort continued until the 1960s. (Tehama County Library collection.)

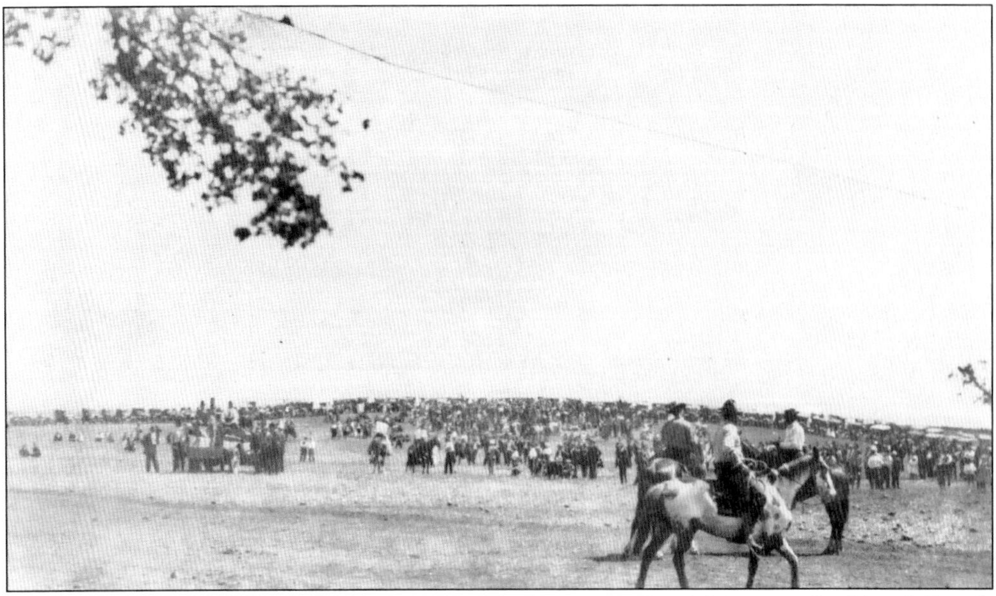

The first organized rodeo in Tehama County took place east of Los Molinos at the Clough Ranch owned by brothers George and Allie Clough in 1918. It was also known as the Clough Picnic. Allie knew the legendary Wyatt Earp, famous from the Gunfight at the O.K. Corral in Tombstone, Arizona. George owned a livery stable in San Francisco where Allie worked for a time training racehorses for Earp. (Frances Leininger collection.)

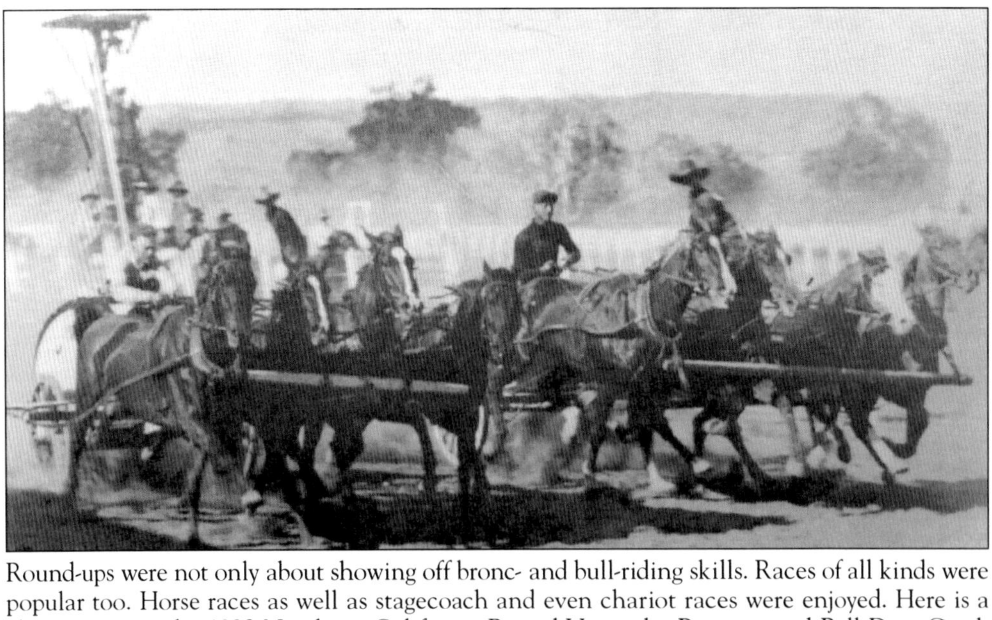

Round-ups were not only about showing off bronc- and bull-riding skills. Races of all kinds were popular too. Horse races as well as stagecoach and even chariot races were enjoyed. Here is a chariot race at the 1923 Northern California Round-Up at the Bennett and Bell Deer Creek Ranch. Usually, only two teams could be raced at one time because the track could not safely handle more. (Frances Leininger collection.)

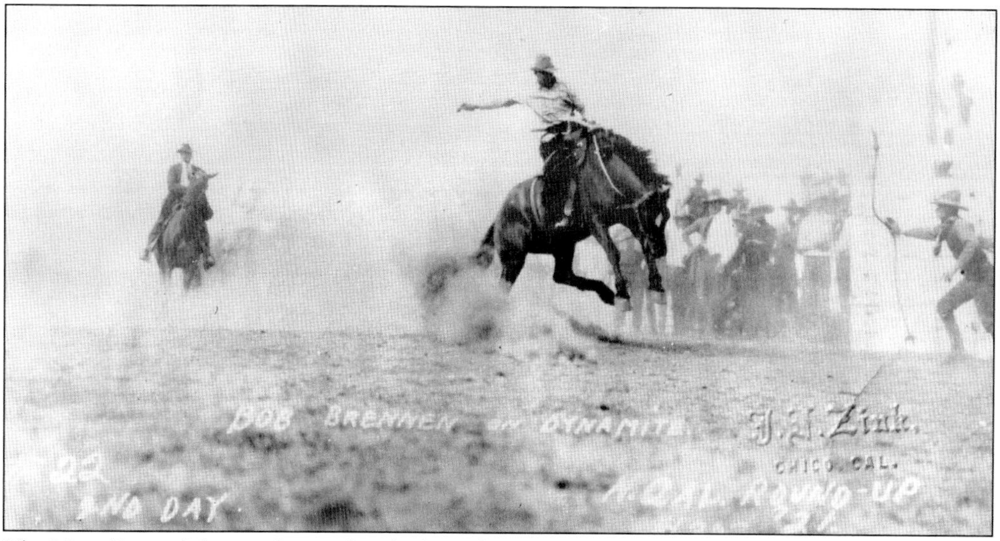


The Vina Festival during the weekend of April 24–25, 1920, at the Bennett and Bell Deer Creek Ranch was advertised as a barbecue and dance "to a good jazz band." Despite a circus in nearby Red Bluff, 5,000 people came by car, horse, buggy, and wagon to enjoy activities ranging from rolling a peanut with a toothpick to riding a wild steer. Here, Bob Brennen is riding Dynamite at the 1921 festival. (Tehama County Library collection.)

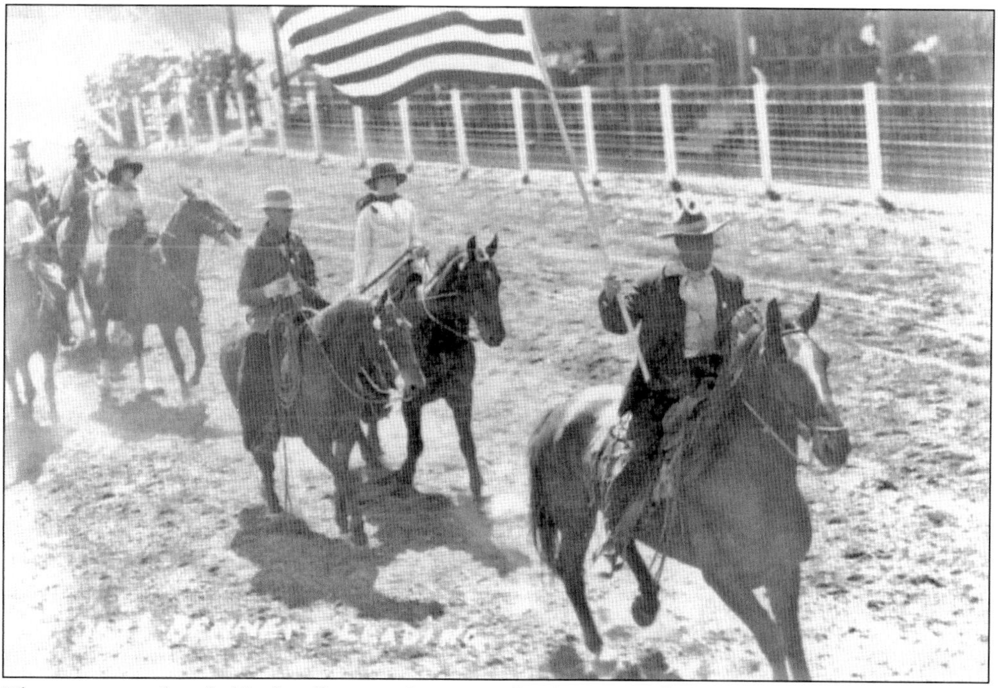

The entry parade is led by Jess Bennett (carrying the American flag), followed by Charles Stover, Lavina Woodward, and Jackie Speegle (in the black hat). The Northern California Round-Up Association formed in 1920. The association built stands, an arena, and a racetrack on the Bennett and Bell Ranch, and the Deer Creek Round-Up was held during the last weekend of April until 1925. (Frances Leininger collection.)

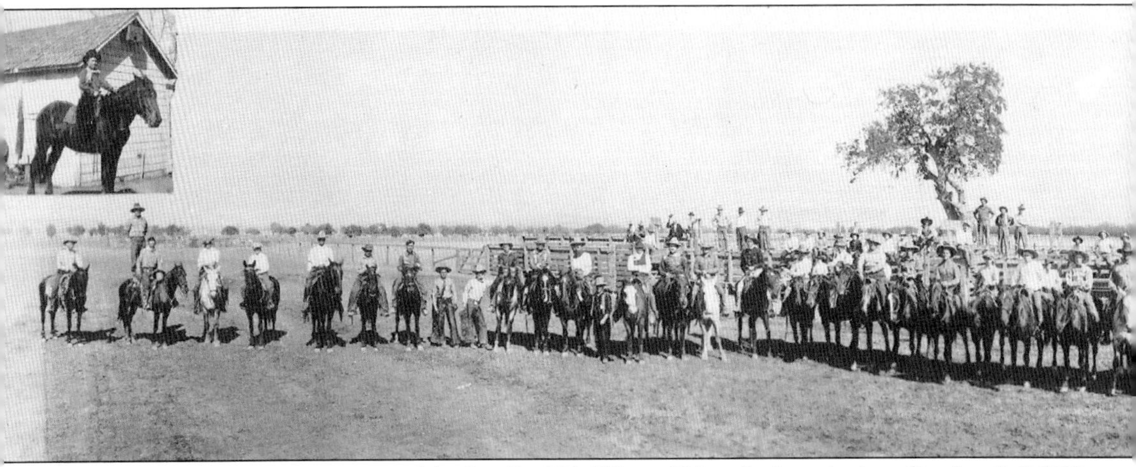

Pictured here are participants of the first Red Bluff Round-Up, which took place October 6–9, 1921, at the fairgrounds and was attended by 7,000 people. First prizes were $300 for bronco busting, $50 for bull riding, and $40 for roping. Mayor G.G. Stice of Red Bluff issued a proclamation that appeared in the *Red Bluff Daily News* on August 23, 1922: "Show your loyalty by wearing a sombrero, colored shirt and handkerchief, with gaudy colors. Turn out for a good time. Let the

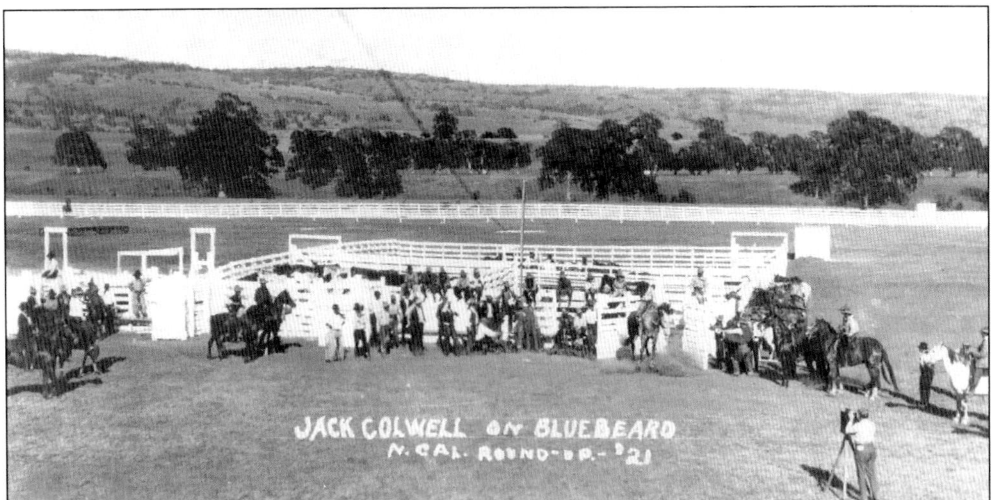


Pete White and Leo Speegle built the rodeo corrals, chutes, and platform on the Bennett and Bell Deer Creek Ranch east of Vina. Here, Jack Colwell is riding Bluebeard at the first Northern California Round-Up at the ranch during April 29–May 1, 1921. In the bucking event, Jim Gilliam won first, John Dobbins won second, and Norman Cowan won third place. (Frances Leininger collection.)

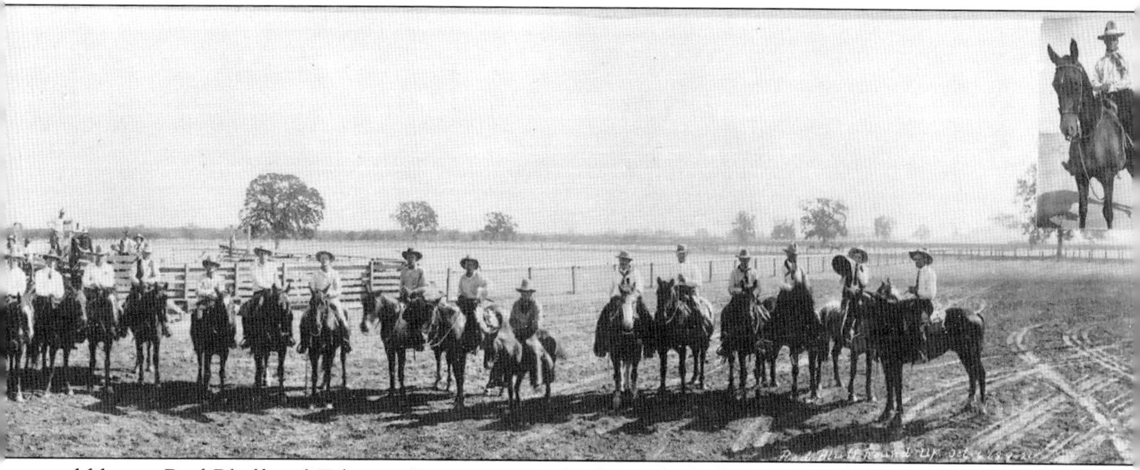

world know Red Bluff and Tehama County never do things by halves. With hearty cooperation the Fair and Roundup can and should be made permanent institutions of this city. Therefore, let us hoop 'er up for both events, and pave the way for a bigger and better time next year." (Tehama County Library collection.)

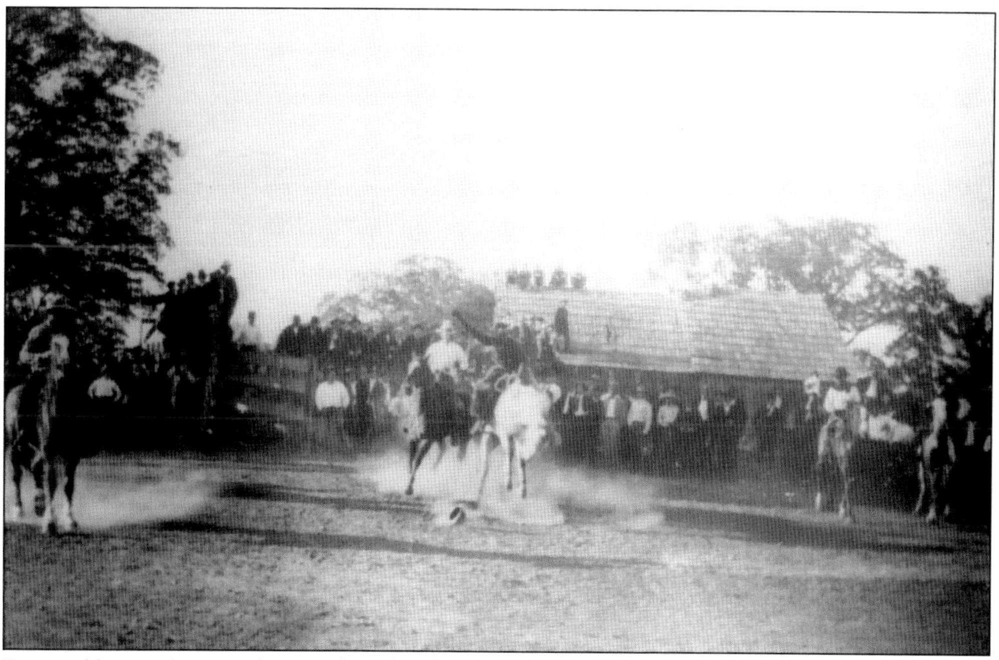

Pictured here is bronc riding at the Clough Ranch in 1918. After the cattle round-ups in spring, local cowboys were invited to picnics and informal rodeos to compete and show their skills at roping, riding, and steer wrestling (bulldogging). In 1919, the Bennett and Bell Dear Creek Ranch held the Vina Picnic, which became the Vina Festival in 1920. These informal gatherings led to more organized events that eventually culminated in today's world famous Red Bluff Round-Up held every April. (Frances Leininger collection.)

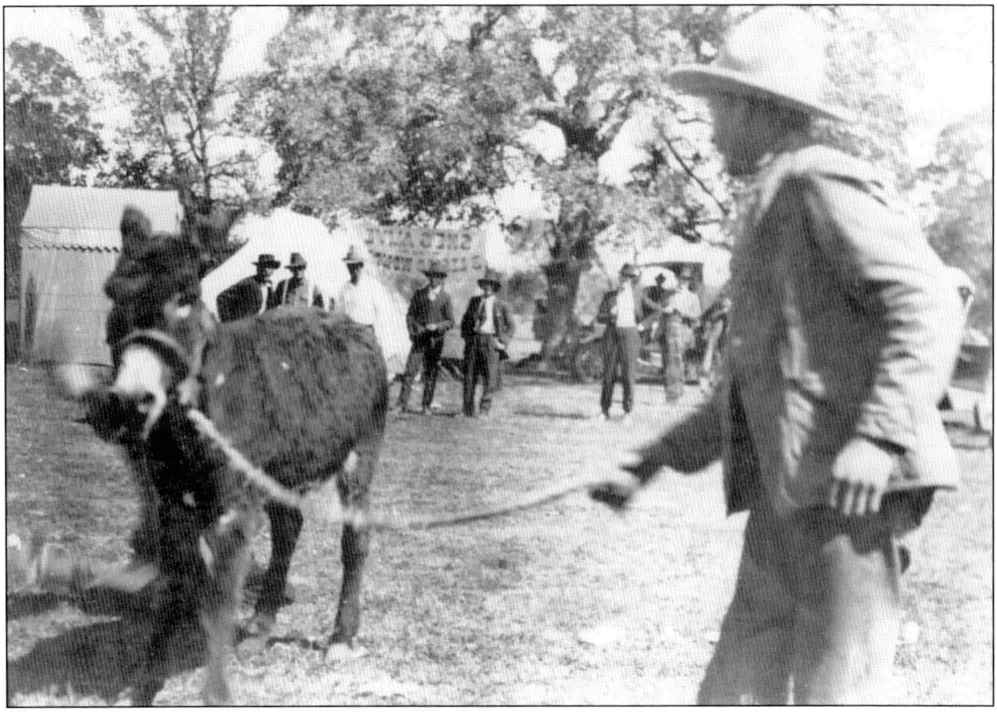

African American cowboy and rodeo rider Thomas "Ty" Stokes (1888–1929) was an expert bronc rider, rodeo clown, trick and fancy rider, and trick roper who could keep six ropes spinning simultaneously. He was also known for the "suicide ride" he did with another famous African American rodeo rider, Jesse Stahl, in which they would sit back-to-back on a bucking bronco. (Frances Leininger collection.)

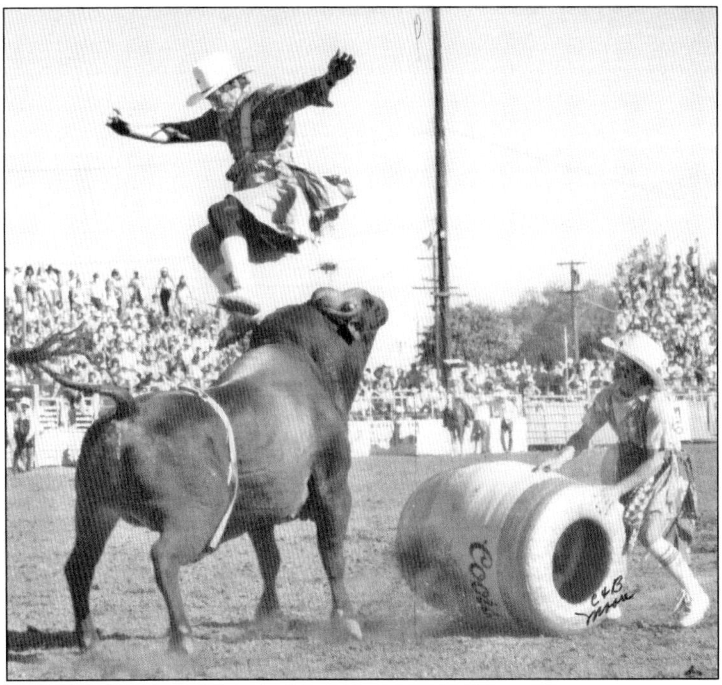

Rodeo clowns Rob Smets (left) and Kenny Watson are pictured bull jumping. Originally, rodeo clowns were performers hired as comic relief. Allie Clough hired Ty Stokes as a rodeo clown to entertain the crowd at his rodeo. Ty arrived with his mule and entertained everyone with his roping and riding skills. Later, rodeo clowns began distracting bulls away from riders who fell or jumped off the animals. (Red Bluff Round-Up Museum collection.)

# *Seven*

# Northwest

This area is home to Beegum, where the promise of gold lured miners to the area only to disappoint; the agricultural communities of Bowman, Dibble Creek, Evergreen, Farquhar, and Hooker; the mighty Yolla Bolly mountains to the west; and the roadside stops of Rosewood, named for the wild roses that grew along its streams, and Thirty Mile, named because it was 30 miles west of Red Bluff for teamsters and people on their way to the Harrison Gulch gold mines in Shasta County.

The largest town in the county, Red Bluff, owes its official existence to a court decision. When California entered the Union, all land not granted to individuals by the Mexican government became public domain. California wanted that land to sell, but the federal government wanted it surveyed first. California disagreed and began selling. This allowed Red Bluff businessman J. Granville Doll to buy the land Red Bluff was sitting on. Suddenly, people became squatters on land they considered theirs, and if they could not buy the title from Doll, they were evicted. It came to a head when Doll tried to evict Meredith Meador in 1859. The case twisted through the courts for more than five years and was finally resolved when the secretary of the interior ruled in Meador's favor.

Legislation in 1868 authorized the issuance of title certificates. All property in Red Bluff was put into the hands of the most trusted person—the county judge. Titles were issued except for the streets and courthouse. County Superior Court judge Curtis Wetter remarked in 1969, "This may be the only county in the country where the judge not only presides in the courthouse but owns the damn thing as well." Title was finally transferred to the county in 1988.

North of Red Bluff is an area that was part of a crazy scheme by Bay Area actor Maurice Curtis (1850–1920), who promoted his play *Sam'l of Posen* by raffling off, selling, or giving lots to people attending his play. He offered to record the deeds for $2 each, which far surpassed the normal filing fee charged by the county. With 9,959 deeds officially recorded, he laughed his way to the bank. One look at the scrub oak, rattlesnakes, gullies, and dry creek bed showed the new owners they had been had. As one reporter quipped in the *Sacramento Sunday Union* in 1891, "The beautiful city of Sam 'l Posen, where the people are invisible, the wonderful scenery is invisible, everything is invisible."

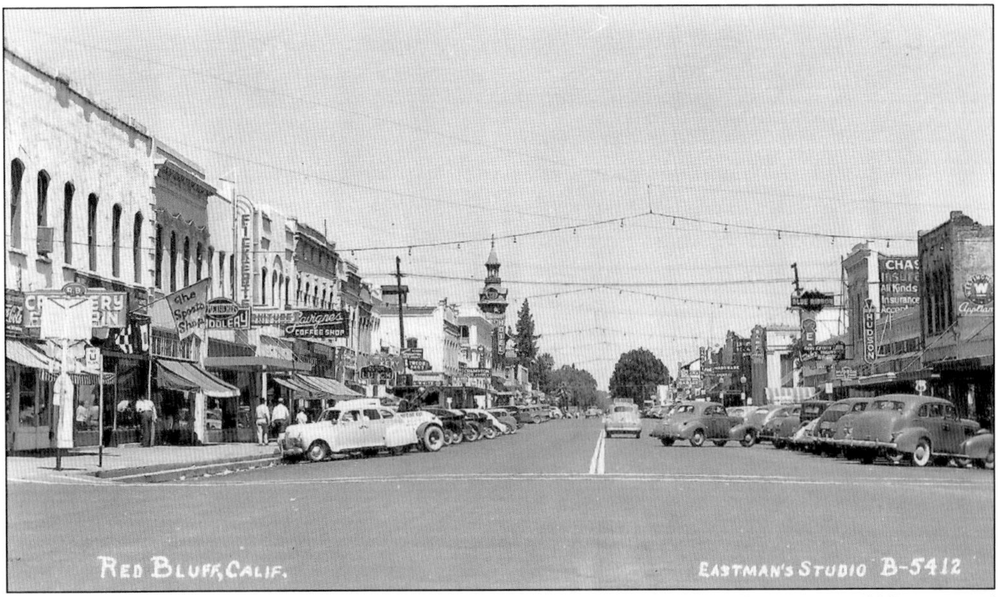


Red Bluff's Main Street is seen here in the 1940s. Before streets were paved, water would be sprayed for dust control. When Red Bluff's Main Street was paved in 1915, it was a cause for celebration. A motorcycle race and daylight fireworks put on by the local Japanese community were just a few of the events that day. The dedication was held May 22 at 2:00 p.m. Lassen Peak upstaged everything with its volcanic Great Blast at 4:45 p.m. (Tehama County Library collection.)

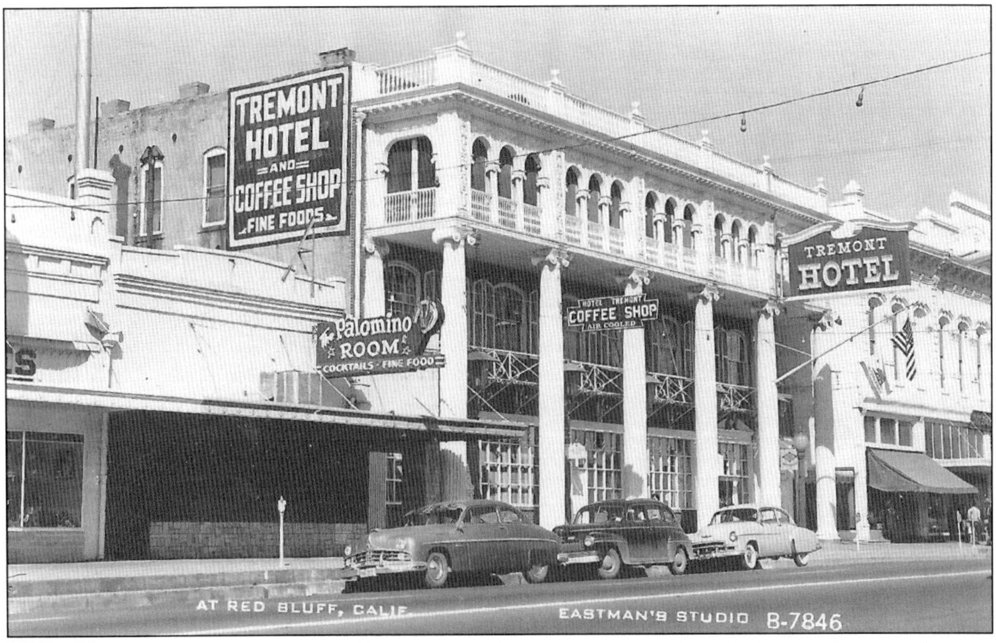


The Tremont Hotel was built in 1861 and rebuilt in 1893 to add a third story, Ionic columns, and balconies. Author Jack London; his wife, Charmian; and their Japanese servant, Yoshimatsu Nakata, stayed there on August 31, 1911. Veterans of the Civil War and Spanish American War would often sit on benches in front of the hotel swapping stories. It was torn down in 1965. (Tehama County Library collection.)

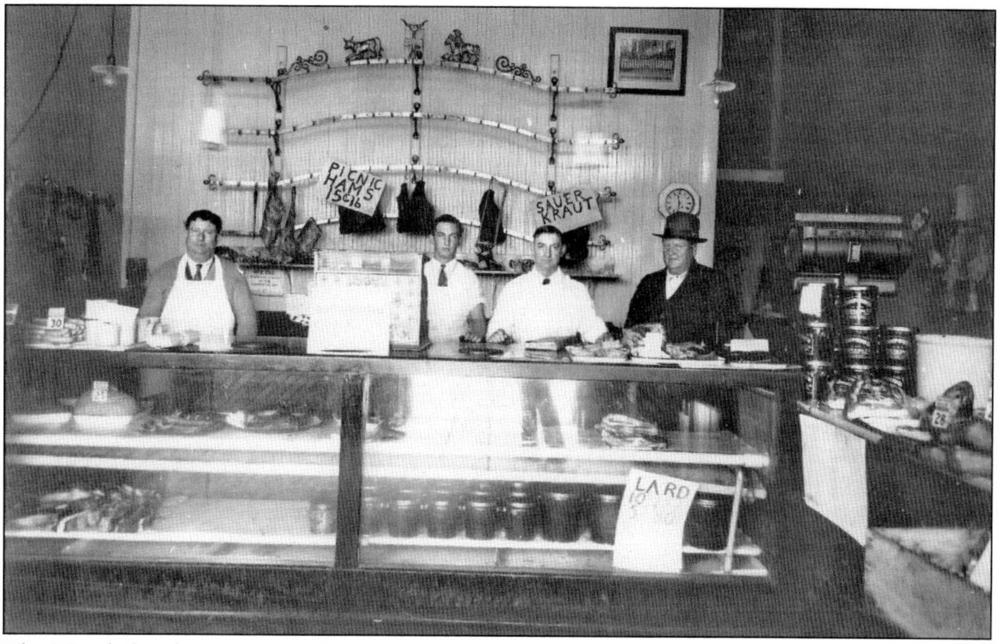


The Minch family came to Red Bluff in 1918. David F. Minch started Minch's Wholesale Meats, which included a meat plant, grocery store, and butcher shop in Red Bluff and a feedlot in Gerber. His son Robert continued it until competition with major meatpackers became too difficult. Minch's Wholesale Meats was a major industry for Red Bluff and Tehama County for 50 years. (Tehama County Library collection.)

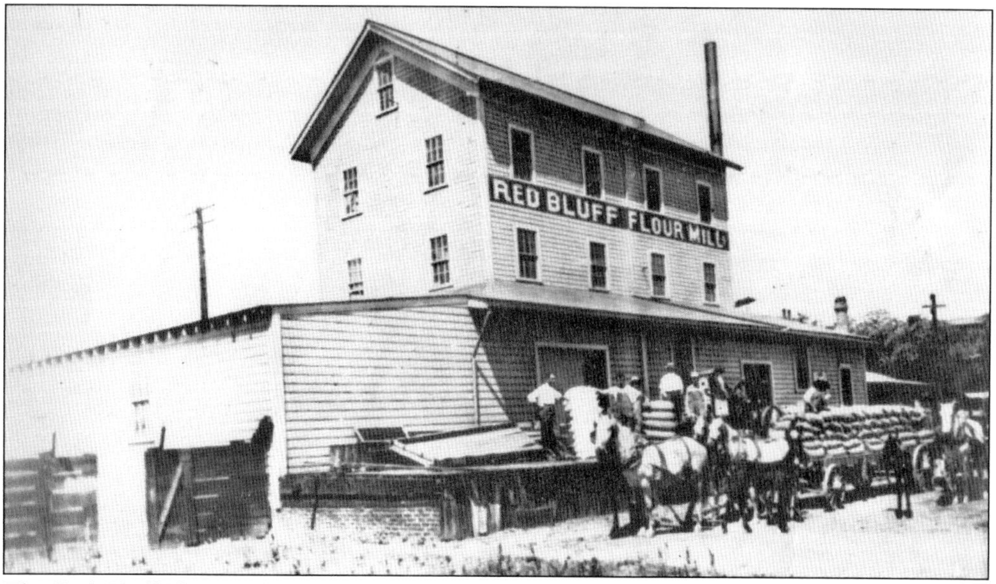


The Red Bluff Flour Mill was steam powered, requiring 1,200–1,500 cords of four-foot wood yearly, until the installation of electricity in 1902. It milled wheat, rye, graham, cornmeal, Germea, middling, bran, and flaked rolled barley. Its French burrs, or millstones, could also mill "substitute flour." During World War I, mills had to sell one pound of substitute flour, which was a mixture of barley, corn, and rye flours, for every pound of regular flour they sold. (Tehama County Library collection.)

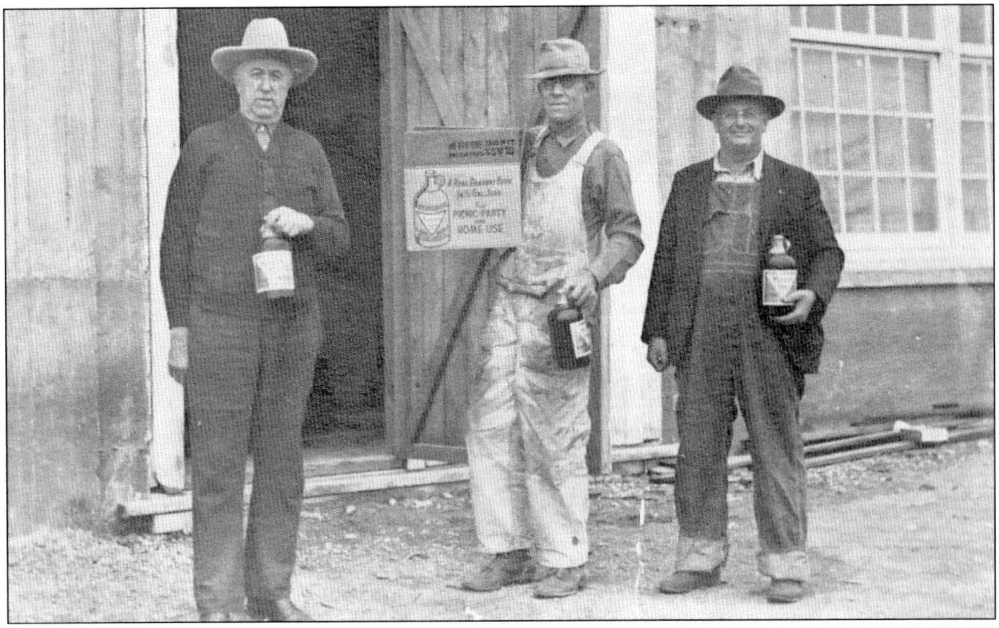

Pete Marinoff had operated breweries in Washington state before moving to Red Bluff and starting the Red Bluff Brewery in 1936. It became the U.S. Brewing Company in 1941. In 1948, the company filed for bankruptcy. A federal court ordered 124,000 gallons (1.5 million bottles) of beer dumped into the Sacramento River to spare the bottling expense. A large crowd of tearful beer drinkers gathered to mournfully watch the "Disaster at Brewery Creek." (Tehama County Library collection.)

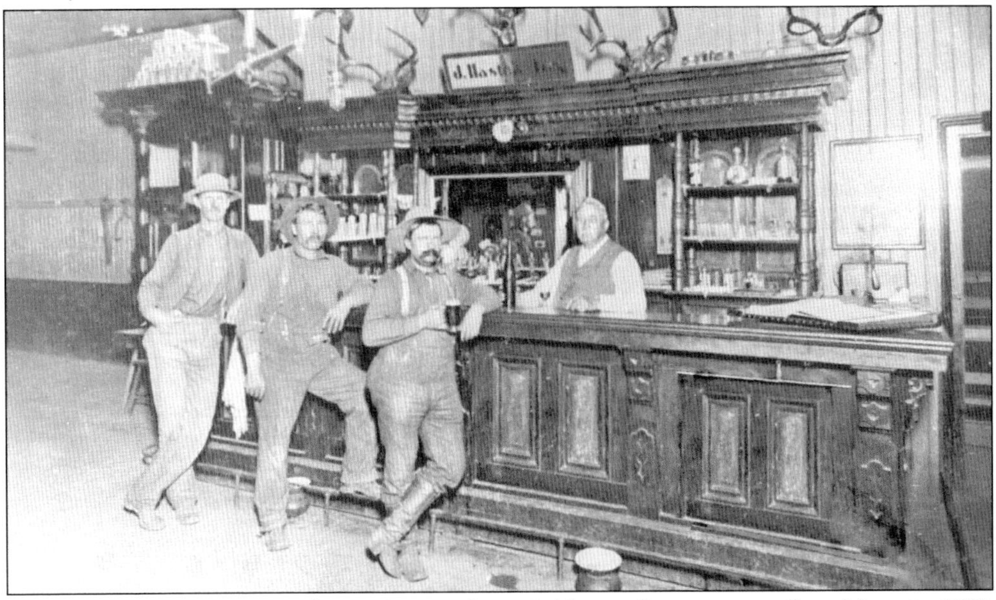

Jacob Hastenplug came to Tehama County from Coblentz, Germany, via Cape Horn in 1870. He worked for the Southern Pacific Railroad before going into the saloon business. He started the Concordia Hotel in 1884. It was near the railroad depot on the north side of the 700 block of Walnut Street. Pictured from left to right around 1907 are Bethel Allen, Bill Nichols, Frank Konover, and Hastenplug. (California State University, Chico, Special Collections.)

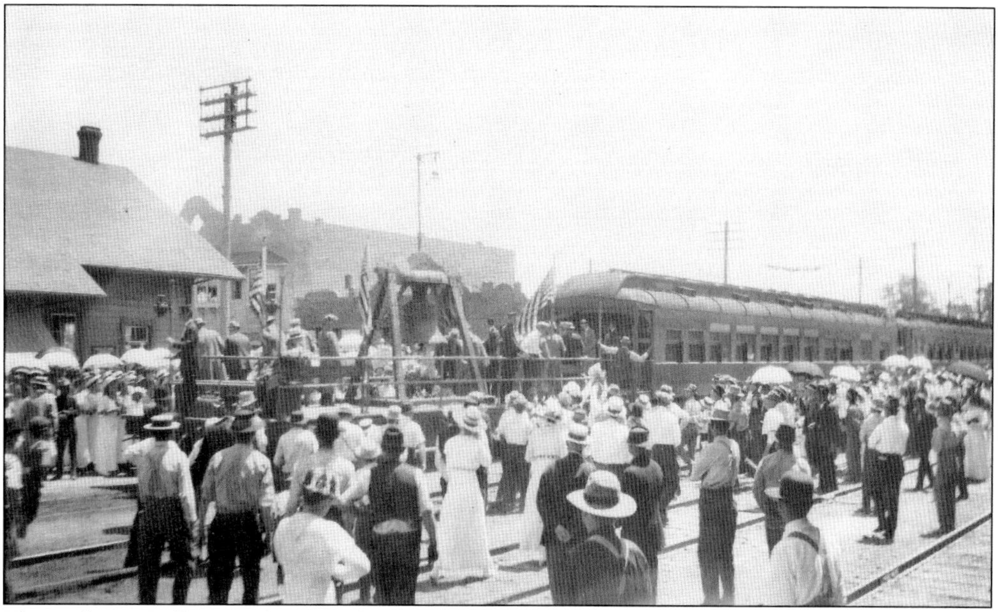

The "Liberty Bell Special" arrived in Red Bluff on July 16, 1915, an hour late and for only five minutes. It was heading to the San Francisco Panama-Pacific International Exposition. The *Red Bluff Daily News* warned, "Don't expect something fancy, for this bell is about 150 years old and was made for service and not for the Panama-Pacific International Exposition." (Tehama County Library collection.)

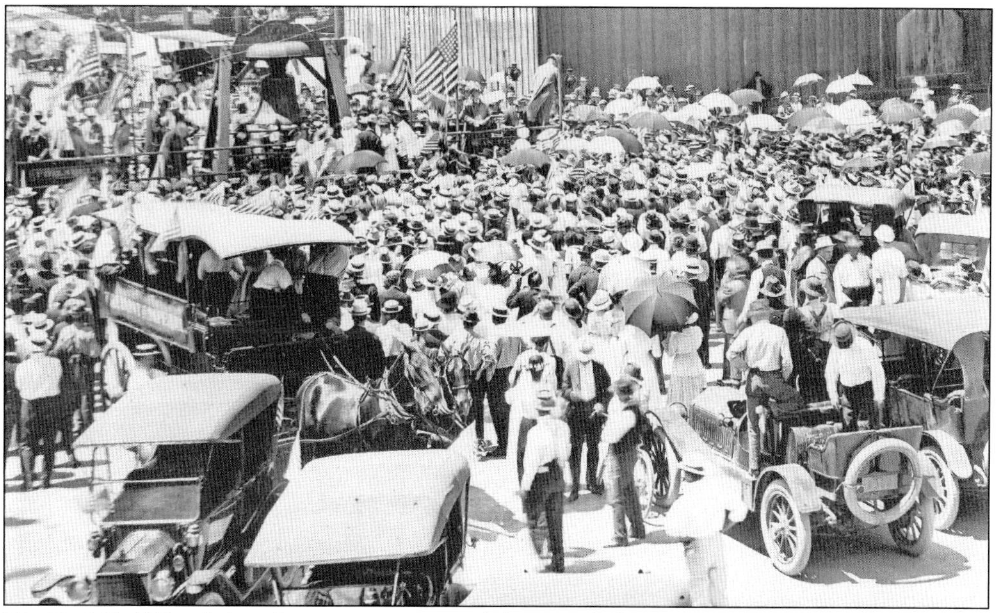

The Red Bluff Band played patriotic songs, and the crowd of 3,000 to 4,000 people maintained a reverent silence as the train pulled into the station. An American flag was unfurled and draped over the bell, the only town to have done this. A week later on July 23, approximately 1,000 people greeted Theodore Roosevelt when he briefly stopped on his way to the exposition. He was given a basket of Tehama County fruit and a large photograph of Lassen Peak in eruption. (Tehama County Library collection.)

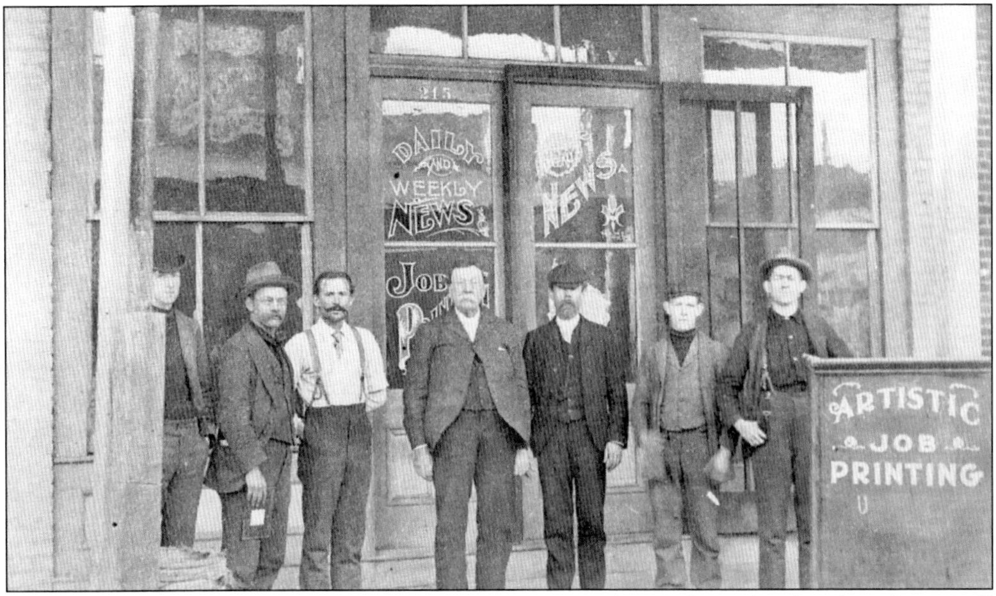


After the Liberty Bell visit, the *Red Bluff Daily News* on July 18 editorialized, "The Liberty Bell crowd was brought to this city through advertising. Local papers brought business for local merchants. No other medium was employed. We call attention to the fact that it's to the interest of Red Bluff merchants to patronize their home papers." The *Red Bluff Daily News* began in 1885 and is still published today. (Tehama County Library collection.)

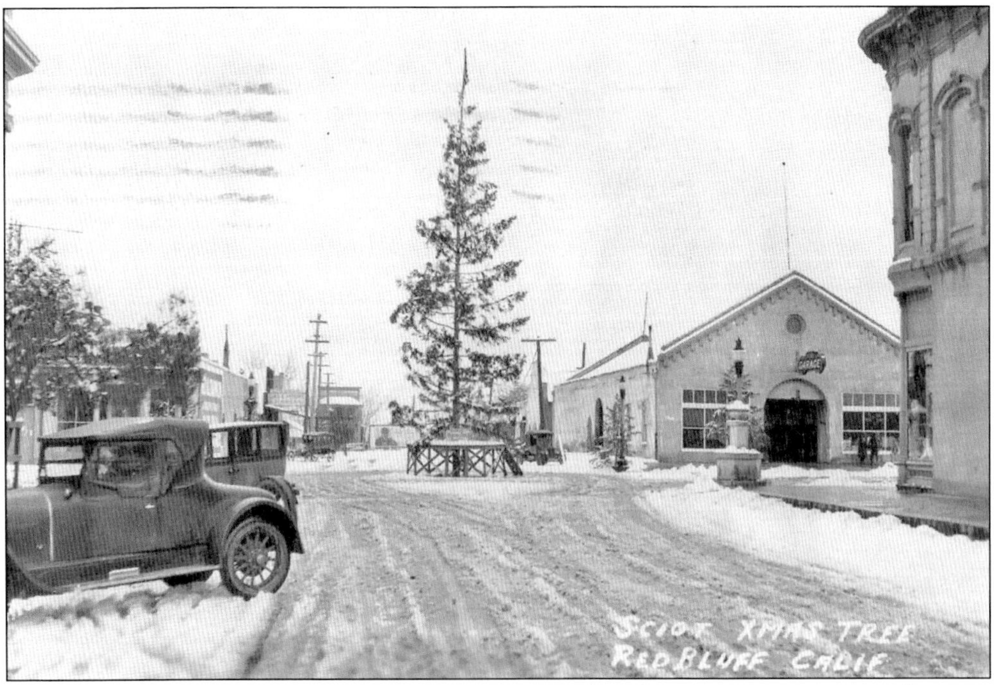


In 1920, the Red Bluff Christmas tree was at Main and Walnut Streets, as seen in this view looking east across Main Street. The Cone-Kimball Mercantile building is to the right, with Buck's Garage facing it. The tree was provided by the Masonic order called the Ancient Egyptian Order of Sciots, Red Bluff Pyramid No. 28. (Dan Bayles collection.)

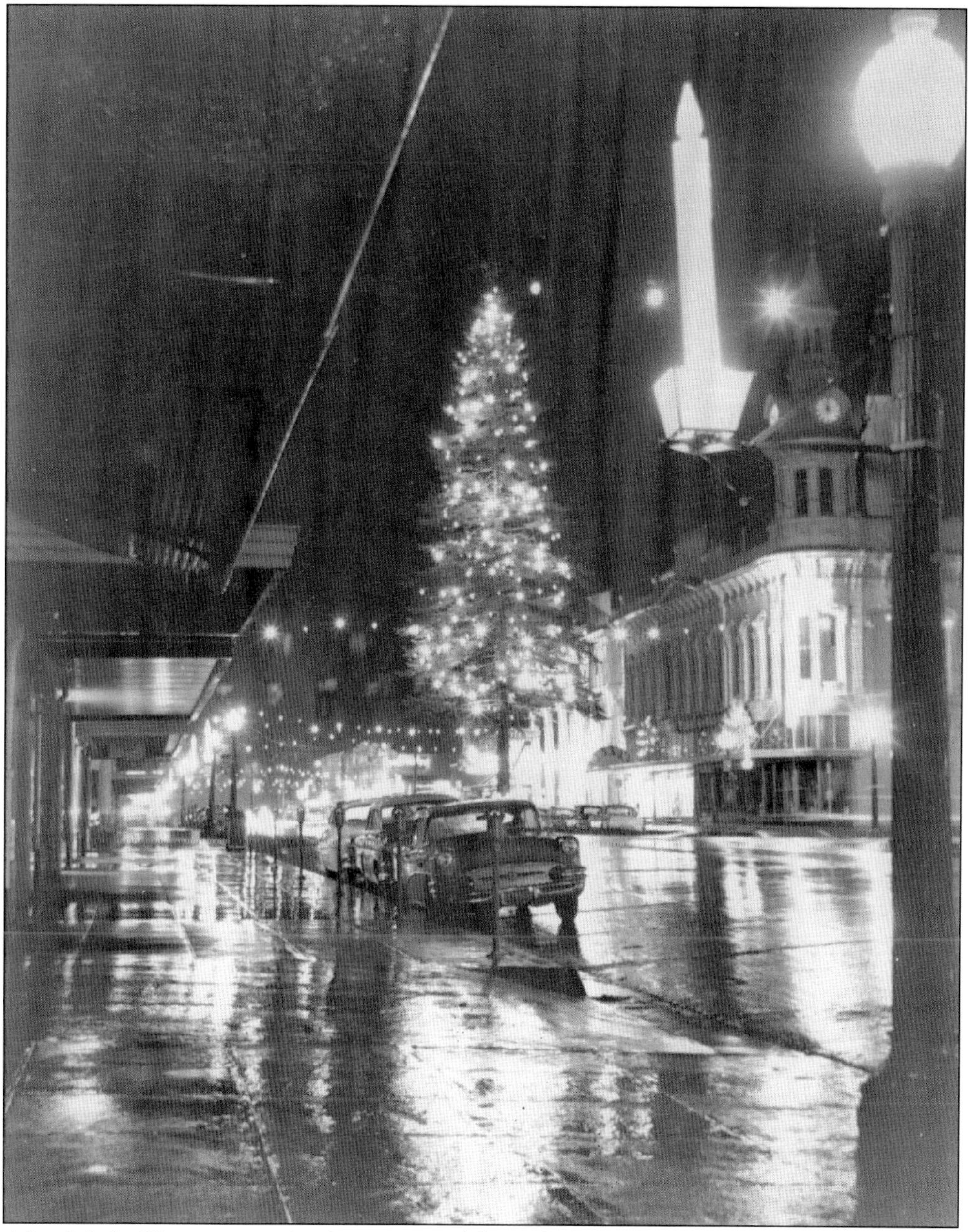

A brightly lit Christmas tree has been a part of the Red Bluff downtown for over a hundred years. Prior to 1980, there were two locations for the trees, both at intersections: Main and Walnut Streets, as seen here, or Oak and Main Streets. The tree would be lifted with a cherry picker from a flatbed truck and placed upright in a manhole deep enough to hold the tree, then braced to keep it level. Despite the bright lights, some drivers still crashed into them. Putting up these trees in the streets was stopped in 1959 because of the traffic accidents and the installation of traffic lights. The current tree is a Deodar Cedar, which does well in Red Bluff's climate. It is located in a small park to the east of Main Street on Pine Street. (Tehama County Library collection.)

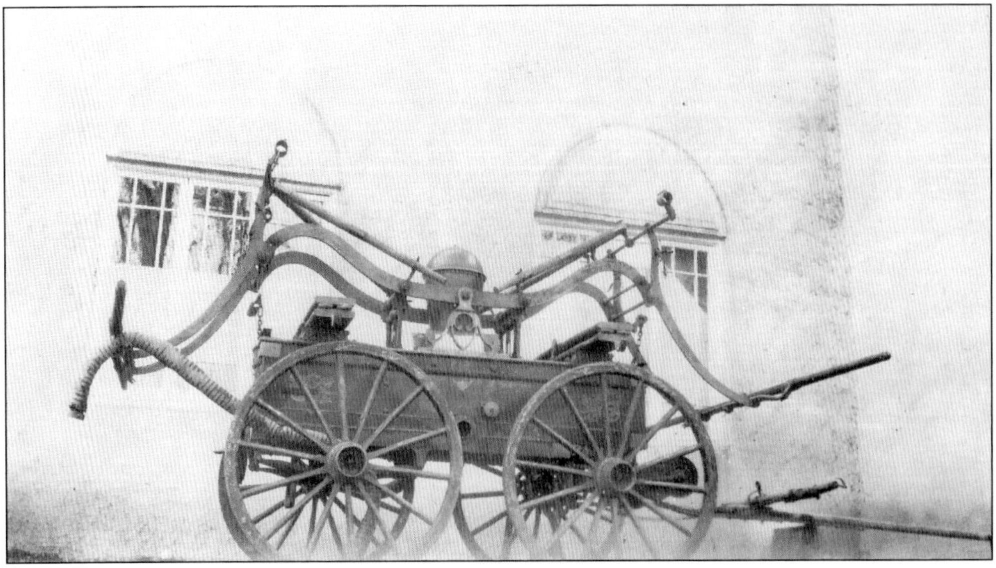

This 1849 LaFayette fire apparatus came around the Horn in 1850. Water was hand pumped through a hose by teams of firemen. Red Bluff bought the LaFayette from Sacramento in 1877. Weaverville bought it in 1906 for $100. When Red Bluff tried to buy it back, Weaverville refused to sell this relic of the "old days." Beautifully restored, it is part of the Weaverville Fire Department Museum and still works. (Tehama County Library collection.)

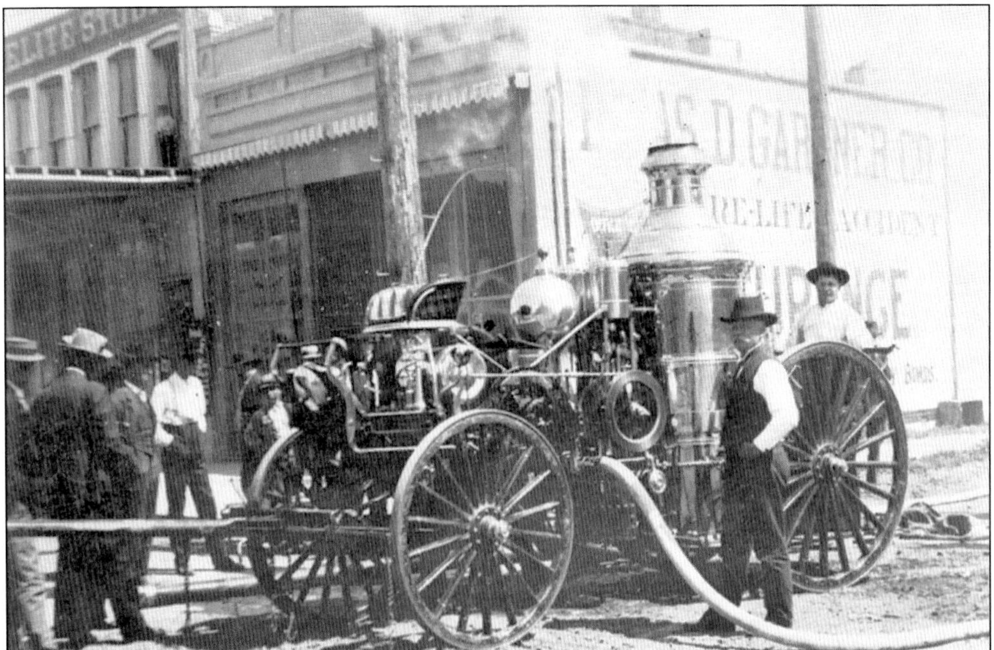

Red Bluff had two steam fire engines: a Silsby and an 1899 LaFrance. Water would be heated inside the engine by a wood fire to create the steam to power it. During a fire call in June 1899, the *Red Bluff News* wrote about the LaFrance: "The exhaust is so great through the smokestack that hot coals were scattered and, at one time, water had to be directed onto a nearby fence which had ignited from one of these sparks." (Tehama County Library collection.)

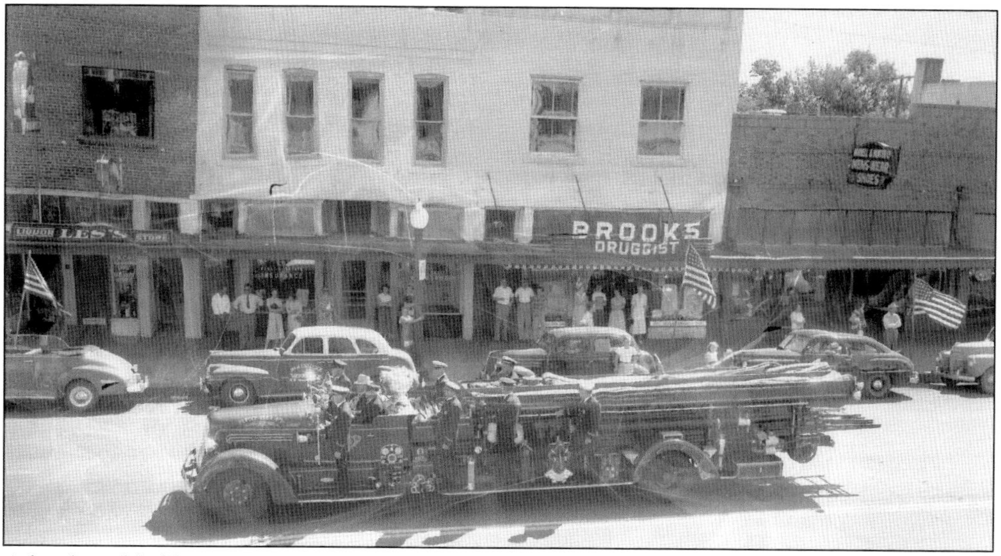


A hook-and-ladder company was formed in Red Bluff on October 2, 1876. It had a Babcock hook and ladder "truck" (more like a wagon) that held four extinguishers, ten canvas buckets, four axes, chains, and hooks and ladders. Uniforms were black pants and red jackets with black belts. A Silsby steam engine was added in 1880 as well as a second hose cart built by the Bidwell Brothers Wagon Shop. This is the hook-and-ladder truck from 1938. (Dan Bayles collection.)

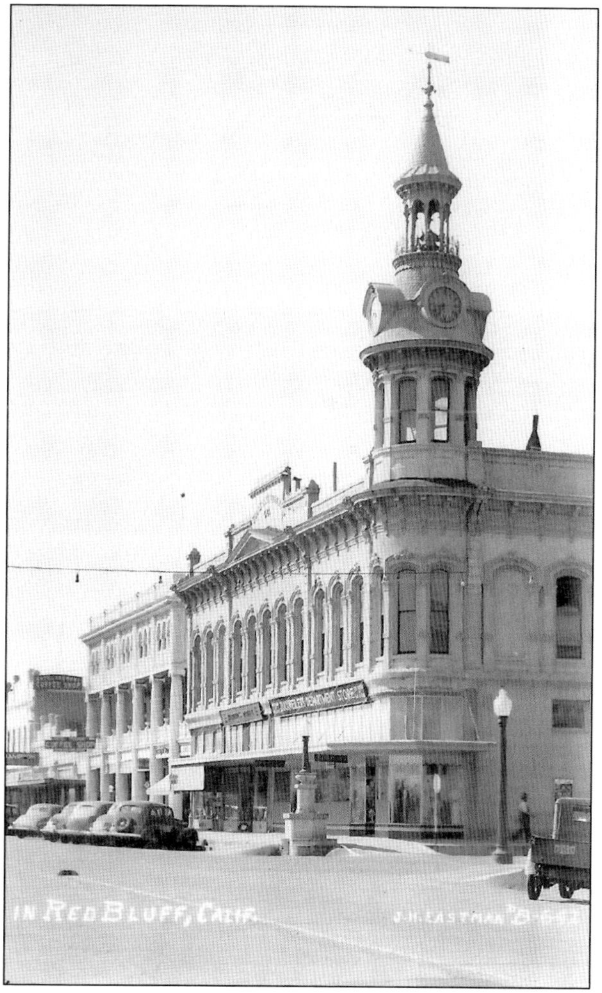


The Cone-Kimball Building had an 1886 Seth Thomas weight clock in its tower. Heavy weights hung from a cable wrapped around a drum that was hand cranked every fourth day. An electric motor replaced this mechanism in 1955. The hands of the clock were made from Sugar Pine. The bell was stopped in the 1930s after complaints from residents of the nearby Tremont Hotel. (Dan Bayles collection.)

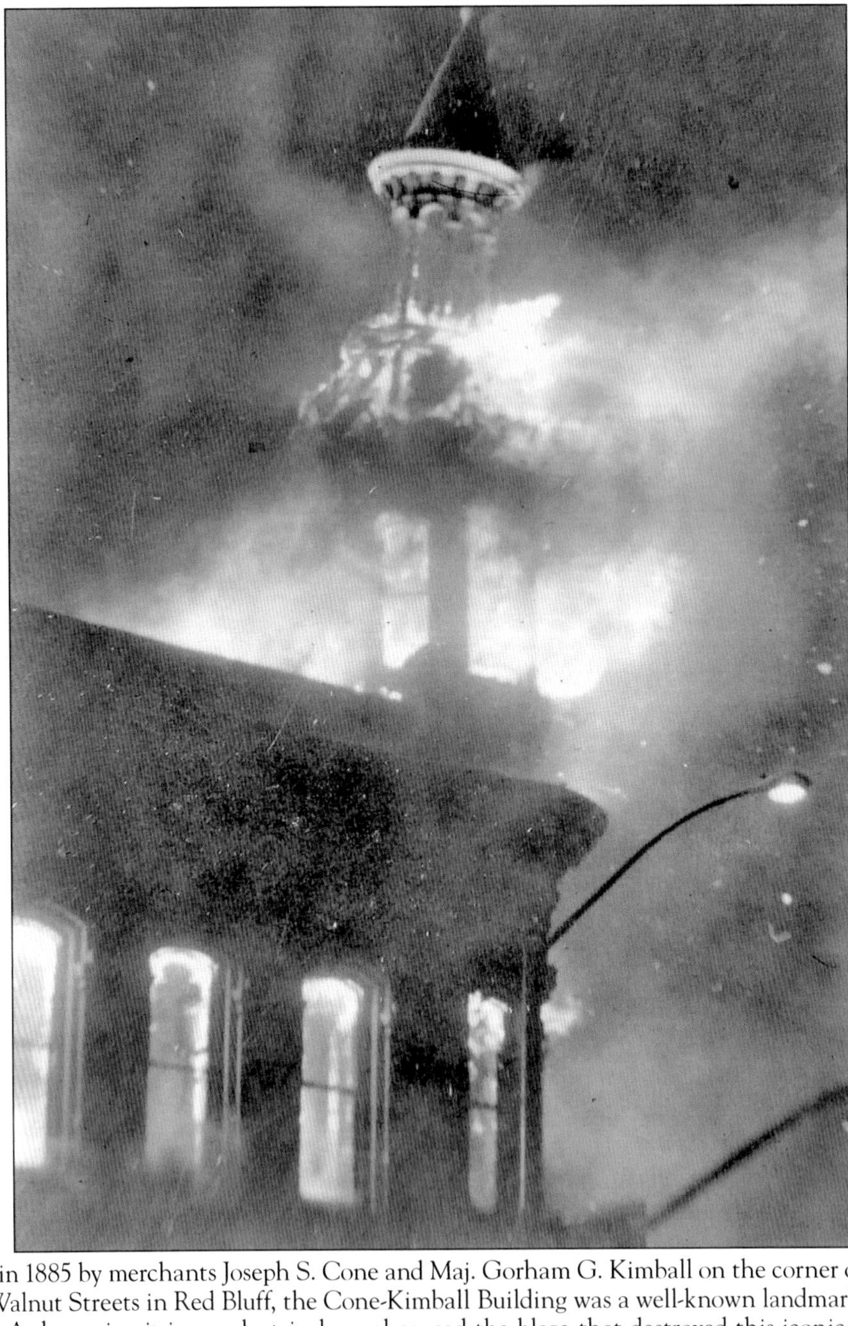

Built in 1885 by merchants Joseph S. Cone and Maj. Gorham G. Kimball on the corner of Main and Walnut Streets in Red Bluff, the Cone-Kimball Building was a well-known landmark for 98 years. A short circuit in an electrical panel caused the blaze that destroyed this iconic symbol of Red Bluff in 1984. Despite the heroic efforts of the Red Bluff Fire Department, departments from Gerber, Corning, and Orland, and the Tehama County Rural Fire Department, the fire destroyed the building in little more than an hour. Later investigation indicated the destruction was rapid because of backdraft—rapid combustion when oxygen is re-introduced. Fire Chief Tom Gauthier explained, "Heat from the fire was filling the entire structure, superheating everything. Finally, fire broke through the roof, oxygen rushed in . . . there was an explosion that blew out the windows. By that time, the flames were out of control." (Dan Bayles collection.)

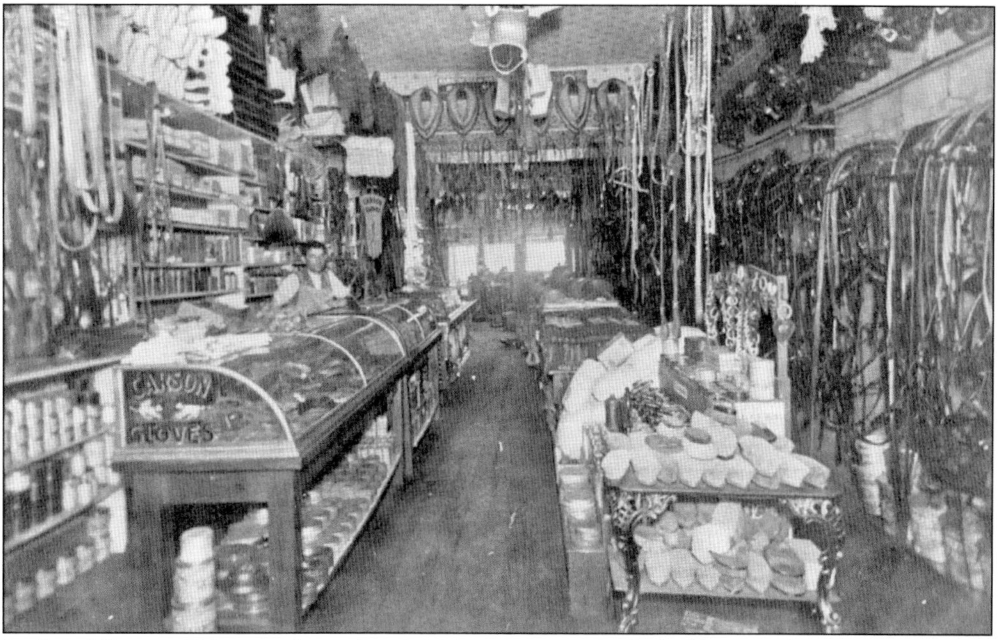


Stoll Saddlery and Harness, located at 649 Main Street in Red Bluff (pictured in 1877), advertised "No man who can afford a spirited horse, can afford a cheap harness. Buy the best. We have it, and at a reasonable price too." Paul Stoll, a native from Bavaria, started the business in 1873 after working for a time in San Francisco and Sacramento before settling in Red Bluff. Saddles were made in the workshop at the rear of the store. Stoll designed several styles of saddles and trees, which is the frame around which a saddle is built, notably the Stoll and Tehama trees. (Tehama County Library collection.)

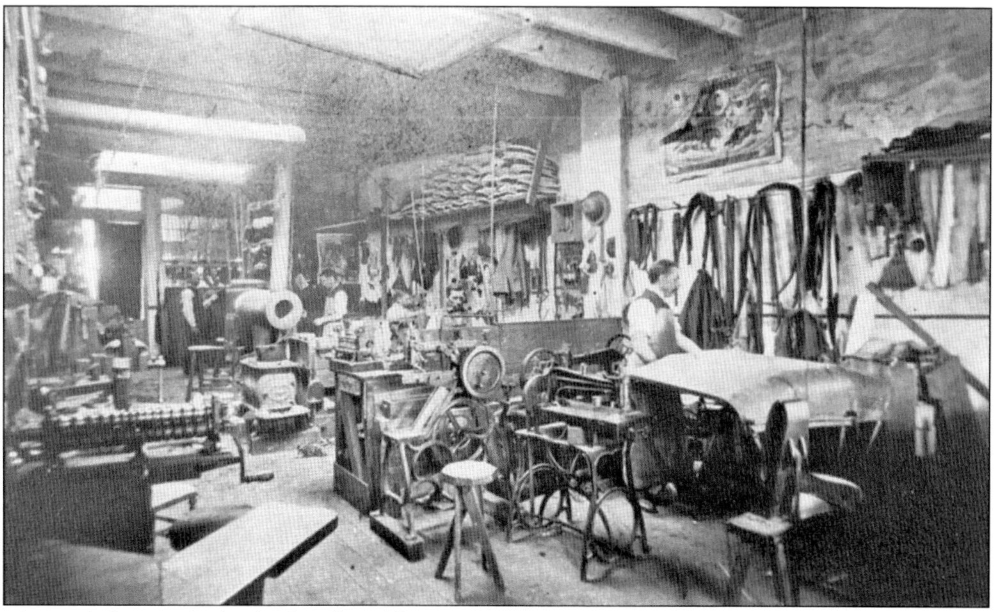

The workshop at the back of Stoll Saddlery and Harness is seen here. Paul Stoll's brother Walter is in the foreground; he owned the first car in Red Bluff. Paul also carried a line of Studebaker buggies and carriages. Later, the store became Stoll Auto Supply. (Tehama County Library collection.)

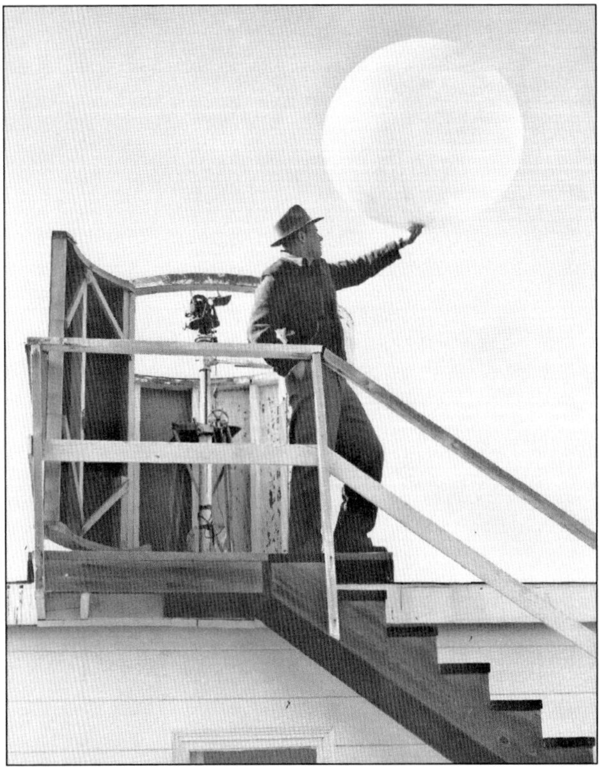

Early weather reports were made by local newspapers noting temperatures, precipitation, wind direction, and unusual conditions. The first barometric station was established in 1866 at Dr. J.R. Bradway's drugstore in Red Bluff. Started in 1870, the National Weather Service began with 24 reporting stations connected by telegraph. The West Coast stations were Portland, San Francisco, and San Diego. A station in Red Bluff was established in 1877. (Tehama County Library collection.)

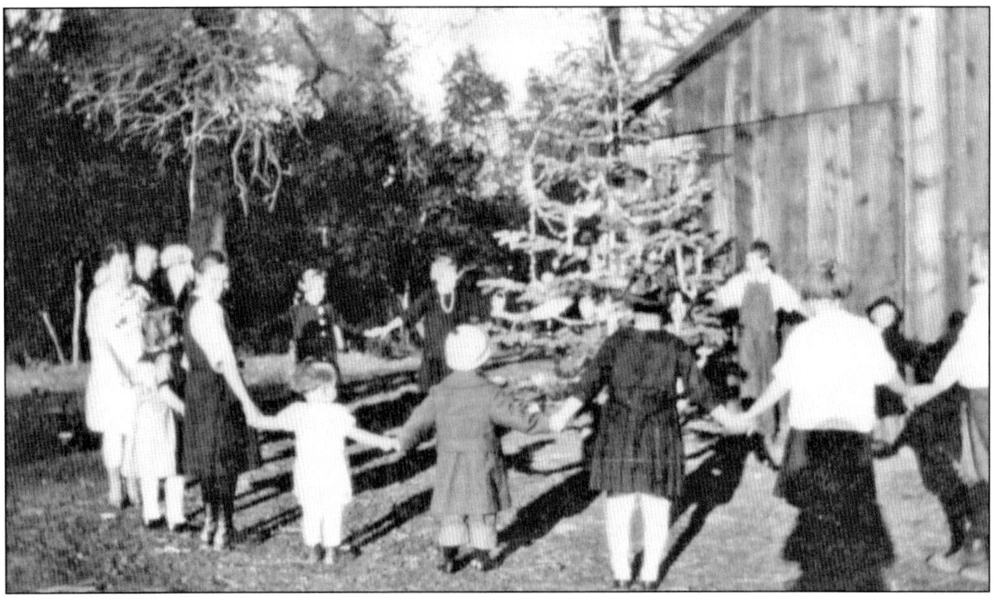

Evergreen is a large agricultural district named because of the many evergreen or live oaks along the banks of Cottonwood Creek. (These particular trees keep their leaves and do not go dormant during the winter.) The Evergreen school was started in 1887, and 12 students were enrolled. It was closed in 1946 when the school district was divided between the Cottonwood and Farquhar school districts. Here, schoolchildren circle a Christmas tree. (Lescher family/Opal Thornton Mendenhall collection.)

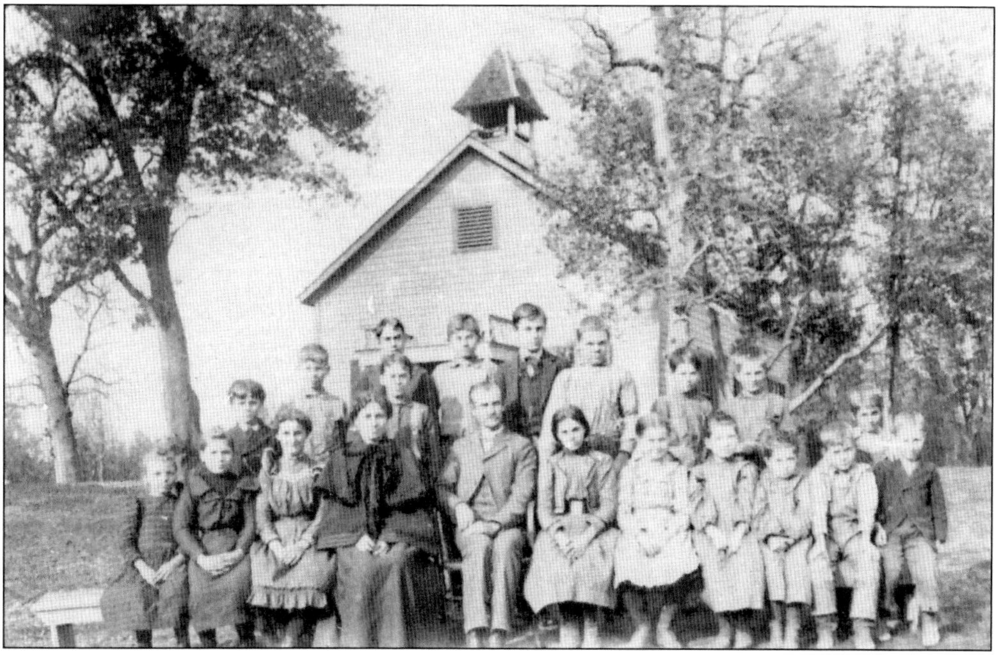

Established in 1879, the Dibble Creek School closed in 1920. Pictured from left to right around 1900 are (first row) Gladys Cummings, Oca Mae Cummings, Jessie Bloxham, Jessie Smith, teacher Jonathan M. Stark, Belle Strait, Gracy Hoy, Neva Smith, Lydia Smith, John Hoy, and Frank Strait; (second row) Ernie Wright, Charlie Hoy, Lee Braden, Jim Stroing, Charlie Smith, Warren Bloxham, and Less Bloxham; (third row) Morris Johnson, Ed Smith, and Marion DuBois. (Tehama County Library collection.)

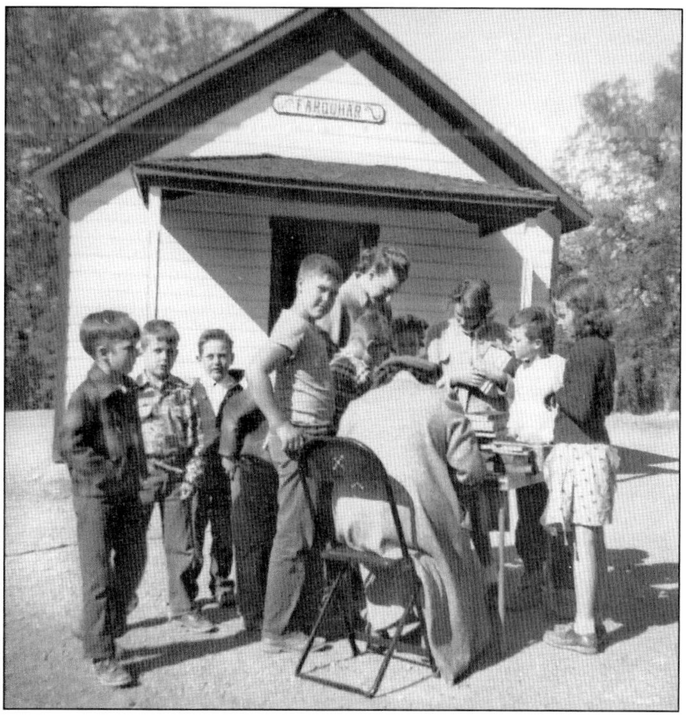

Bookmobiles were owned by the Tehama County Schools but operated by the Tehama County Library. Seen from left to right are Tony Durrer, two unidentified persons; Douglas Blunkall (tall boy), Noel Hulseman (short boy), Malia Livingston (standing, perhaps the teacher), Bonnie Garvey (short girl); Lillian Altman (seated, most likely the bookmobile operator), Mary Ann Hulseman (girl with books in arms), Jimmy McCollister, and Margaret Durrer. (Tehama County Library collection.)

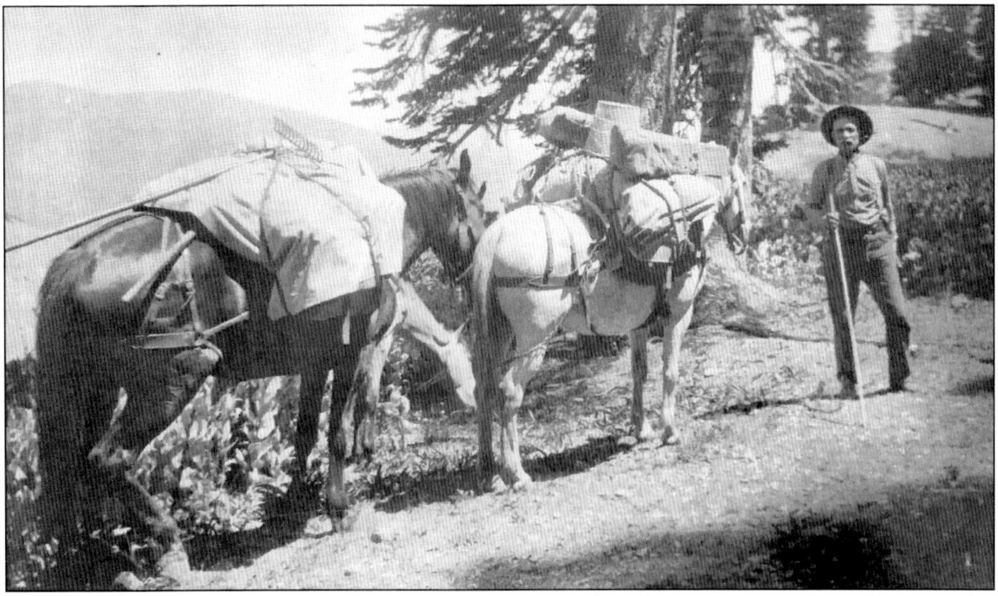

Pack trains brought supplies to remote, roadless sheep and cattle summer camps. Pack trains also carried freight from river landings and warehouses to distant homesteads and isolated communities. These early trails were the first "roads" in the area. In this c. 1920s photograph are Thomas E. Cameron and his pack string in the Yolla Bolly Mountains. Rakes helped keep the campsite—and especially, the campfire area—clear of debris. (Wilson family collection.)

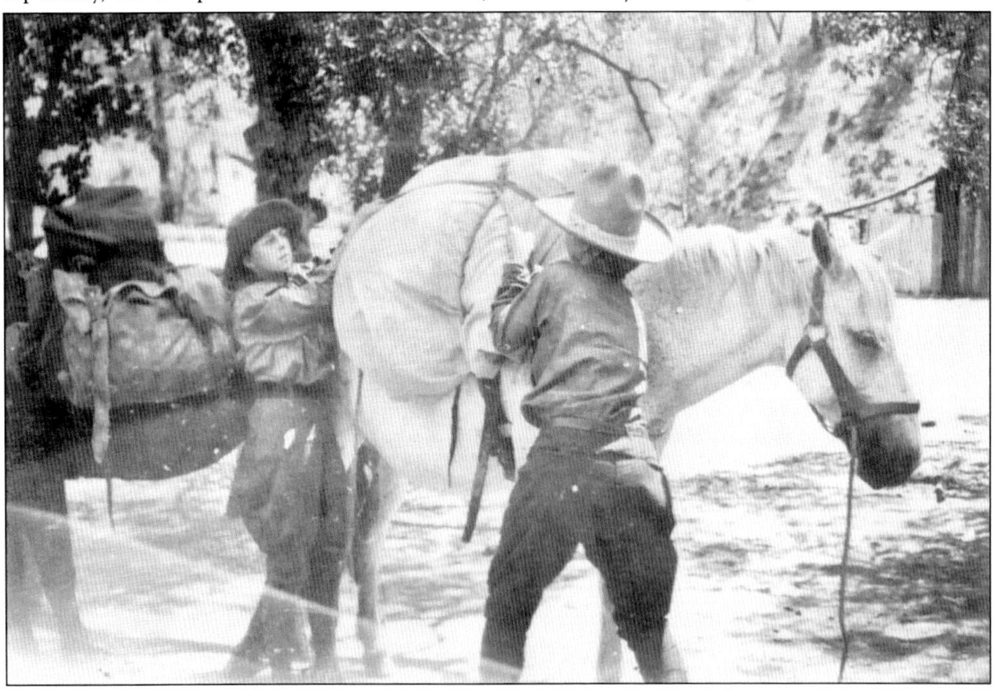

Pictured around 1920, Almeda (Irish) Johnson, 17 years old, and Ethleen (Irish) Hall, 15 years old, "throw the diamond" (tie down the packs with a diamond hitch) at the Carroll Irish Ranch on Balis Bell Road, west of Red Bluff. The Irish girls are getting ready to go to the Yolla Bolly Mountains in the Mendocino National Forest with their sheep. (Wilson family collection.)

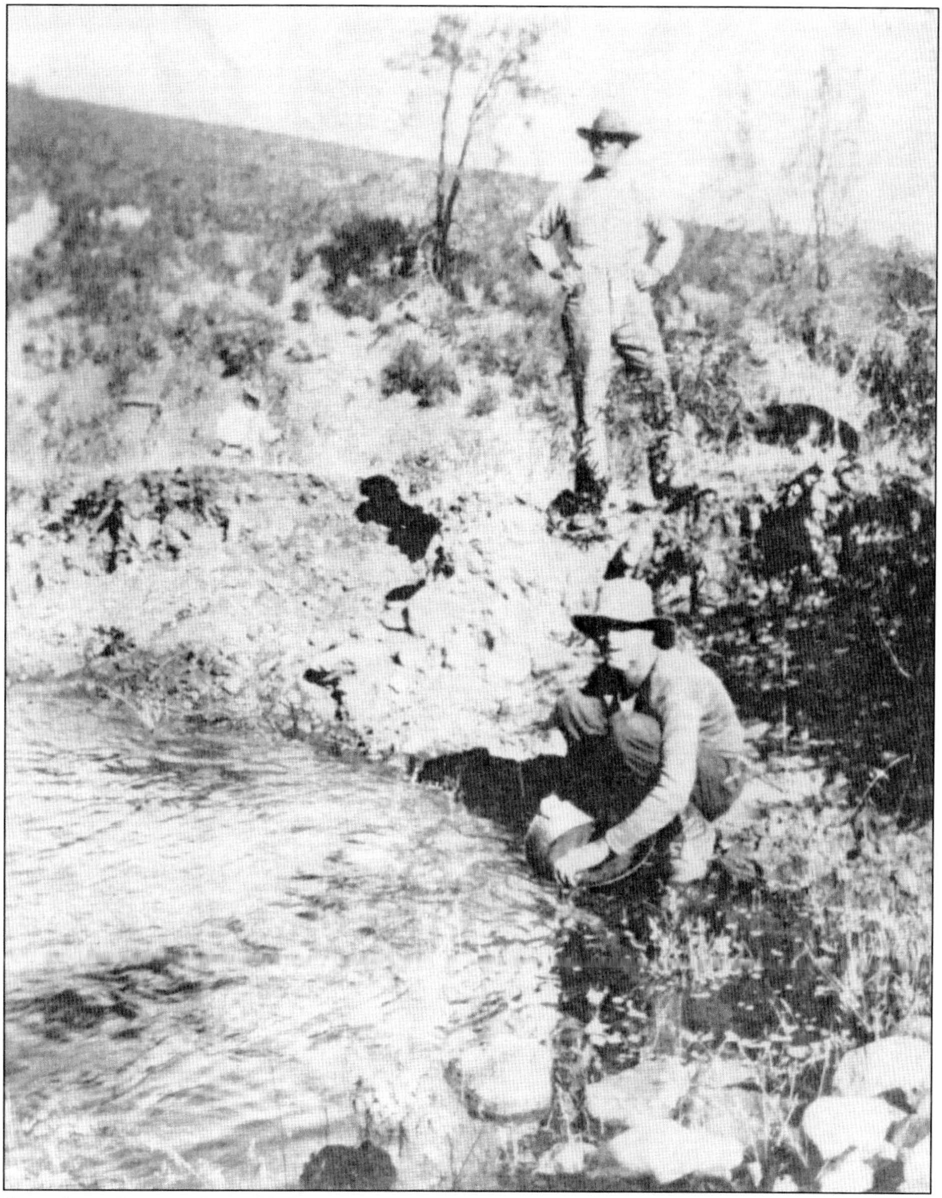

Although not known for gold deposits, hopeful miners, seen here at Beegum, still tried their luck in Tehama County. Chromium was more common and economically feasible to mine than gold. Chromium gives steel strength, toughness, and durability. It is also used for dying, tanning, leather products, bleaching, paint pigments, and photographic printing. The earliest chromium mining in Tehama County was in 1886, when high-grade ore was mined by the Tehama Consolidated Chrome Deposit Company. Ore was shipped to San Francisco and then Philadelphia. Nine mines produced chromium in western Tehama County. At Tomhead Mountain, copper mining was attempted in 1906. The California and Massachusetts Copper Mines Company purchased a number of private mining claims in the area and formed the Red Bluff Mining District. But plans to develop a road from the coast to the mines fell through, probably due to the ore's low copper content and fluctuating prices. Mining in western Tehama County from the late 1880s to the 1960s included oil, natural gas, manganese, asbestos, clay, sand, and gravel. (Jack Schneider collection.)

# Bibliography


Bancroft, Hubert. *History of the Life of Leland Stanford*. Oakland, CA: Biobooks, 1952.

Bauer, Margaret. *History of the Los Molinos Land Company and Los Molinos*. Tehama, CA: Tehama County Museum, 2004.

Colusi County Historical Society. *Wagon Wheels*. 1951–2015.

Froome, George, and Marie Froome. *50 Years of Rodeo: A Pictorial History of the Red Bluff Round-Up*. Red Bluff, CA: Walker Lithograph, 1972.

Grimes, Mary Lee. *The First Fifty Years (1856–1906): A Pictorial Essay of Tehama County*. Red Bluff, CA: Impressive Print, 1998.

Haase, Cheryl Conard. *Too Many Irons in the Fire*. Red Bluff, CA: Impressive Print, 2005.

Hislop, Donald Lindsay. *The Nome Lackee Indian Reservation: 1854–1870*. Chico, CA: ANCHR, 1978.

Hiskin, Clara Hough. *Tehama: Little City of the Big Trees*. New York, NY: Exposition Press, 1948.

Hultgren, Ellen. *A Brief Early History of Corning and the Maywood Colony*. Red Bluff, CA: Walker Lithograph, 1989.

Leininger, Frances L. *Vina's History in Photos and Stories*. Red Bluff, CA: The Copy Center, 2010.

Mark, Andy. *The West Branch Mill of the Sierra Lumber Company*. Charleston, SC: The History Press, 2012.

Mendenhall, Opal. *Olde Time Country School Reunion and History*. Red Bluff, CA: The Copy Center, 2002.

Moulton, Hobart. *We Are Not Forgotten*. Self-published, 1987.

Moulton, Larry. *Sawmill and Lumbering History in Northern California*. Self-published, 2015.

Muffler, L.J. Patrick, and Michael A. Clynne. *Geologic Field-trip Guide to Lassen Volcanic National Park and Vicinity, California: U.S. Geological Survey Scientific Investigations Report 2015–5067*, dx.doi.org/10.3133/sir20155067.

Osborne, A.J. *J. Granville Doll and the Formative Years of Red Bluff*. Chico, CA: ANCHR, 1985.

Peninou, Ernest P. *Leland Stanford's Great Vina Ranch, 1881–1919*. San Francisco, CA: Yolo Hills Viticultural Society, 1991.

Serr, Gene. *Mineral-Mill Creek Place Names*. Red Bluff, CA: Walker Lithograph, 2002.

Tehama County Genealogical & Historical Society. *Memories*. 1983–2015.

Tehama County Genealogical & Historical Society. *Tehama County: 1856–2006*. Red Bluff, CA: Paragon, 2007.

Willendrup, Alan. *The Lassen Peak Eruptions and Their Lingering Legacy*. Chico, CA: ANCHR, 2015.

# About the Organization

*Preservation engages the past in a conversation with the present over a mutual concern for the future.*

—William Murtagh

History and its truths must be preserved to protect it from preconceived notions or inaccuracies. When history is lost, it cannot bolster or dispel claims, especially those that add nothing to the body of knowledge, but if repeated enough times, becomes entrenched as a historical "fact."

Historians must keep an open mind, ask questions, develop credible sources, avoid bias, encourage dialog, revise where needed, and seek the truth in order to strengthen the historical record, not confuse it. We must provide a firm base for future historians and honor the people and events that gave us our history in the first place.

This is what the Tehama County Genealogical & Historical Society does. It is a nonprofit dedicated to collecting, preserving, and fostering the history and genealogy of Tehama County. Organized in 1980, the society strives to:

Encourage valid research relating to the rich history and genealogy of our area;
Preserve this history for future generations;
Share it through publications, presentations, and other programs; and
Collaborate with individuals, the Tehama County Library, and local museums to collect and preserve items of historical and cultural significance.

The society relies on membership dues and donations to continue its mission of preserving and promoting the historical and cultural heritage of Tehama County. You can make a difference by joining us. Our members share a vision, dedication, commitment, and passion for history. Reach us through Facebook (www.facebook.com/TCGHSOC) or the society's website (www.tcghsoc.org). The author can be reached at memorieseditor@gmail.com.

History is best when shared!